Kenealy and the Tichborne Cause

KENEALY
and the
TICHBORNE CAUSE

A Study in mid-Victorian Populism

MICHAEL ROE
Reader in History
University of Tasmania

MELBOURNE UNIVERSITY PRESS
1974

First published 1974

Printed in Australia by
Wilke and Company Limited, Clayton, Victoria 3168 for
Melbourne University Press, Carlton, Victoria 3053
USA and Canada: ISBS Inc., Portland, Oregon 97208

THE PUBLISHER ACKNOWLEDGES THE ASSISTANCE
RECEIVED FROM THE AUSTRALIAN LITERATURE BOARD

ISBN 0 522 84057 4
Dewey Decimal Classification Number 322.430942

PREFACE

'J UST THINK . . . OF THE FLOOD of human idiotism that spent a couple of years or so of its life in writing, printing and reading the Tichborne trial—the whole of that vital energy and time being not only a direct loss, but loss in loathsome thoughts and vulgar inquisitiveness'. My text quotes this passage from John Ruskin at an appropriate point, but perhaps now is the moment really to ponder it. Since August 1965 I have spent more than two full years in pursuing my subject. The result does seem rather puny in terms of the effort and aspiration. Yet at least the task is done, which at times seemed impossible enough, and it has given many moments of pleasure.

At the centre of this book lies 'the Tichborne cause', that is the popular movement supporting a claim made to the Tichborne baronetcy by a man whom in 1874 the law declared an imposter. Various authors have studied the issue in terms of the claim's legitimacy. A climax came in 1957 with the publication of three such books: M. Gilbert, *The Claimant*; G. MacGregor, *The Tichborne Imposter*; and D. Woodruff, *The Tichborne Claimant*. The last of these is wonderfully detailed and solid, probably as close to a definitive history of the episode *qua* case as circumstances allow. I add a little to this story—most importantly at the end of chapter 6—without aspiring to solve all the mysteries although with the authority of alone having scrutinized vital documents held in Australia. Conversely Woodruff in particular gives data relevant at point after point to my study, including its central concerns. A thorough reader of the extant literature could already draw a picture something like that offered in chapter 2. But whereas that is almost as far as earlier writing takes 'the cause', it is the base

v

for my work. From that base I have pushed into several contiguous areas.

First is the life of E. V. H. Kenealy, counsel for the Claimant in his criminal trial of 1873–4. Kenealy so benefited from his client's popularity that he became a member of the House of Commons, 1875–80. Chapters 3 and 4 describe these years of fame. Both the earlier stages of Kenealy's life and his posthumous impact on the world—especially through his children—are interesting, and my first and last chapters explore these subjects. Thus the book incorporates the biography of a man more extraordinary than significant, yet significant enough.

Kenealy was chief, but not the sole protagonist of the Tichborne cause. At all appropriate points, and especially in chapters 5 and 6, I refer to other notable supporters. Chapter 5 delves into the underground of mid-Victorian radicalism in Britain, while chapter 6 spreads across the globe to Australia. The relationship between Britain and Australia is a constant subject of debate among my fellow-Australian historians. I hope to have contributed to this debate, from an unusual angle.

The most ambitious part of the book, chapter 7, attempts to synthesize what has gone before in terms of a concept, 'populism'. Definition of this concept is the first and hardest task of the chapter; briefly, populism is best described by way of negatives—it ran counter to the precepts of commonsense, of progressive liberalism, of Karl Marx, of trade union labour, and of much else. My argument is that the Tichborne cause was a paradigm of populism, and that its strength both drew from and contributed towards the extent to which Everyman's politics of that day were populist. Doubtless most readers will leave chapter 7 with their personal reservations against the argument. But most might agree that 'there is something in it', and perhaps my own effort will encourage more expert and refined analysis of that something.

This *apologia* cannot conceal that the book, like its title, sprawls in rather messy way. Amorphous though it is, the populist concept does not embrace all the material I offer, and if that concept lacks validity the book becomes merely a collection of essays. Even then, however, readers may find the central topic so fascinating as to justify all flaws.

I am especially content that the book should have been prepared in three of the cities—Cambridge, Hobart and Canberra— that have shaped my life, and is being published in the fourth. My primary debts are to universities in each of those places. Of all libraries in the world, that at Cambridge was uniquely suited to my basic research, allowing as it does extraordinarily easy access to its stacks. Without that access I would not, for example, have come upon the biography of Zoe Thomson, which—for no logical reason—might give the clue to the Tichborne mystery. I would not have been in Cambridge but for study leave granted me by the University of Tasmania, the chief but not the sole respect in which that institution has been a good employer. The Australian National University honoured me with a short-term appointment at a vital stage; I thank especially Professor J. A. La Nauze for his assistance in this respect. Melbourne University Press has accepted the risk of publishing a rather peculiar study.

Beyond that my thanks are due to a great number of persons and institutions. My endnotes indicate many, but not all, of these obligations. In some compensation for default, may I say that it has been a privilege and inspiration to work within a world-ranging network of scholarship. Yet in the end my greatest debts are near to base: on the one hand to my wife, on the other to colleagues in Hobart. Among the latter I think especially of Diane Caulfield and Mary Nicholls. To them I offer the book.

M.R.

Hobart
1974

AUTHOR'S NOTE

K ENEALY HIMSELF SPOKE OF 'the Tichborne cause' in the sense of my title, and his warrant also permits 'Tichbornite' to describe a supporter of the cause.[1] My text uses 'Tichborne' as an adjective referring to the cause and its supporters, while 'the movement' is an occasional synonym for 'the cause'. I do not dilate on errors by previous commentators; where I have noticed discrepancies I have checked my facts with particular care. The majority of references have been traced back to originals, but Antipodean distance has prevented this in some cases, for which I beg pardon. In quoting from various sources, I have imposed some minor conventions of spelling and capitalization so as to accord with the text generally. Bibliographic detail is given for books and articles at their first mention in the notes to each chapter, but thereafter reference is by author and/or short title. The bibliography does not repeat these details: instead it lists Kenealy's important writings, and those of his daughter Arabella, and indicates the nature and location of my more esoteric sources. The only abbreviation used is MCA for Magna Charta Association.

CONTENTS

ILLUSTRATIONS

I

KENEALY

K ENEALY'S LIFE WAS FANTASTIC. That became obvious with
his involvement in the Tichborne cause, but earlier years
determined such a climax. Ability and achievement mixed
with pretence and opportunism. Ambition was constant, yet wayward—ranging from literature to politics, from this world to the
next, from materialism to mysticism. Until 1873, this ambition
experienced torment rather than satisfaction, yet stayed alive.

Edward Vaughan Hyde Kenealy was born in Nile Street, Cork,
southern Ireland, on 2 July 1819, son of Catherine and William
Kenealy. The latter was afterwards described as 'a R.C. whisky
shopkeeper',[1] and a directory of 1824 confirms this. Edward was
the first son among two boys and two girls (Christina and Annamaria). Relatively free of a brood, and ministering to man's thirst,
the father maintained his family in solid comfort. He had some
eccentricities, his particular conceit being genealogy. As well as
claiming to be chief of the clan Kenealy, he cherished family
portraits and heirlooms and laboured 'to demonstrate that he was
descended in direct line from the Arkite Patriarch, through a
splendid roll of monarchs, heroes, saints and conquerors, in whom
the blood and passions of many mighty families were grandly
blended'.[2] So the son wrote in the 1850s, but already he noticed his
mother's claimed descent from Charlemagne and Edward III, and
in later life his own pride of family waxed strong. Likewise he was
as much serious as satirical in telling of paternal hopes that he
'was to be something wonderful', a priest of the Church, whose
devoted member the father was. Many an Irish publican has
had that dream for his progeny, but Kenealy's account of his

1

father and of the family's introversion suggests that there prevailed a peculiar intensity.

Kenealy portrayed himself as a strange child, 'idle, quiet . . .
reserved, solitary and silent, dull of observation but quick to
learn'. He listened to folk-stories, had his daydreams, read beyond
his years, and played with a puppet theatre. He shared in the
family's ardent religiosity. Family deaths, especially that of his
younger brother, left a heavy imprint. Fun played some part in the
boy's life, but solitary walks were his greatest outdoor pleasure.
Once he shot a bird, and revulsion at the blood that spurted from
its eyes turned him from hunting forever. This story told more of
the autobiographer of the 1850s than of his younger self, but its
outline was probably true enough. His account of schooldays
stressed the sadism of teachers, which crippled his intellect.

Kenealy entered Trinity College, Dublin, on 6 July 1835. The
university's younger blood included some names notable in Irish
history: poet Thomas Davis and politician Isaac Butt, for
example. In retrospect Kenealy equivocated about his peers. The
autobiography of the fifties scorned them as 'word-splitters and
grammarians', falling far short of 'any exalted confraternity of
youths aspiring to the beautiful', but earlier Kenealy had recalled
exciting debate at the College Historical Society.[3] He himself
affirmed the execution of Charles I and, in nice contrast, the abolition of capital punishment; and he won a poetry prize sponsored
by the society. Memoirs speak of roistering and extravagance, but
he enjoyed only one friendship and generally found the college
banal and barren. The son of a Catholic tradesman probably
needed a thicker skin and a more imposing presence than were
Kenealy's to feel comfortable at Trinity of that day. The college's
one great virtue was its library. Kenealy, moreover, had entered at
King's Inn and spent much time among its books. He claimed to
have read virtually everything, save items for the classical syllabus
and contemporary 'dull and vulgar sermons'. Allowing for hyperbole, this was probably when Kenealy gathered much of his literary and linguistic knowledge—more ostentatious than profound,
but still remarkable enough. He missed honours even in classics,
scorned science and maths. Examinations were overcome, however, and in six terms Kenealy met qualifications for his subsequent degrees.

At Dublin Kenealy suffered a crisis of faith. He studied the Old
Testament 'with a sacred resolution to scan it as I would any

other ancient volume', and determined that it was no holy writ but blended good precepts and bad. Liberation from belief allowed Kenealy to adventure in vision and fantasy, yet respect for his father and somewhat perverse loyalty to the Church thwarted any direct break. In politics the O'Connellite sympathies of his home were overlaid by doctrinaire republican radicalism. Paine, Rousseau and Burke were among Kenealy's favourite philosophers, while he dreamt of emulating the practice of Bolingbroke and Pitt. His literary heroes were Lamb, Byron and Shelley. These mentors taught vigour rather than consistency.

Kenealy spent the second half of 1837 in Cork as a trainee-surgeon, answering his father's desire that he learn anatomy. In January 1838 parent and son crossed the sea to England. 'Now was I indeed in land classic to me', remembered Kenealy. He entered at Gray's Inn, to fulfill residential qualification for the bar, and then spent the first half of 1840 at a lawyer's office, still in London. Visits to the House of Commons left Kenealy with contempt for most members, but praise for Daniel O'Connell. Horizons opened through making acquaintance with William Maginn, founder in 1830 of *Fraser's Magazine*. Like Kenealy, Maginn—born in 1794— was a son of Cork, a graduate of Trinity, and a strange man. He had wit and facility, but drink and debt cursed his later days. He much influenced Kenealy, who for the next few years at least pretended to accept Maginn's scorn of O'Connell and Repeal, and at once began writing verse in the Maginn manner. 'The Wonderful Life and Adventures of a Jontleman Attorney',[4] evidently Kenealy's first published work, told of some young man who secured his education at Maynooth by pretending vocation, and then departed for the joys of secular carnality.

Next Kenealy returned to Ireland, graduating as Bachelor of Arts and in November 1840 joining the Irish bar. An oddity of this occasion was his correcting newspaper reports that implied he was not a Catholic. To a London friend Kenealy boasted 'what magic there is in a wig'; 'I cock my hat at every pretty girl, and my nose at every law student'.[5] But soon he admitted ennui and frustration. He yearned for England, and to escape from his native land where 'politics are so much a staple that not to trade in them is to be an unknown'. Distrusting both politics and demagogues, Kenealy saw no future in Ireland for that 'goddess to whom I would sacrifice—no matter what—Ambition'.[6]

To slake that thirst, Kenealy soon could boast publication in

Fraser's, the numbers for May and June 1841 carrying his 'Table-Talk of the Late John Boyle'. In this and following work Kenealy reconstructed conversations of the Deipnosophists, a group of Cork wits of the 1820s. Members included Maginn, Boyle, and a priest named Francis Mahony who as 'Father Prout' had won a reputation with his Maginnish whimsy. Kenealy followed the same model: 'What is an Irishman but a machine for converting potatoes into human nature' was one shaft, characteristic of a humour that has dated beyond aeons. When a Cork journalist criticized the effort, Kenealy replied with venomous force, anticipating many a future passage.

In September 1841 Kenealy left Cork for Furnival's Inn, London, and a taste of literary fame. The next January *Fraser's* published 'A Letther from Mr Barney Brallaghan', which continued the Cork fantasy in heavy dialect; another followed in February. By now the allusions to living persons had become crude. G. W. Nickisson, editor of *Fraser's*, called halt, and deprecated the articles generally; Kenealy answered that Maginn, Mahony and W. M. Thackeray had each been suggested as authors of the pieces.[7] Nickisson remained firm, but in 1842–3 published Kenealy's version of 'The Love Epistles of Aristaenetus', a Greek author (*c.* 500) of ordinary erotic verse. The translator remarked that love had ever been a favourite theme in literature and that Aristaenetus would impress all who had 'themselves experienced the passion'. The verse was turgid, except where flippant. Nickisson found some lines 'much too amorous'. The relationship survived, even to *Fraser's* publishing more Irishry.

Meanwhile Kenealy's work appeared elsewhere. W. H. Ainsworth was generous not only with rather facile praise but also with space in *Ainsworth's Magazine*. The first offering, early in 1842, showed Kenealy's skill at presenting a classical version of some famous English poem and playfully suggesting that this was an original from which the moderns copied. His 'Songs of Italy' were more in the Aristaenetus vein, and prompted editorial remonstrance on behalf of 'the straightlaced public'. In 'A Venetian Romance' Kenealy wrote from self-fantasy, his hero enjoying both 'the Talisman of Omnipotence' and a beautiful lover. Most other contributions to *Ainsworth's* were lyrical verse. Through 1842 Kenealy also wrote for *Bentley's Miscellany*, and to much the same pattern—occasional conventional poems and one major series, 'The Life and Songs of Anacreon'. Kenealy extolled the

poet for celebrating 'love, beauty, and wine'; his translations
sometimes caught this gay hedonism. Again the author prided
himself on rumour attributing his work to famous wits, and he
considered publishing the whole as a book. Richard Bentley seems
not to have responded.[8] He too chided Kenealy for indelicacy,
while a sharper tension resulted from his paying less than top
rates.

Kenealy's life in London from 1841 to 1843 did approach that
romantic blend of delight and despair, such as his reading and
temperament idealized. Especially was this so in his relations with
the Maginn family. With William Maginn he had some quarrel
early in 1842, but on overcoming this he became a frequent visitor
to the family house at Walton. Maginn, however, was drifting towards his death, which occurred in August. Kenealy established
himself as trustee: he published a ballad that Maginn had been
writing at the end, and began organizing a testimonial fund. At
some stage he became enamoured of Annie Maginn, the family's
elder daughter. Annie already had an attachment; Kenealy persuaded Mrs Maginn that the man was philandering, and thus
disrupted the romance. After turmoil, this relation resumed,
although but temporarily. Kenealy and Mrs Maginn became
enemies. The woman was at least difficult, perhaps half-mad;
when she quarrelled with her young son, Kenealy gave him shel-
ter. Meanwhile he continued preparing a memoir of Maginn.

Soon afterwards occurred an episode that was more deeply to
colour Kenealy's life with scarlet and black: an affair that resulted
in the birth of a bastard son. The girl, said Kenealy's memoirs,[9]
was the daughter of an army officer and the victim of a peer's seduction. She went on the stage, and thereby crossed one of Kenealy's
interests. Kenealy took responsibility for the child, who evidently
was born in about March 1844. Meanwhile, to complete his
troubles Kenealy signed a 100 guinea bill on behalf of a friend,
who defaulted. Threat of legal proceedings probably determined
him to withdraw to Ireland in summer 1843. Next he toured the
Rhineland, before returning to the family home, now in Cork's
King Street. One sister, Christina, had died in 1840, the second entered a convent in February 1843. Always the favourite, and now
virtually the only child, Kenealy withdrew into the parental
cocoon.

As author, Kenealy soon stirred several brews. In September
1843 the *Dublin Review* published his review of a biography of

Henry Grattan, complementing his earlier study of a life of Henry Flood. He found Grattan culpable of truckling to Britain in 1782, and an infidel hedonist as well. For Kenealy—contributor to *Fraser's Magazine* and *Dublin University Magazine*—to uphold the nationalist cause was strange; to present himself as its curator against Grattan's pollution doubled this contradiction in one sense, but in another cancelled it. Daniel O'Connell repudiated the *Review* in anger at the article. H. R. Bagshawe, the journal's editor, shunned Kenealy's offer to contribute regularly so that the *Review* might better uphold the noble Catholic cause against English acrimony.[10] More explosive still was a memoir of Maginn which appeared in the *Dublin University Magazine*, January 1844. There were references to the grimmer side of Maginn's life, to rivals and enemies, and to the shrewishness of Mrs Maginn. Charles Lever, editor of the *Magazine*, told his publishers that the original memoir included eighteen insults and four libels.[11] Kenealy accepted some cuts, but in the aftermath still challenged Lever to a duel. The literati gossiped. John Blackwood, son of Maginn's publisher and friend, surmised 'that this little vagabond has prigged my father's letters'—a charge which Kenealy's own papers leave in doubt. Blackwood reported general feeling that 'the particularly bad part of it was the little brute attacking Mrs Maginn'.[12] The lady's brother considered legal action, but to no effect.

Yet the journals continued to use Kenealy's work. *Fraser's Magazine* published two articles about the continental tour of 1843, including a long apostrophe to nature in which Kenealy declared his love of mountain and valley, ocean and lake, stars and sky. *Ainsworth's Magazine* also took prose and romantic verse. Early in 1844 appeared Kenealy's first contribution to *Punch*: 'The King of the Cannibal Islands'. It was an ode in clever verse, both Greek and English.[13] He determined to collect his work in a substantial volume. The title, *Brallaghan, or the Deipnosophists*, indicated its emphasis on the tales of Cork a half-generation before. A Cork printer charged Kenealy senior £80.0.0 for 1050 copies. A slip quoted comments from reviewers, praising the original pieces.[14] Who was to publish? Nickisson was the obvious hope, and Kenealy felt that the obligation had been accepted. But Father Mahony learned that the collection included a scandalous description of himself, and so threatened action. For this reason, Kenealy believed, Nickisson and several other London publishers refused the book. Kenealy's strictures against Mahony and the

Jesuit Order—for which the priest had trained, although not continuing to be a member after 1830—grew strong. At length the offending page was rewritten and a publisher, Churton, issued the work late in 1844.

The Irish whimsy which bulked large in *Brallaghan* falls more heavily on the modern ear than does Kenealy's work generally. More impressive is the verse. Linguistic dexterity was its chief virtue, whether in comic mode, in translation of modern giants into the classics, or in English versions of European work—Portuguese, Italian, Spanish, German. Most of Kenealy's own poems offered an occasional line or stanza of worth, but dross usually smothered the gold. Perhaps 'A Hint' succeeded best in its lyric of love and laughter:

> A fair lady once, with her young lover walked,
>   *Gillyflower, gentle rosemary;*
> Through a garden, and sweetly they laughed and they talked,
>   *While the dews fell over the mulberry tree.*
> She gave him a rose—while he sighed for a kiss,
>   *Gillyflower, gentle rosemary;*
> Quoth he, as he took it, 'I kiss thee in this'
>   *While the dews fall over the mulberry tree.*

And so it went on for seven stanzas. In different mood, 'Dreams of My Youth' almost overcame the mawkishness of its writer's self-musings:

> In times of old
> Angels came down from Heaven's starry floors
> And walk'd on Earth and knock'd at poor men's doors,
> And entered and sat down in earthly guise
> But brought bright revelations from the skies—
> So to my soul came Dreams of lovely things;
> Dear Angel-dreams; alas, why had ye wings
> Ye times of old?
>
> At Evening's fall
> By the dark Ocean I would slowly pace,
> Watching the star-beams mirror'd on its face;
> Or stretched along the strand, sedgy and damp,
> Until the Moon lit up her crystal lamp,
> Gaze upward to the Heaven and pray that some
> Celestial shape thence to my side would come
> At Evening's fall.

Brallaghan fell flat. Kenealy reported that only eleven copies had sold in Ireland by February 1845. *Ainsworth's Magazine* was the only major journal to give a favourable notice: 'the mantle of Greek lyrical excellence has descended on worthy shoulders'.[15] This was puff, yet *Brallaghan* prompted some later appreciation of Kenealy. S. A. Allibone described him in 1859 as the Irish Longfellow,[16] while S. M. Ellis, poetaster of the early twentieth century, believed Kenealy 'could have attained a very high position in the ranks of literature' had he fulfilled early promise.[17]

For the moment, Kenealy could only taste the bitterness of failure, and spit out its acid. He upbraided Thomas Davis—who was giving his life to Young Ireland as chief writer of the *Nation* —for that journal's failure to notice *Brallaghan*. So sweet was Davis's response that even Kenealy admitted faults in his own work. But a few weeks later all was dark again as *Punch* criticized Kenealy's anonymous articles in the *Dublin University Magazine* concerning the Scottish poet Thomas Campbell. The latter appeared as mean and narrow, while Kenealy—not for the first time is such circumstances—applauded his own work. *Punch* berated the sickly egotism of the writer and the scandal of his pen.[18] To Shirley Brooks, one of his correspondents and future editor of *Punch,* Kenealy vowed his anger against 'that Jew pot boy', Mark Lemon, whom he presumed wrote the critique. Brooks said this was not so and advised his friend to avoid 'these infernal "private shindies" '.

Punch was acute in suggesting a morbid strain in Kenealy's life. The house in King Street was silent with the long, fatal illness of the mother, while Kenealy senior devoted himself to religious duties. Kenealy's puny efforts to win briefs brought little return. He showed more vigour in seeking a chair at the university college then in formation at Cork: he lobbied Sir Robert Peel and gathered testimonials, but without avail. He abused himself for idleness in words that suggest a manic-depressive tendency, and brooded upon the grimmer passages of his past. Telling Brooks of his erstwhile gaiety in London, the young recluse remarked that a certain way of overcoming first love was to take the girl to bed, 'as I well know': a grim hint of his attitude to sex.

Some brightness lifted the gloom. Kenealy's favourable review of the Flood biography brought friendship with its author Warden Flood, a grand-nephew of his subject. So he entered into the fairly high society of Flood's home outside Cork. Long, good letters passed between Kenealy and several English correspondents: Brooks, T. J. Ouseley (a minor poet, editor of a Shropshire journal), Aldborough Henniker (companion on the continental tour of 1843), and others. A local correspondent was John Windele, renowned for his studies of Irish antiquity. Appearances on circuit could be entertaining if not remunerative.

Above all remained the spur of ambition. It was two-edged, and Kenealy often smarted at his failure to fulfil youthful dreams; but no less did he still hope. Success at the bar, which might lead to the bench, was one ideal. Another way led to politics. Kenealy sometimes railed against his exile from England, indeed against his non-English birth, but Irish affairs offered some chance. Writer for the *Dublin Review* on one hand and the *Dublin University Magazine* and *Fraser's Magazine* on the other; admirer of Flood and O'Connell, while critic of Grattan and Irish demagoguery; unbeliever, yet Catholic fellow-traveller; romantic revolutionary and ardent self-seeker: Kenealy could follow any path with some consistency, none without some contradiction. Late in 1843 he not only courted the *Review* but hoped that Peel's continuing ascendancy would benefit himself 'as a loyal Papist'. In September 1844 he repeated that many Repealers were rascals, but endorsed their demand for an Irish parliament. Excitement was rising:

then hey! for the game of political ambition, which is the only game in the world worth playing, and which will be played in Ireland to an extent you dream not of. The people of this country I can tell you pant to be independent; they are loyal so long as you are at peace, and have a hundred thousand unemployed bayonets. The first hostile shot fired in Europe they will hail as a signal of their liberties; and the people led on by a host of young men filled with the mad but powerful spirit of the men who organized the French Revolution and revelled in the Reign of Terror will strike . . .[19]

Kenealy approved the temper of the Young England group in the House of Commons, and apparently felt some affinity with Young Ireland.

For the present Kenealy engaged in more practical affairs, with explosive effect. In mid-1845 he met O'Connell, and was proud to report the latter's compliments. (Evidently the Liberator had never learned who wrote the *Grattan* review.) Coincidentally he

received an approach from Father Theobald Mathew, leader of
the Irish temperance movement—a movement that eschewed formal politics but complemented Repeal by attacking the image of
Irishmen as feckless fools, incapable of self-government in every
sense. Mathew was a man of Cork and an associate of the Kenealy
family, having guided the second daughter into her vocation. Now
he asked Edward, 'my dear friend', to attend a special meeting of
the local temperance group. Kenealy accepted, for all his erstwhile
roistering; presumably he saw temperance as the liveliest social
force of the time and place.

Hence developed an Institute of Literature and Science,
affiliated to the temperance club. Mathew was president, but as
vice-president Kenealy was the guiding genius. His *Inaugural
Address,* given on 1 September 1845, dealt in conventional terms
with the power vouchsafed by knowledge.[20] Kenealy praised the
Catholic bishops' recent approval of Peel's scheme for establishing
university colleges in Ireland. Meanwhile the institute would be a
place where sectarian differences might dissolve and whence 'a
little Scotch prudence' might enter the Irish character. Kenealy
enthused over 'the senate house of England, that mighty congress
of the greatest minds on Earth', and presented oratory as Ireland's
best contribution to political skills 'notwithstanding the prover-
bial warmth of the Irish imagination and our Eastern brilliancy
of fancy'. He warned against use of this art in low demagoguery.
Mayor Richard Dowden, temperance supporter and Repealer,
took this as an insult. At a special meeting he moved Kenealy's
expulsion.[21] The factions raged, with Mathew attempting peace.
When Dowden found the numbers against him, he stamped out
'amidst deafening shouts from the Kenealyites'. The latter told
their hero that 'we are proud of having given our humble support
to the man whose genius we honor, and to whose kindness we are
so largely indebted'.[22] Among the institute's students was future
parliamentarian and writer, Justin McCarthy. He recalled that
the charismatic Kenealy 'perfectly dazzled us young fellows', who
found him 'fascinating and forcible'.[23]

Kenealy hungered for grander things. On 9 April 1846 he wrote
to Ouseley of a project

calculated if well carried out to achieve the two objects of immortal name or fame, and great temporal power . . . It is merely to
found a new religion which is to supersede all others. . . . I know
I have all the elements of success in me, and I don't despair of

triumphing yet. Indeed I am persuaded that I sometimes have revelations from the spheres on the subject.

Hints of such aspiration appear throughout Kenealy's earlier work. From childhood he had pondered on the infinite, and for almost as long had narcissist-dreamed of himself as superman. His study furniture, he said, included 'queer cabalistical instruments', aids to his study of alchemy.

For the present this was a by-way, which Kenealy soon passed. He graduated as Bachelor of Laws from Dublin and in June 1846 returned to London. This might have been the occasion of a daguerrotype which is his first photographic record. It concealed his right wall-eye but hinted at that aggressiveness which Kenealy's word-portrait of the time underplayed:

I am a small body, not at all frightful in appearance, but as grave and reverend-looking as a dean . . . Nature intended my face for a bishop's, the only character it presents being that of gravity and religion and deep thought . . . I wear gold spectacles, a white neckcloth and long coat, and I am mistaken everywhere for a clergyman.[24]

McCarthy hints at 'troubles' that might have forced this shift to London: possibly legal action with a doctor who had been treating Kenealy for venereal disease.[25] Anyway, the move's significance was small; although joining the English bar in May 1847 as a member of Gray's Inn (the least esteemed of the day), and giving some time to gaieties, Kenealy concentrated still on Irish politics. Discarding most of his earlier ambiguities, he strove to identify himself with Young Ireland and radical nationalism.

The first move in this campaign was to offer for Trinity's seat in the Commons in June 1847. Charles Gavan Duffy wrote afterwards that Young Ireland had its backing sought at this time by several candidates of apparent enthusiasm but dubious sincerity.[26] Kenealy he placed first in this class, his scorn encouraged by a letter from Father Mahony which attacked *Brallaghan* as a 'depraved collection of blasphemy' and Kenealy as seeking 'notoriety of any kind'. Mahony pointed to Kenealy's recent attack on Thomas Davis as a 'dog-faced demagogue'. Receiving support from neither Young Ireland nor elsewhere, Kenealy withdrew from the poll. Next he applied for membership of the Irish Confederation, vanguard of Young Ireland, while apologizing for his attack on Davis. On 29 July he received membership ticket num-

ber 4541 of the confederation. Kenealy became president of London's Davis Club, but Duffy still resisted him. The confederation
appointed a young barrister and parliamentarian, T. C. Anstey,
as Inspector General of the Repealers of England and Scotland,
so as to diminish Kenealy's standing; then his election to the
council of the confederation was opposed, as people referred to
his literary squabbles and other personal troubles. Of all this
Kenealy wrote to John Mitchel early in 1848, pledging support if
Mitchel would challenge the Duffy group, and offering to write
for his projected journal, the *United Irishman*. On the way
Kenealy argued about how Ireland might gain independence. A
Continental war could create conditions in which Irishmen might
win that boon by their own effort; otherwise, English support was
essential. Kenealy now hoped for the latter situation:

The Irish people in their present state of ignorance and mutual
distrust would not be fit for freedom achieved by a revolutionary
outbreak. I hope they will never try it, for if they failed they were
indeed undone; and should they succeed they would until educated and rescued from ignorance and bigotry be a curse to
Europe and to themselves.[27]

Mitchel replied in tepid tone. In February-March 1848 Kenealy
vainly floated himself as a Repeal candidate for a by-election in
the Kinsale electorate outside Cork.

Kenealy continued as president of the Davis Club in London
and so became involved in the turbulence of 1848. In April the
London chartists staged their demonstration, in July-August the
Irish nationalists attempted a rising. Kenealy afterwards told that
he had hovered on participating in the latter, and so might have
suffered the same sentence of transportation to Tasmania as did
other Irish leaders. London also had its trials, less dramatic but
revealing an affiliation between the two insurgent forces. In July
five rebels were charged, among them Francis Looney, secretary of
the Davis Club. Kenealy was defending counsel in his trial which
began on 8 July. Two months earlier he had withdrawn from
dining at his circuit's mess, and Looney's trial confirmed eccentricity in his professional behaviour. He later said that the association
with 1848 lost him 'respectable' business in London, but if so it
was probably his style more than the subject which was decisive.
Very early, Kenealy remarked that he had known Looney from
childhood; the judge said counsel must not give evidence; Kenealy

disagreed.[28] He stated that he stood at disadvantage, having heard 'that anything he might say upon the subject of the repeal of the union would be watched by the Attorney-General with lynx eyes, and that ulterior proceedings would possibly be taken against him'. The Attorney-General, who was prosecuting, denounced such aspersions, and the judge added his rebuke. Kenealy continued at length, antagonizing judge and counsel. Looney received two years on two separate charges. 'Very well, that will do', the prisoner laughed; a generation later he avowed himself a devotee of his erstwhile counsel.[29] Meanwhile Kenealy received an ode extolling his effort 'To crush injustice, perjury, and wrong'.

The government brought another batch of charges in September, and Kenealy again defended.[30] His client was William Paul Dowling, a portraitist of some ability and respectable Irish family. In association with chartists, Dowling had planned arson of such points as police and railway stations; the great day was to have been 16 August. Evidence revealed that within the Davis Club, Dowling and Kenealy had split, the latter having argued against extremism. Yet in court Kenealy argued with enough spirit to provoke rebuke for slandering the police. He alleged that government was increasing its armed forces so as to restrain free discussion at home, and in similar context he reviled the use of informers. In reply the Attorney-General scoffed at Kenealy's verbosity and pseudo-learning. Dowling received a sentence of transportation for life.

In late 1849 Kenealy tried again for the Commons—in Cork.[31] His address sought the Liberal-Repeal vote and told of his long-held conviction 'that Heaven has armed me with a Divine Mission . . . to work out the freedom of my countrymen'. A newspaper report said that 'he denounces, ridicules and defies his opponents with a *gaité de coeur*, pluck, pungency and exuberance . . . the nearest approximation to the O'Connell vein which has, since the departure of the Liberator, appealed to an Irish multitude'; McCarthy, now resuming acquaintance with Kenealy, saw him as brilliantly impressive still. Kenealy failed to arouse much response however, and soon retired, apologizing for the extremism of some assertions.

Since 1845 Kenealy had contributed to the reviews at diminishing rate. *Ainsworth's Magazine* published his most ambitious project to date, the novella *Edith Carleton*. The hero of this autobiographical fancy

was a strange, perhaps a wayward young man. Books were his
passion, poetry his divinity. He had the most thoroughly poetical
intellect of any one I ever saw. He looked at the whole world with
a fine and noble enthusiasm. He dreamed great dreams; he luxu-
riated in visions of the beautiful, and the grand, and the useful.

Concern for his future fame was another passion of Edgar Hyde,
albeit it jostled with contempt for the mundane world. Likewise
Edgar oscillated between a view of men as 'naturally enemies . . .
in a state of warfare with each other' and the belief that the
human soul at its brightest proved the existence of God, omnipo-
tent in his benevolence. Kenealy extolled the Catholic ideal, and
also introduced an interest in the Oriental religions—interest
hitherto suggested only in references to the Irish possessing
Eastern characteristics, but which was to develop into obsession.
Mixed with all this was a romance, but that diminished as the
writer's reveries grew, the story finally tailing into a non-end.
Much of Kenealy's poetry at this time was also heavily contempla-
tive. He kept up his speaking in tongues, going beyond western
Europe and the ancients to present work in Swedish, Bohemian,
Friesian and Guipuzcoan (Basque)! His longest essay was another
memoir, that of Laman Blanchard, who was also a member of the
London literary circle in about 1840. 'Charming and sympathetic',
Michael Sadleir wrote of this in 1938; 'what a master-hand was
Kenealy's at tributes to the minor dead!'[32] The essay indeed did
pay respect—mixed with condescension—to Blanchard, but a
more persistent theme was Kenealy's railing at the drudgery and
rancour of literary life. Kenealy still wrote for the *Dublin Review*:
of Prescott's *History of the Conquest of Peru,* he remarked that it
'not unskilfully' put together facts which everyone knew. His
knowledge of genealogy enabled him to correct John Burke's
Landed Gentry and to win an invitation to contribute to Burke's
journal, the *Patrician*.

Kenealy maintained other cultural interests, especially the
theatre. An actress, Anna Mowatt, enthused him and deepened his
interest in religion; Swedenborg now became an influence.
Writers, talkers, and artists of a little standing, were among his
acquaintances. Closest to him was Richard Birnie, who later won
some fame as an essayist in Melbourne, Australia. Kenealy could
hope yet to establish himself in the great world.

But 1850 brought cataclysm. On 15 February a child, Edward
Hyde, came before the magistrates of London's Guildhall; he

bore, said the *Times*, 'bruises of a most sickening character', the sight of which 'created a great expression of horror and disgust'.[33] A domestic claimed the boy and, under pressure, named his parent: he was Kenealy's love-child of 1843-4, and currently had been living with his father. Other newspapers reported the case yet more luridly than did the *Times*. Rumour alleged that the father had thrashed the boy. *Punch* forecast that if he should be guilty, 'we know of no process that can return the learned gentleman, sweet and wholesome again to the fraternity of barristers'.[34] The preliminary hearing was on 18 February; hissed by the crowd, browbeaten by the magistrates, Kenealy appeared in a nasty light. He was committed. At his trial in mid-May, evidence modified earlier reports; possibly the police were avenging Kenealy's charges in the Dowling case. Lord Chief-Justice Campbell emphasized the less damaging aspects of the situation and Edward Hyde himself averred that his father had often shown kindness and showered kisses, albeit losing temper at fibs and slowness in lessons. The jury found Kenealy guilty of common assault; Campbell sentenced him to one month's gaol. Having served this, Kenealy could not meet costs and therefore spent seven more weeks in prison.

The man went through hell. His memoirs raged especially against the early newspaper reports and the mob scenes at the Guildhall.[35] He saw the aldermen as exorcizing their status-envy: 'those low traders were glad to obtain a vulgar notoriety at my expense; a gentleman, a barrister in practice, a scholar of some reputation, and a writer of some name'. Years later a journalist recalled a current joke—'Lines on a Boy's Back by Dr Kenealy'—expressing precisely such vindictive jealousy.[36] Simultaneously, and to some extent consequently, Kenealy's family background shattered. His mother had died in January 1847. Thereafter his father became poorer and more eccentric; for a time he lived with Edward in London, but then set off in search of some monastery that might accept him. Frustrated in this, and grieved by his son's disgrace, he died in September 1850. Early in 1851 Annamaria Kenealy died, also in torment: she had been expelled from her convent, allegedly at Father Mathew's instigation.

The year 1850 had another, more ambiguous, significance in Kenealy's life. The *Dictionary of National Biography* gives that as the date of his earning a Doctorate of Laws, by implication from Trinity. Records do not confirm this award, then or ever. That

Kenealy would dare assume the title without warrant is scarcely more likely than that he could do so with impunity. Yet the possibility remains.

Kenealy struggled against his troubles. On his behalf a fellow lawyer, P. J. Nagle, wrote a pamphlet, *Parental Authority,* upholding the right of a father to punish and lauding Kenealy's 'universal celebrity' as a scholar. In prison Kenealy began writing his memoirs. On release he planned theological treatises which might 'change the very nature of the present religious world', and published an epic in verse, *Goethe: A New Pantomime.* The opening scene was Goethe's death-bed in Weimar, whence Mephistopheles led the poet's spirit on a tour of hell and the universe.[37] The prologue introduced the story as a pantomime with the moral that 'man's an ass', but the strongest mood was bitter despair. Among the targets for Kenealy's venom were priests, princes and lawyers:

> There the black and viperish lawyer
> Robs, protected by King Law;
> Widows, orphans, men, and infants,
> Daily fill his dragon maw.

Aspersions on wealth had the same sting:

> There the monied man grown fetid
> With the pride of wealth and state,
> Thanks his God so many people
> Yearly starve to make him great.

Another political theme, evoking better verse, was the nationalist cause of Europe's subject peoples. Kenealy spoke for Ireland:

> I too am of an isle whose emerald plains
> Have been thrice wet with heroic blood of men
> Who loved her, as Christ loved mankind, to death.
> The scaffold, dungeon, gibbet, gyve and stake
> Have not subdued us, nor our holy hate
> Of the oppressor.

The work's highest achievement was in creating a sense of the horrific, Kenealy again calling upon his own experience:

the base brood
Of those who ruled in human hells called jails,—
Policemen, warders, turnkeys, brotherhood
Of Beelzebub.

The length of the epic, its variety of forms, and also the verse it-self, created a force which imposes itself upon the reader. Prosi-ness, crotchets and obscurity out-balanced these virtues, but not too grossly. Scarce-concealed attacks on legal-literary persons again aroused Kenealy's friends to urge that he avoid thus adding to his enemies. Reviewers appear to have ignored the work. The *Dublin University Magazine* did so lest its notice of other versifiers suffer from 'the expression of unqualified astonishment which we could not restrain at the frequent bursts of power, splendour, and wit, which illumine this brilliant but detestable performance'.[38]

The child-beating case struck at Kenealy's career, assuring that he forever would fail the standards of that mid-Victorian profes-sional society to which he nominally belonged, and wherein he might have been happy to rest had opportunity offered. A weaker man might have withdrawn altogether; Kenealy was tough enough to stay. His sister's death brought some money, which he spent in furnishing chambers at Gray's Inn. He joined the bar on the Western, or Oxford, circuit, working chiefly in the county courts of Stafford and Shropshire. His diary echoed the old ambi-tion and egotism—as when noting refusal to register in the census of 1851—and he retained nerve enough to criticize bench and bar to appropriate authorities.[39] In November 1851 Kenealy married. His bride was Elizabeth Nicklin of Tipton, Stafford. The girl was but sixteen, and Kenealy had to persuade her into marriage, after very brief courtship. Later years were to show her capacity for a self-made career, and Kenealy depended on wifely support even more than do most men. The first child was born in April 1854 and eleven others followed over the next twenty years. This fecun-dity suggests that Kenealy was too passionate to heed his own precepts and experience as to the double-edge of sexual pleasure.

Professionally, the next years were humdrum when not difficult. Kenealy found no joy in the everyday life of the bar, and this period offered little but drudge work. The man's heart was with his books either at home or in the British Museum. Recollections tell of him as suffering ostracism because of the child-beating and 'other delinquencies'; as being 'the most unpopular man in the courts' in consequence of his extreme rudeness; as enjoying 'some request when a slashing speech rather than prudent strategy or scrupulous fairness was what a case required'. Yet the virtues of *Goethe* softened some colleagues towards him, and he returned to mess dinners.[40]

Kenealy's political ambitions still lived, and in the early fifties received some encouragement from Benjamin Disraeli. The pair had many points in common, although one was as sensitive to political and human realities as the other was oblivious. In January 1851 Kenealy wrote to Disraeli suggesting that Tories oppose the Whig government's proposal to outlaw the Catholic assumption of episcopal territorial titles. Thus the unnatural union of Whigs and Irish would end, and there flower 'the real spirit of old Toryism'. By this Kenealy seemingly meant social paternalism such as *Fraser's Magazine* and Young England had advocated. He presented himself as having influence among both people and priests of Ireland. Disraeli voted for the government's measure, but Kenealy persevered. On the creation of the Derby ministry in February 1852 he congratulated Disraeli on gaining the Exchequer: 'you are destined to triumph over all, and eventually become Prime Minister of England'. Later in the year he called for Disraeli to ally with the Tenant League men in the Irish party, whom he saw as genuinely concerned for reform unlike the rabble of the Irish Brigade. The Tories should abandon 'no popery' as they had protection, and 'cut the ground from under the feet of the Whigs and Radicals by promoting education, an ocean penny postage, libraries in towns, and social measures of improvement, a fair extension of the franchise'. The next letter fished for a job in India. Disraeli responded with a morsel—an invitation for Kenealy to contribute to the *Press,* a journal he was planning as a vehicle for progressive Toryism. Kenealy reacted by seeking a share in copyright, co-editorship, and scope to develop his Irish policy. Disraeli and the editor, Samuel Lucas, wanted Kenealy merely to write satirical verse. The association ended before the first issue appeared in May 1853, although Kenealy may have written some of its squibs. In September he again urged Disraeli to appeal through himself to 'the Irish who impelled by their hot Eastern blood, were ready to enrol themselves like Arabian fanatics under your banner twelve months ago'. Lucas advised Disraeli to be careful in answering: 'he *is* useless and may be dangerous'. Kenealy withdrew in anger, convinced that Lucas's

The Young Kenealy: from a daguerro-type made when aged about twenty-six

The Prime Kenealy

[A. Kenealy, *Memoirs of Edward Vaughan Kenealy LL.D.*]

Kenealy (*right*) and Disraeli
[A corbel on Chester Cathedral]

The Claimant—or his Tussaud Model? With ambiguity symbolic of the Claimant's mystery, Tussaud's themselves are unsure whether this photograph from their files represents man or model

Roger Tichborne: from a daguerrotype made at Santiago in 1853. The gap between this youth and the Claimant is that which the fantasy of the latter's supporters had to bridge

[D. Woodruff, *The Tichborne Claimant*]

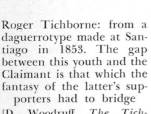

jealousy had thwarted Disraeli's goodwill and readiness to elevate him to parliament.[41]

A bizarre break from routine offered with the case Darby *v.* Ouseley, March 1856. Darby was a tide-waiter at Liverpool who brought an action against Kenealy's old friend, briefly editor of the *Liverpool Herald,* for charging that his membership of a Roman Catholic society for the conversion of England rendered him a traitor. Ouseley retained Kenealy, enticing him from the Western circuit. Darby offered to withdraw if Ouseley retracted; the judge urged this solution, but Kenealy refused, creating animosity. He called no witnesses, but instead gave an historical exegesis on Church-State relations. The judge interrupted, declaring that he would prohibit any 'great Protestant speech'. Following the verdict for Darby, Ouseley appealed for a new trial. Kenealy claimed that the judge's interruption had disturbed him. 'I don't think it would be very easy to stop you', responded the bench. Laughter in court; case dismissed.[42]

A few weeks later Kenealy appeared as junior counsel for the defence in one of the most sensational of all murder trials, that of William Palmer the medico-sportsman-poisoner of Rugeley, Stafford. So partisan was local feeling, the poor being Palmer's sympathizers, that the case was tried in London. The presiding judge was that same Lord Chief-Justice Campbell who had heard Kenealy's case. Then he had tempered justice; in Palmer's case his favour went to the prosecution, although he observed the proprieties. On 27 May Palmer was sentenced to death and he hanged at Stafford on 14 June. Kenealy played a very subordinate part in the trial itself, but was active in its aftermath. Palmer's sentence provoked not only his friends and family but also opponents of capital punishment at large to campaign for a remission. In consequence there appeared *A Letter to the Lord Chief-Justice Campbell,* nominally written by the Reverend Thomas Palmer, William's brother, but actually by Kenealy; Thomas Palmer soon disclaimed any connection, but presumably he authorized the use of his name. Kenealy began with appropriate emphasis on the dubiety of the scientific evidence and on past errors in capital cases, but soon deviated. You and your brother judge both showed prejudice, he told Campbell. The pressure you put on the jury destroyed the liberties of Englishmen. The absence of any right of appeal in criminal cases allowed that 'a wicked man may commit almost any conceivable crime upon the bench, and gratify his love of blood to the utmost without restraint or fear'.[43] Campbell's diary referred to this product of 'a blackguard barrister . . . ; for the sake of example he ought to be disbarred'.[44] Kenealy's autobiography repeated his strictures on Campbell, but affirmed Palmer's guilt. Meanwhile the capital abolitionists made their efforts through parliament, public meetings and the press. Respectability took its stance. The *Times* believed that no man had ever deserved execution more and that mercy to Palmer would be cruelty to the nation. The *Saturday Review* lamented that 'a party, fanatically or foolishly opposed to capital punishment, discreditably permitted itself to tamper with eternal justice'.[45]

The events of 1856 scarcely improved Kenealy's chances for conventional success. Perhaps in compensation, he determined eventually to publish his theological musings. Increasingly absorbed in this ambition he yet hankered for worldly prestige. In 1858 he returned to lobbying Disraeli, now back in office. On hearing a rumour that Disraeli planned to become Governor-General of India, Kenealy sought a post in his service. 'The glittering Orient dazzles my imagination and inspires my heart . . . but I am chained like a galley slave to the oar of a profession, which makes me indeed independent, but fails to fulfil the ardent longings of my spirit'.[46] More prosaically he cast for Disraeli's backing in further parliamentary venture, for a place as recorder or county court judge, or even as a circuit treasurer at £700 a year. In 1862 he hoped to stand for Stoke in the House of Commons, but withdrew—according to his later story—when the Liberal council there refused to back him.[47]

Yet Kenealy's position in about 1860 was less than desperate. As he said, his labours achieved independence. His diary referred to constant, admittedly extravagant, purchase of books, furniture, pictures: *Aut Caesar Aut Nullius* proclaimed his book-plate. Mrs Kenealy and the family lived at Portslade, near Brighton, whither Kenealy resorted as often as possible to court nature and to ponder his theology. The home appears to have been happy. Now too Kenealy resumed his busyness with the pen. The first fruit may have been a version of the Palmer trial in mock-classical Greek, which appeard in 1860.[48] That year Kenealy supplied the English translation to a Gaelic epic;[49] it was mundane, but witnessed some continuing association with his native land. More ambitious was a volume of *Prayers and Meditations,* issued anonymously lest knowledge of the author's absorption in theology lose business.

The work has not been seen, but the same or similar poems are extant.[50] Romantic verses, they speculate about the mysteries of the eternal and infinite, postulating that through communion with nature and scrutiny of ancient religions, man could understand God. Kenealy's letters to Disraeli mentioned work for the *Dublin Review* and law quarterlies. He submitted an item and subscribed his money for a memorial volume to the Consort— *Albert the Good* (1862), edited by W. T. Kime—but that horrendous collection omitted his verse. (He later told Disraeli otherwise:[51] was he bluffing, deluded, or just forgetful?)

Above all, Kenealy prepared a new edition of his poetry in two volumes: *A New Pantomime*, which presented *Goethe* in more articulate form, and *Poems and Translations*, a collection of other work of the past twenty years. The latter volume was meant to appear first, but some complication caused *Pantomime* to be published early in '63, and *Poems* almost a year later. If ever a reception was mixed, these volumes knew it. *Pantomime* had such a trouncing in the Presbyterian *Weekly Review* that Kenealy considered a libel action. The *Reader* found *Pantomime* weird beyond explication yet said of *Poems* that their author 'presents this infallible mark of a good writer, that he always rises with his subject and makes the felicity of his diction keep pace with the elevation of his sentiments'.[52] The reviewer noticed the unevenness of Kenealy's performance, as did the *Athenaeum* in a more critical notice. Yet no verdict is permanent. In 1874, when Kenealy was out of favour in literary circles, the *Gentleman's Magazine* published a critique of *Pantomime* which spoke of 'lines of exquisite beauty . . . the tenderest pathos and sweetness . . . moral beauty and vigour'.[53]

The volumes had interest beyond their verse. *Pantomime* bore dedication to Disraeli and *Poems* to Sir Alexander Cockburn, Lord Chief-Justice. The wording was florid, indeed sycophantic. Kenealy cultivated Cockburn's patronage with vigour and effect: 'the best wish I can make for him is that he may have his father's genius', wrote the judge in agreeing to stand godfather and give his name to Kenealy's fourth son, born in 1864.[54] (The earlier sons were Ahmed, Charlemagne and Maurice, honouring their father's spiritual and physical forebears.) For such occasions Kenealy used the Church of England: probably another indication of social climbing. In his preface to *Pantomime* Kenealy recognized that the work had puzzled many, but apologized not: 'for the Wise and

True and Learned it was written, and they alone can understand and appreciate it'. He advised the reader interested in his message to consult *Prayers and Meditations*. In introducing *Poems* Kenealy remarked that many of the newly published verses reflected his growing interest in the East and fulfilled his almost lifelong veneration of Britain's finest Orientalist, Sir William Jones. He finished by saying farewell to the poetic muse.

In the mid-sixties Kenealy appeared in several trials of national repute. Overall, they confirmed his reputation as a hard, wild fighter for lost causes. A variant arose in his association with the defence of two Fenian extremists in 1867. The employment of Kenealy reflected his pugnacity and perhaps even his work for Looney and Dowling in 1848. Early in the trial, however, an attempt was made at forcing Clerkenwell Prison and so releasing the prisoners. A bomb killed twelve and injured many others. Kenealy abandoned his brief, arguing that retention of a lawyer committed a client to the rule of law. Both the outrage and the withdrawal provoked excitement, debate over Kenealy's step becoming very heated. His career brightened when he became a Queen's Counsel early in 1868. For months he had badgered Disraeli to assist in winning this honour. 'This is a troublesome fellow', noted Disraeli; but he added 'must not altogether be neglected', leaving posterity to surmise just why he so felt.[55] Cockburn's patronage might also have helped. As a Q.C., Kenealy became a 'bencher'—committeeman, more or less—of Gray's Inn. The honour aroused protest from someone who recalled the 1850 case.[56]

Also in 1868, Kenealy sought parliament once more, standing for Wednesbury at the general election. His correspondence with Disraeli showed that he still cherished progressive Toryism: he urged that the government establish the Catholic Church in Ireland so as to win 'Poor Papist fanatic Paddy' for the Conservative party and undermine Irish militancy. 'Your ordinary demagogue is destroyed by going into parliament', he said. Dissenters and radicals would object, but they were hostile to Disraeli anyway.[57] At Wednesbury Kenealy stood as a 'people's candidate' with an appropriate grab-bag policy: secret ballot, retrenchment of armed forces, reduction of rates and taxes, national education and open entry to universities, uniform rail freights and penny carriages for all trains, protection for trade unions, better public amenities, justice for Ireland. 'I love the working man', he called in raucous voice. The legislation of 1867 had created Wednesbury as Britain's

largest single-member constituency, and the election was lively
enough to bring 300 policemen to town. The Liberals accused
Kenealy of being in Tory pay and attempting to split the radical
vote. The charge may have been true, but the Liberal won easily
enough.[58]

Two cases of 1869 again brought Kenealy into prominence, the
first involving defence of Frederick Hinson for murder of his de
facto wife. It was a crime of passion, responding to the woman's
intent of leaving Hinson for another man. Hinson was of prepossessing appearance and evident sincerity; the great popular interest in the case expressed itself primarily in sympathy for him.
Kenealy argued that Hinson had acted at the moment of learning
his lover's intention, that statement of this intention constituted
adultery, that ancient or common law accepted a man's killing
his wife found in adultery, and therefore that manslaughter was
the appropriate charge in this instance. The argument failed, and
agitation failed to stay Hinson's execution.

Kenealy's second great appearance of 1869 was as prosecuting
counsel in a charge of criminal conspiracy against the directors of
the Overend, Gurney finance house. This company, a cornerstone
of English business, had been recklessly ill-managed for years before a reconstruction in 1865 attempted to save the situation. The
attempt failed; and the crash on 9 May 1866, said the *Annual
Register,* created excitement in both London and the provinces
such as living memory did not know. Shareholders' shock and
grievance prompted the establishment of a 'defence committee'.
Dominant in this was one Adam Thom, a wealthy Scots-Canadian
resident in Aberdeen who ultimately was to publish books of in-
comprehensible mysticism. Thom and his followers cited the firm's
directors for criminal conspiracy. When the preliminary hearing
came before the Lord Mayor's court early in January 1869, public
feeling supported the prosecutors. Jubilation met the aldermen's
verdict that a prima facie case existed. Thom rejoiced in this blow
struck by 'a court of justice which, under purely popular auspices,
has just won, by universal acclaim, a place by the side of the professional tribunals of the country'.[59]

That, however, was the zenith. The case did not return to the
courts until the end of the year. Part of the delay resulted from
Thom's claim to fight the prosecution in person. The judge, Cockburn, refused him permission to do so. The resultant search for a
counsel ended only a few days before the hearing, with Kenealy.
In a case that demanded exact knowledge of a financial subject,

Kenealy was at his worst. His speeches were long, emotional, abusive and ineffectual. Cockburn, summing up, sneered that Kenealy 'notwithstanding his remarkable ability' should have argued as he did.[60] When the jury determined 'not guilty', the reaction in court was as enthusiastic for the directors as that at the Guildhall had been hostile. The voices of righteousness modulated accordingly. Whereas commentators earlier had cited the case as showing the need for a public prosecutor who might have acted against the company, now the *Economist* saw his putative role as being 'to save us from such vulgar exhibitions on behalf of the public as those of Mr Thom and Dr Kenneally'.[61]

Reproof of the clamour that the trial created, and that helped create the trial, became very insistent. Its most fluent expositor was W. F. Finlason, law reporter for the *Times* and author of a book on the case. The great object of English procedures, Finlason argued, was precisely to negate the influence of popular feeling on the administration of justice. 'Of late years a notion has unhappily arisen that this sacred principle does not apply where public interests or public questions are involved', the prosecution of Governor E. J. Eyre for alleged mass murder of natives in the West Indies being a notorious example. 'There is only one sense in which it might be said *vox populi vox Dei*', continued Finlason, 'and that is in the sense of *power*. In its dread portentous *power*, popular clamour is, for the time, terrible'.[62] The Overend, Gurney case illustrated the lesson; happily, in this instance truth had won.

The case hit Kenealy hard. To lose was no novelty, but the cheers for his opponents, the criticism of the press, must have echoed his agony of 1850. After the trial he and Thom quarrelled with their solicitors and junior counsel, R. D. Yelverton. At Thom's request, the benchers of the Middle Temple enquired into Yelverton's behaviour. Among the young man's defenders was Sir John Coleridge, the Solicitor-General and counsel for the Overend, Gurney directors. During the case Coleridge had sneered in correspondence at Kenealy's ineptitude, and now he criticized openly. Kenealy responded in letter and in verse, anonymously circulated:

> The long, lean lumbering, ugly Bald-pate drew
> His fetid life from Styx's stagnant spew;
> Satan himself gave shape uncouth and make
> To this new reptile of the Infernal Lake.

A hideous correspondence culminated with Coleridge declaring he would submit it to the judges.[63] Kenealy's relations with Cockburn also worsened. On 10 December 1871 the lawyer wrote to his erstwhile hero, tracing their growing enmity down to a clash on the previous day. He would never enter Cockburn's court again: 'I think you know that I have a soul sensitive in the highest degree; a soul of fire and pride that cannot brook aught like insolence or injustice'.[64]

Meanwhile Kenealy's pursuit of supernatural truth and joy had exploded into voluminous print. *Edward Wortley Montagu* pretended to be the subject's autobiography, but in fact was a three-volume novel embodying Kenealy's own musings and experience. Published in London in 1869, it met indifferent response, although an American edition followed. Between 1866 and October 1870 Kenealy issued a massive trilogy, *The Book of God*, which was sub-divided into *The Apocalypse, An Introduction to the Apocalypse* and *Commentary on the Apocalypse*. Some two years later appeared *Enoch, the Second Messenger of God* in two volumes. To find clear, consistent meaning in these volumes is impossible, but certain themes did recur.

Kenealy saw himself as a Messiah, twelfth in a chain reaching back into the ancient past. The first messenger had been Adam, the true author of the Apocalypse, and thereafter new messengers arose every 600 years, that being the mystic 'Naronic cycle'. Enoch was the second messenger, while Christ, Mohammed and Ghengiz Khan were Kenealy's immediate precursors, with Swedenborg in a sort of John the Baptist role. Adam's message had been vouchsafed to disciples whose teachings inspired the various mystery cults of the past; these cults had been strongest and closest to truth in the East. However the Druids were one Occidental variant of some authenticity, and all the great religions of the world, East and West, traced to the one divine source.

Kenealy's theology was amorphous. He believed in free will, and in a God of vengeance. The doctrines of atonement and justification by faith were monstrous, encouraging men to believe they could sin with impunity. Divine punishment expressed itself through the reincarnation of souls: a sinner of the present might well find himself a hyena or jackal henceforth. Not only animals operated in terms of spiritual force: all living matter was invested by God with his 'immortal essence' as he created the universe some 10 000 years ago. Darwinism was wicked and false. So was religion as conventionally taught, especially in the West where the terrible influence of Paul had corrupted Christianity. Priests and rabbis had a vested interest in maintaining falsehood, and were evil alike. The Old Testament was a mendacious hotch-potch.

Kenealy's sources would take a lifetime to trace, and on his death-bed the researcher probably would have to hypothesize that invention played some considerable part. The *Apocalypse,* to take the simplest case, bore similarity to the conventional version, but passages adapted from the Old Testament appeared indiscriminately, and Kenealy's own message overlaid all. To determine the books' sincerity is a teasing problem. They sometimes appear a mighty linguistic leg-pull. Scores of pages rambled over transpositions, textual comparison and verbal analysis, while references ranged from the most abstract to the most prosaic. Kenealy's letter to Ouseley in 1846 suggested calculation, if not chicanery, in his Messianic mode. Yet the passion and vigour of his writing persuade acceptance of its good faith. Maybe Kenealy convinced himself as he wrote.

The scriptures delivered opinions on contemporary society. Kenealy believed England to be uniquely wretched. 'Our political system, which accumulates all the wealth in the coffers of the rich, while it makes the poor every day poorer, will end one day in a volcano of fire, of blood, and ruin'.[65] In consequence of ill-government, moral evil flourished. Kenealy was more than Victorian in his horror-fascination with sex. He harped upon infanticide, seeing it as the ultimate horror inflicted by poverty. Civilization itself seemed to breed vice. 'Sin exists everywhere; adultery is the fashion; seduction is universal; prostitution pollutes every street; half our surgeons derive their income from abortion'.[66] The degradation of women to serve male sexuality was a feature of the Paulite West. European imperialism, based upon the falsehood of Western superiority, was another fulfilment of the more horrendous prophecies of the Apocalypse. Britain was especially to blame, but the United States would emulate her in 'cruelty, spoliation, selfishness, and superstition' just as domestic evils there already outdistanced those of the Old World.[67]

What did the future hold? The day would yet come for the disparate sections of God's church to unite as one flock under one shepherd. Hitherto the initiated had been reluctant to declare this faith, recognizing that 'thousands of fanatics or imposters would arise, every one of whom would lay claim to the mystic character of the promised Messiah . . . Men of vast ambition and towering intellect would usurp the name, would mislead mankind, and wrap the earth in turmoil'. So the faithful waited until one should appear whom instinctively they recognised as leader. Kenealy did not publish his own name as author, but the text pointed to him as the new Messiah and supplied a paean of welcome:

> Hail thou who art Parasu Rama,
> In the golden plains of beauty;
> The chosen child of lightning and of truth;
> Long have I looked for thine arrival.
> Hail thou who are Imaum Mahidi,
> Fiery-cinctured by the Word of Heaven:
> Long have I looked forth from the mountains,
> To behold the sunlight of thine advent.

How different ran Kenealy's everyday life. His short, stumpy figure suffered scorn and failure within the legal profession; when his harsh, rasping voice achieved a national audience, it seemed always on the losing side. His religious books, sold at however low a price (ten shillings for the two massive volumes of *Enoch*), made no impact, popular or scholarly. 'For them I have sacrificed and indeed have lost everything'.[68] Patrons had failed, illness was constant, and his brood increased. On 21 March 1873 at about one o'clock this Messiah without a following received a call from Lord Rivers inviting him to act as defending counsel in the forthcoming criminal trial of the Tichborne Claimant.

2

THE TICHBORNE CAUSE

ROGER TICHBORNE WAS BORN in 1829 into an old and wealthy family. His uncle was the eighth holder of a baronetcy that dated back to the seventeenth century. The family's seat was in Hampshire, a handsome exemplar of landed solidity. An idiosyncrasy was the family's membership of the Roman Catholic Church; Roger's immediate background also was peculiar in that his mother, Henriette Felicité, was the illegitimate child of an English Seymour and a French Bourbon Conti. She abhorred the Tichborne family, her husband almost as much as the rest, and spent most of her time in Paris. Young Roger became a victim of these circumstances, his parents squabbling over his education and allegiance. The mother won most of the battles until 1845 when Roger sailed for England and the Catholic school, Stonyhurst. In that year the eighth baronet died, to be succeeded by his younger brother, Edward (who had earlier assumed the surname of Doughty); as Edward had no sons, Roger's father and he (as elder son) became likely heirs. On leaving Stonyhurst Roger prepared for the army and in 1849 took a junior commission with the 6th Dragoon Guards (the Carabineers). He served in Ireland until 1852 and then briefly in Canterbury before resigning his commission.

In these years Roger became involved in family matters, despite his mother. Vacation and leave passed with relatives; in consequence romance developed between Roger and his cousin Katherine Doughty—born in 1834—the daughter of the ninth baronet. The girl's parents shunned the match: as a potential husband, Roger had several flaws, including fondness for liquor, a yearning to see the world, and a moody disposition. He further angered his uncle by obstructing the reorganization of family property. In February 1852 Sir Edward forbade the couple seeing one another, but soon all agreed that marriage was ultimately possible if Roger changed his behaviour.

In December 1852 Roger resigned his commission and prepared for foreign travel. He sailed on 1 March 1853 from Le Havre for Valparaiso where he arrived on 19 June. The next ten months passed in South American travels, including a trip across the Andes to Buenos Aires. Thence Roger moved to Rio de Janeiro. His money ran short as liquor consumption ran high. On 20 April 1854 Roger took passage for Kingston on a ship named *Bella*. It disappeared, evidently with the loss of all aboard. The incident was part of a paroxysm in Tichborne affairs. Sir Edward died in March 1853, and Roger's father succeeded. Family quarrels raged, with the new Lady Tichborne as cantankerous as ever. For years she had feared some catastrophe befalling Roger, but declined to believe that he had drowned with the *Bella*. This itself added further bitterness to relations with her husband, even until his death in June 1862. The baronetcy then went to Roger's younger brother Alfred, recently wed to Teresa, daughter of the house of Arundel with which the Tichbornes had already intermarried. Alfred was remarkably profligate. His mother, now Dowager, responded with yet more ardent hope of Roger's survival. In 1863 she placed advertisements throughout the world's press in hope of contacting her son.

In October 1865 one such advertisement sent back an echo that became the mighty roar of the Tichborne case. Its origin was Wagga Wagga, a country town in southern New South Wales, Australia, more than 500 kilometres from Sydney. A local man known as Tom Castro claimed to be Roger—or at least he accepted the speculation of William Gibbes, a solicitor, that this was so. Castro was a butcher, considerably in debt; he had recently married Mary Ann Bryant, an illiterate girl of second-generation Australian birth, a washerwoman, and already the mother of another man's child. Gibbes wrote on Castro's behalf to Arthur Cubitt of Sydney, agent for the Dowager; Gibbes wrote to her himself; and he persuaded Castro to do so also. The letters added to another spasm of family drama: in February 1866 Alfred died and in May his wife bore a son, the twelfth baronet. In the interim, Mary Ann Castro also gave birth, to a daughter.

Ponderously, events carried Castro, 'the Claimant', back across the world. In June his entourage left Wagga Wagga for Sydney, in September Sydney for Panama, thence to New York for an extended spell; not until Christmas Day did it reach London. The Claimant engaged as his solicitor John Holmes, a youngish man of unknown background. The two went to Paris on 10 January, where the Dowager recognized the Claimant as her son. But already the Tichborne family had begun to join in repudiation of him. The matter first reached the courts in July-August 1867, in a Chancery dispute over the claim. Over three days the Claimant elaborated his story of the years from 1854. The *Bella,* he said, had indeed sunk, but two lifeboats escaped. Another vessel, the *Osprey,* had rescued one boat's passengers, including himself, and disembarked them at Melbourne, Victoria, in July 1854. There he had found employment on a cattle station in Gippsland, eastern Victoria, and had taken the name, Castro, of a family he had met in Chile. He remained in Gippsland for four or five years. Then followed odd-jobbing, droving, gold-mining and mail-riding in Victoria and southern New South Wales. From early 1864 he had been settled in Wagga Wagga.

The Australian chapter of the saga drew the lawyers' attention. From early in 1867 both sides put sleuths to work there. They soon made suggestions that formerly the Claimant had the name of Arthur Orton, and as such arrived in Hobart, Tasmania, in April 1853. Further research indicated that Orton left Tasmania for Gippsland late in 1855, that the Claimant wrote to the Orton family from Wagga Wagga in April 1864, and that on the very night of his arrival in London from Australia he sought Orton's sisters in Wapping, the London dockside suburb where their father had been a butcher of modest prosperity. Later, Orton was found to have spent June 1849 to February 1851 in Chile. A fundamental of the Tichborne family's case became the identity of the Claimant as Orton. Against this, the defence argued that Orton and Castro had known each other from Gippsland to Wagga Wagga, and that ties between the two only bespoke their intimacy. The Orton question dominated the next legal proceedings: commissions of enquiry authorized by Chancery in both Chile (late 1868) and Australia (middle months of 1869). In Chile the focus of attention was the Castro family, with whom Orton had lived and whose name the Claimant had adopted. Language and cultural barriers hindered the commission, but at least its proceedings filled out Orton's biography. In Australia the balance of testimony fell against the Claimant, but there was ample confusion and counter-evidence.[1]

Events in Britain deepened the enmity of the contenders. In November 1867 the family hinted at compromise: that the Claimant be accepted on condition that he grant £50 000 to the infant baronet. The offer appeared a signal of weakness, and the Claimant spurned it.[2] His cause suffered in March 1868 with the death of his outstanding witness and financial support, the Dowager. Each side suspected the other of having caused her death. Her funeral at Tichborne was grotesque, family and Claimant jostling for precedence. The lawyers fought with every weapon and rancour.

Not until 11 May 1871 did the root issue come before the courts.[3] In this civil action the Claimant sought to eject the lessee of Tichborne House; paradoxically, the gentleman concerned, Colonel Franklin Lushington, supported the plaintiff's cause. The judge was Sir William Bovill, Chief-Justice of the Common Pleas, a man of average ability. He sat in Nisi Prius before a special jury: special in that its members had to own substantial property. Chief counsel for the Claimant was William Ballantine, whose reputation then stood high; higher, probably, than it deserved. His junior, Hardinge Giffard, was to rise in stature, ultimately to become Earl of Halsbury, Lord Chancellor. Leading for the defence was a yet more distinguished pair, John Duke Coleridge and Henry Hawkins. Coleridge, still Solicitor-General in W. E. Gladstone's government, was able, rational, superior, ambitious. Hawkins was the average sensual man, extrovert in a rather noxious fashion, yet with the knack of presenting his case as alone worthy of consideration. The Tichborne case proved too much for all the lawyers involved in it.

The civil proceedings lasted until early March 1872. That duration was fantastic, and so were many other aspects. Ballantine opened with various old associates of Roger who accepted the Claimant: officers and other ranks of the Carabineers, residents of the neighbourhoods where Roger had spent his English sojourns, random friends and acquaintances. The last group included A. J. W. Biddulph, Roger's second cousin and the only member of the family known to stand for the Claimant, and Anna Mary Braine, governess to Katherine Doughty in about 1850. In cross-examining, Hawkins and Coleridge strove to indicate that the witnesses had little knowledge of Roger, or were exaggerating their conviction, or were responding to the coaching of the Claimant's organizers. On the fourteenth day appeared the Claimant himself. He gave evidence to Giffard for more than four days, again telling his alleged adventures. Drama—albeit tedium also—came with Coleridge's cross-examination. Day after day he niggled at the Claimant. Some points were more important than others, especially that concerning 'the sealed packet'. On his departure from Britain for South America Roger had left this packet with Vincent Gosford, agent for the family and his own close friend. Gosford said that it held Roger's vow to erect a chapel at Tichborne should he ultimately marry Katherine. Now, in cross-examination, the Claimant said that it spoke as to his seduction of her in mid-1852. Later the Claimant added that the packet also referred to the cousins' secret marriage.

Even with the ending of the cross-examination, the tempo scarcely quickened. The time had come for the courts' summer vacation and, after much discussion, the full spell was taken. Then Ballantine continued with his witnesses. One was F. J. Baigent, antiquarian and genealogist, absorbed in the history of the Tichborne family and a virtual courtier in its service before 1867. Even more striking was Andrew Bogle, a West Indian Negro who had served the Tichbornes for decades before migrating to Sydney in the fifties; there he had met the Claimant en route from Wagga Wagga to Britain, and remained in his train until death. In the New Year Coleridge opened with a massive presentation of the family's case, stressing the weaknesses of his opponents' submissions and exaggerating the failure of the Claimant under cross-examination. Coleridge's opening witnesses spoke especially of Roger having been tattooed. This was a surprise development and in its introduction the family seems to have been guilty at least of craft. Ballantine and Giffard were by this stage not receiving payment, and the former especially was defeatist. The jurymen doubtless were still more exhausted. On 4 March they declared that they had heard evidence enough. Ballantine responded with a 'non-suit', that is, withdrawal of the plaintiff's case. This avoided an outright defeat, but Bovill declared that the Claimant had perjured himself and that the Crown therefore should prosecute. On 7 March followed arrest and imprisonment in Newgate. The Crown secured true bills charging both perjury, on two separate counts, and forgery.

The next year broadened the case, as the Claimant presented himself as the victim of malice in high places. On 25 March he issued from Newgate an 'Appeal to the British Public'. This called for support and money; a defence committee would mobilize all offerings. The Claimant won bail, but only on appeal and against the plea of Coleridge, now Attorney-General. On release the Claimant began a tour of the country which succeeded in remarkable manner. While the Claimant's cause thus brightened, his advisers found difficulty in employing counsel. Relations with Ballantine were poor; Giffard was none too keen. Other barristers declined. Then Serjeant W. C. Sleigh accepted, but soon quarrelled with his clients. Nevertheless he felt that Kenealy's acceptance of the brief offended protocol. 'If Sir Roger Tichborne will not have you for his Counsel, why should I force him to do so', came Kenealy's response. The Claimant joined in the roundabout of recrimination.[4]

Maybe more Victorian Britons felt more interest in the Claimant than had so many people in any one individual before. At the very beginning the *Wagga Wagga Express* boomed the local boy's story, and excerpts from that journal appeared throughout Europe. British newspapers gave the affair considerable notice from its earliest days, so that when the Claimant left for Paris in January 1867 numbers gathered at London Bridge to see him. At the Chancery hearings a few months later, crowds pressed their gaze and persons onto the Claimant. Ballantine objected: 'I never saw such a scene; it is more like what one hears of as taking place in an American court than in an English Court of Justice; it is perfectly scandalous'. Such episodes as the birth in June 1867 of an heir to the Claimant, and the Dowager's death, sustained excitement. On 1 February 1870 the *Echo* declared that by now the case was becoming stale, 'everybody' having pondered its mysteries 'a thousand times'. If ever a write-off was premature, this was it.

The civil case brought a new boom. 'The world was divided this year into the believers and the unbelievers', declared the *Annual Register* of 1871 in review of the case; 'we know as we write that no jury's verdict will ever set the vexed question at rest'. To the court thronged masses, including the Prince and Princess of Wales, the Emperor of Brazil, the visiting emissaries of the King of Burma. To sight the Claimant became an excitement of London life. Newspapers gave long reports: the *Illustrated London*

News, for example, establishing a regular weekly column on its progress. Bovill bemoaned his receipt of hundreds of anonymous letters. The success of the Claimant's tour of 1872 reflected and continued the story.

The case became one of the institutions of the country; comment upon it the stock of everyday talk. One example was the popularity of catch-phrases derived from the suit. In his cross-examination Coleridge prefaced many of his questions with 'Would you be surprised to hear', hoping thus to force the Claimant either to admit ignorance of Roger's early life, or to show it by failure to set the incident in context. The phrase became a preface for the most conventional of remarks; thus, 'Would you be surprised to hear that it's a fine day', spiced meteorological conversation with modish wit.[5] John Bright's parrot learned the phrase, and popular song took its chance:

> Would it surprise you to hear,
>   Though now big, you are really small?
> Would it surprise you to hear
>   That you never were born at all?

This continued for fourteen verses. 'Just like Roger' was another phrase of contemporary appeal. *Judy,* a comic paper, especially played with this expression; 'So Like Roger' was the caption for a cartoon spread which showed him 'As a tattoed Savage, in a Wagga-Waggy mood' and 'As a Jolly Butcher-boy in "Hostray-lier" '.[6] When the Adelphi Theatre presented a burlesque on the case immediately after its completion, 'Just Like Roger' was the chosen title. Other catch-phrases were 'No Tich', meaning 'enough of the case' and 'Wagga Wagga guards' or 'Tichborne's Own' for the Carabineers.[7] At least one baby took the nickname, 'Tich', for his chubby resemblance to the Claimant.[8]

There were numberless points at which the case provided public entertainment. 'Theatrical managers, authors of burlesques and pantomimes, singers of topical songs, and clowns, what would you have done without your Claimant', asked *Fun* in March 1872. H. G. Clarke & Company of Covent Garden, manufacturers of parlour games and cardboard cut-outs, issued various comic books of sixteen sketches each, presenting aspects of the case; regard for truth was spasmodic, but their black and white simplicity retains charm and effect.[9] Alphabets, anagrams and conundrums, all took

Kenealy in Caricature
[*Vanity Fair*, November 1873]

'The Westminster Tragedy'
A popular cartoon of February 1874
[E. V. H. Kenealy, *The Trial at Bar of Sir Roger C. D. Tichborne*]

'The Bleeding Heart of Dr Kenealy'
The Trial's caption goes on to describe Kenealy 'with his heart ripped out of his body, and the Judges preparing to dash his brains out with an iron mace, and to flagellate him with their Fury-whips'
[E. V. H. Kenealy, *The Trial at Bar of Sir Roger C. D. Tichborne*]

fantastic inspiration from the case. Photographs of participants had much the vogue later enjoyed by portraits of sportsmen and film stars. The litigation gave material for Arthur Sketchley to produce two more of his Mrs Brown monologues in the mass-selling Yellow Book series.

Epecially interesting was the representation of the case in popular balladry. This was one of the last spasms of activity in the genre, which began to decline from about 1850 after three or four vigorous centuries. The sheets were in traditional form: crude typography, rough and often irrelevant illustrations. Most of the extant London ballads hailed from the Disley Press, St Giles, always prolific in such output. Adding to the volume were Liverpool and Manchester at least. The words were sung to popular tunes like 'Perhaps She's on the Railway' and 'The Flying Trapeze'. Many ballads made little sense, but rather expressed that fun-fantasy which characterized the comics and conundrums:

> Oh did I not stand it well,
>   Against the rum old codgers,
> But never mind my boys,
>   I yet shall be Sir Roger.
> And when I have a son,
>   He shall be a gentleman of Tichbourne
> He shall have horses, pigs and cows,
>   Yes, the glorious Sir Roger Tichbourne.
>
> Oh! did they not rail at me,
>   I am sure they did like fury,
> I could swallow all the wigs,
>   Counsellors, Judge and Jury,
> Well I suppose awhile
>   In quod I must be stopping,
> And when I get discharged,
>   I'll have a butcher's shop in Wapping.[10]

'Just Like Roger' was far from the only dramatic representation of the case. The *Pall Mall Gazette* remarked in March 1872 that whereas the press necessarily had refrained from prejudical comment, the stage had known no such control. 'The Chamberlain, it is true, forbade all reference to the Claimant and his affairs in the Christmas pantomimes, but as the clowns were faithful to their old custom of saying and doing more than was set down for them, the results of his lordship's prohibition were inappreciable'. W. B. Donne, the Lord Chamberlain's examiner of plays, exorcized reference upon reference to the case, even 'Australia' becoming a forbidden word;[11] nevertheless, as the *Gazette* said, censorship didn't stop everything. At Hanley a melodrama, 'The Lost Heir', presented the case ending as Arthur Orton appeared incarnate before the court. At the Britannia Theatre's pantomime 'the Claimant' wore an india-rubber nose, at one point stretched right across the stage, which proceeding 'the Attorney-General' described as 'pulling the long bow': this so excited three spectators one night that their laughter provoked a riot.[12] From Paris came reports of *Le Procès Tichborne,* and Neapolitans later enjoyed *La Causa Ticciborni.* A secondary effect of this art-form was the production of mock playbills, full of puns and whimsy: 'Sir J. D. Coleridge, a man of few words, who "Would you be surprised to hear" is like Othello, *a tawny general*'; 'Miss Braine, who, though a Spinster, has some *little Brains* of her own'; 'Lady Tichborne and her False Hair'; 'The Carabineer Band of Lyres', appearing at the 'Lies-see-'em'.[13]

Representation sometimes took more static form. China figure-ware presented the Claimant in several variants. Dinner sets and clay pipes bore his face, while toys were made in his image. French interest showed again in the production of plaster figurines of major personalities.[14] The Claimant won a stand in Madame Tussaud's waxworks: preparation of his model, late in 1871, took place at his own residence, not in Tussaud's galleries, as was normal. On display from December, it attracted unusually, if not uniquely, large crowds. The Claimant dressed the figure from his own wardrobe.[15]

Why did the case cause such a stir? A mystery—and this was a mighty one—will always attract; so will stories of life among the upper classes; so will contemplation of the human memory and mind. Contemporaries often referred to the case as 'romance', both the *Times* and the *Saturday Review* later suggesting that the Claimant himself had been encouraged in his fantasy by indulgence in novel-reading. The returning wanderer and the prodigal son are recurrent figures throughout literature, just as imposters and claimants have evoked fascination throughout history. The Tichborne case offered other characters, who transcended models of permanent delight: Bogle, the faithful coloured servant; Baigent, the nincompoop intellectual; Miss Braine, the virago spinster-governess; Mary Ann Bryant, the girl of humble heart who (almost) won a coronet. The Claimant's Australian life contributed especially to 'romance'. Whether Orton or Tichborne, he was an archetypical outback worker: station-hand, gold-digger, rouseabout, mailman, with a whiff of bushrangery and violence. This was the career-line that Australian romantics were to glorify, using it as the core of national mythology, 'the Australian Legend'. Outback life has always been the aspect of Australia of greatest interest to the outside world. The Claimant and his supporters stressed the idea of Australia as barbaric, strange, mystic, thus explaining the change of Roger Tichborne of Hampshire into Tom Castro of . . . Wagga Wagga. Those euphonic syllables clinched the theme: anything wonderful could have happened there, something wonderful must have. 'Wagga Wagga' became a shout that hailed the Claimant in the streets; a watcher at the courts was heard to mutter 'Wagga Wagga' as he slept; and an inventor offered 'The Wagga-Waggagraph: a patented speaking indicator, for carriages'.[16]

A corollary of the case's romantic quality was its appeal for men of letters. Charles Reade, who had already written on Australian themes, was first to exploit the case, his *Wandering Hero* appearing as a serial in the *Graphic* during 1872. George Eliot found a day at the civil hearing 'of great interest',[17] while Edward Fitzgerald thrilled to the reading of its daily accounts. Mark Twain, then in London, also became engrossed; years later, he included Wagga Wagga in his Australian itinerary. A. C. Swinburne and G. M. Hopkins were other enthusiasts. Coral Lansbury's study, *Arcady in Australia: The Evocation of Australia in Nineteenth-century English Literature* specifically recognizes that the Claimant's story accorded with the image of Australia that Dickens, Lytton, Reade and others presented to their readers: the image, that is, of 'Arcady' where glorious nature returned man to pristine innocence.[18]

Sex was a further ingredient that ensured the case's fascination. The alleged seduction of Katherine Doughty would have had all the greater impact in that by 1871 she was Lady Radcliffe, a wife and mother of utter respectability. More recherché was the story —not advanced in evidence in 1871-2, but widely told—that final evidence in the Claimant's favour was an oddity of his genitals, the penis totally retracting. Stories of the Claimant's lustiness, even the slang usage of 'Roger' and the onomatopoeic suggestions of 'Wagga Wagga', all strengthened the sexual theme, which was most evident in the constant, if mild, bawd of the ballads. 'Old Jolly Roger' included such verses as:

> He kiss'd his cousin once or twice,
> Of course its naughty, but its nice,
> He was cast away like Robinson Crusoe,
> It was not right for him to do so.
>
> Let's hope like Cambridge he will win, sir
> To beat him now would be a sin, sir,
> He fed on birds, and whales blubber,
> Yet he was known by his own mother.
>
> She swore to her child, the rightful heir
> How she knew will make you stare,
> She stript him of course, she'd not neglect it,
> She found the strawberry where she left it.[19]

The middle stanza involved yet another of the case's qualities, its function as sport and contest. Several ballads developed affiliated themes, such as 'Roger, or not Roger, or, the Race for the Tichborne Sweepstakes'. Perhaps the most elaborate cartoon provoked by the case was a double-folio nicely-tinted depiction of 'The Hampshire Hunt', showing the Claimant just ahead of his pursuers. Another, 'The Tichborne Handicap', showed him astride Ballantine while the infant heir jockeyed Coleridge, and in 'The Cleverest Jockey of the Day', the Claimant was about to mount 'Gullibility'. Life followed art when one owner of the day named a horse 'Tichborne'.

The Claimant's person added much to the sporting theme. His appetite for liquor and food was as great as for women, and equally notorious. A later account of his weekly consumption was thirteen pints [more than seven litres] of spirits. Presumably he was at least half drunk most of the time. Still more obvious was his bulk: this developed in the early years of the claim, carrying him to twenty-seven stone [171 kilograms]. The 'Old Jolly Roger' refrain drew some of its inspiration from his size. The Claimant was a fine sportsman: especially in the gentlemanly arts of shooting and fishing. He used the former skill by entering, and usually winning, shooting matches held in conjunction with his appeal to the country. Henry Labouchere's description of the man's voice fitted this context: 'He speaks in that low, wheezy tone which is peculiar to those who have had much to do with horses, and generally before commencing a sentence, he pants like a seal'.[20]

The Claimant was the supreme character, the ultimate focus of romance. Atop his obesity and alcoholism were other illnesses, including venereal disease. Supporters often feared for his life; yet he survived all. What went on in that mind; what was the history of that flesh? How could Arthur Orton know so much of Roger Tichborne's early life; how could the true heir know so little? If genuine, had he undergone such experience in Australia as almost to create a new man in the frame of another? If false, what balance of personality enabled him to persist, and even to impress, while appearing contemptuous and bored at the whole proceedings?

Study of support for the Claimant, as distinct from interest in the case, can begin with recognition that by the end of the civil hearing, respectability had largely decided against him. 'Largely' is a necessary qualification: of 'respectable' people already mentioned, Fitzgerald knew not what to think, J. R. Tussaud found the Claimant full of suave gentility, and Labouchere thought his manners better than the average. His witnesses included Sir T. C. Constable, a Yorkshire squire, and several Carabineer officers. After the non-suit, the Junior Gun Club still resolved against expelling 'Sir Roger'. Examples of such sympathy continue to the present. Douglas Woodruff, born of the high bourgeoisie and a Catholic scholar of distinction, inclines towards the Claimant, stressing that vested interest, class allegiance, and emotion played ample parts in determining respectability's stand.

However, that stand remains the significant fact. The *Times, Morning Post, Punch*, and the great bulk of the press, scorned the man and his friends. As early as February 1872 Disraeli wrote of the Claimant as 'the most infamous imposter since Titus Oates'.[21] Bovill, with all his mediocrity, probably expressed the consensus of the ruling-professional class in calling for criminal trial of the Claimant, and that the government responded to his call speaks for itself. Similarly, the special jury represented Everyman of property. As censor, W. B. Donne upheld established order: in censoring Tichborniana he reflected the attitude that the case did involve, and even threaten, established order.

To some extent a consequence of respectability's stand, but

transcending it, was popular support for the Claimant. Some ordinary folk wagered against the Claimant, some of the posters, cartoons, conundrums, laughed at him, but these qualifications were minor. Cheers always outdid jeers; ballads, more expressive of opinion that the other ephemera, sometimes were cynical but never condemned the Claimant. The class confrontation on the case was as sharp as the historian is ever likely to find. Popular support might trace back to the earliest days of the Claimant's return to England. On 5 January 1867 Vincent Gosford badgered the Claimant at his hotel, telling the landlord to beware lest his bill never be paid. An attending waiter afterwards said 'that if he had possessed the money he would have cheerfully lent it . . . so satisfied was he that the Claimant was a gentleman in every sense of the word'.[22] At the Dowager's funeral, so Holmes claimed, a crowd of five hundred expressed sympathy and recognition: certainly many of the Tichborne tenantry, and local people at large, rallied to the Claimant. In retrospect, the *Times* saw public opinion as operating in the Claimant's favour from 1868 or 1869; the *Nonconformist* pushed back to the Chancery case, saying that it had 'seized hold of the imaginations of imaginative people'.[23] The civil hearing gave vent and focus for this opinion. Crowds not merely gathered but applauded from June 1871; one report put their numbers at five thousand and commended their appearance.[24]

Beyond reasonable doubt, the spontaneity and force of these demonstrations, rather than any pre-ordained scheme, prompted the Claimant and his advisers to summon popular backing. His 'Appeal to the British Public' from Newgate said that only with reluctance did he so proceed; his sole hope of achieving 'justice and fair-play' was to call for public aid against the resources of government. After release on bail, applauded by a waiting concourse, the Claimant wrote again to the press: 'To whom I am indebted for my release? To the British public!'[25] From his first public meeting the Claimant showed demagogic capacity: kissing babies, waving to pretty girls, making short, extravagant speeches, all of which evoked laughter and enthusiasm. His supporters wore coloured rosettes, and bands played in welcome and farewell. The *Spectator* asserted that the Claimant would easily win an election for national President.[26]

Subscription lists and news items agreed that 'workmen and such like' gave generously to the 'Appeal'.[27] Group efforts were

frequent: from Huntley and Palmer's, for example, and the Pitt
Press, and non-commissioned officers of F Battery, 11th Brigade,
Royal Artillery. Cabmen—probably more indicative of opinion
even than their taxi-driver successors—were conspicuous. Of similar but greater import were publicans, and their contribution to
support for the Claimant is the most telling evidence of its popular nature. The trade's paper, the *Morning Advertiser,* vehemently
upheld his cause. John Hotchkiss, licensee of the Farmer's Arms,
Old Kent Road, used its columns to propose that collection boxes
labelled 'The Tichborne Defence Fund' be put in 'the various
public and private establishments in the metropolis',[28] and this
did become general practice. At a mighty meeting addressed by
the Claimant at Bristol, the occupations of those who expressed
support were accountant and auctioneer, commercial traveller,
outfitter, corn-factor, tobacconist.[29] Presumably such were the
more elevated and articulate Tichbornites. W. E. Adams, whose
Memoirs of a Social Atom convey a sense of responsiveness to
atmosphere, declared that among his peers 'it was almost dangerous' not to uphold the Claimant.[30]

Journals other than the *Morning Advertiser* advanced the
movement. *Reynolds's Newspaper* was one, particularly interesting because of the journal's off-beat radicalism, ever indignant at
pretension and privilege yet disdainful of conventional working-
class politics. Its proprietor, G. W. M. Reynolds, was a veteran
chartist and novelist; his first book had been entitled *The Youthful Imposter!* At least two small ventures, the *Tichborne Gazette*
and the *Tichborne News and Anti-Oppression Journal*, based
their appeal on the cause. Both referred to working-men's interests of various sorts: crime, gossip, the eight hours' movement,
the agricultural labourers' union. They reported Tichborne meetings in detail, and the beginnings of quasi-political organization.
Leeds had the first local Tichborne Defence Committee, and it
circularized all parliamentarians:

A firm conviction has taken hold of the public mind, that the
Claimant has been the victim of a foul conspiracy, and has not
had a fair trial. A movement is now on foot which it would be
dangerous to ignore. It is daily, and we may say hourly, acquiring
fresh force, and will never cease until the chief actors in this conspiracy are discovered and punished, and restitution be made to
the man who has been so cruelly robbed of both his honour and
his inheritance.[31]

A few other such committees began in 1872 and early 1873, as did use of that other form of grass-roots Victorian politics, the mass petition to parliament.

To describe the movement in favour of the Claimant is easier than to explain its strength. The facts of the case, both as apparent to contemporaries and as knowable to historians, go against him. He had one mighty item in his favour, the Dowager's recognition. The opposing case was shaky at important points, the tattoo most obviously. Some facts indicated that Roger did have malformed genitals; there was no such indication about Orton. Buttressing these peaks was a mass of lesser data, some impressive. Yet all this falls short of the countervailing evidence. The failure to establish that an *Osprey* ever had arrived at Melbourne with shipwreck survivors; absurdities written by the Claimant into a will which Gibbes had him make at Wagga Wagga; the unlikelihood of Roger ever having met the Castros of Chile; the certainty that Orton had done so; other evidence linking the Claimant and Orton—these were potent facts.

So far as this study has revealed more data than the contemporary public knew, it further indicates the Claimant's guilt. Holmes's withdrawal from the case in February 1869 always seemed a black mark against the Claimant. His papers are an important source, as are those of other solicitors including Anthony Norris who acted for the Dowager. Evidence of Orton's sojourn in South America, coupled with the Claimant's failure to participate in the commission there, broke Holmes. An incident arising from a talk with one of the Orton sisters struck him especially, as he told his client: 'she explained that Arthur Orton had once crossed the Mountains from Valparaiso to Buenos Aires and had to eat onions on the way which was the very circumstances you had mentioned . . . to . . . myself'.[32] In commenting on the South American commission to his solicitors, the Claimant denied various incidents in Roger's sojourn there which, beyond all doubt, did happen.[33] Australian data is most significant for supporting the authenticity of a confession published by the Claimant in 1895. Later chapters discuss this document, offer further evidence in support of the Orton identification, and suggest how the imposture developed. Explanation for the Tichborne movement has to be sought elsewhere than in the appearance or the reality of truth.

Interest in the case fed upon, and so itself fed, belief in the Claimant. For a historian the case is probably most remarkable if seen as an imposture, but for contemporaries that would not have applied. To gain full romance from the case, it had to weigh in full seriousness. This argument is unprovable, but it makes sense. It might be even more true, although less logical, that maximum interest in the case resulted from simultaneous belief in both the truth and the falsity of the claim.

This comes to the brink of saying that the Claimant's supporters were romantic fools. Some contemporary critics did suggest this, almost in as many words. Coleridge often spoke with patronizing contempt of the 'glamour' that caused his opponents to take a wrong view of the case. The *Spectator* also invoked 'that capacity for wonder always so great in uneducated mankind', but offered a more thoughtful analysis of the process of judgement in the Claimant's favour.[34] 'Popular opinion in matters of justice is impatient and far too credulous . . . when it has got any apparently simple clue, it repudiates almost violently the idea that that clue is a misleading one, which you might account for on a principle directly opposed to that to which it seems to point'. In this instance the crucial item was the Dowager's recognition. Thus the favourable verdict formed, based on some evidence but not on intelligent balancing of the whole evidence. These hypotheses, too, are beyond test yet make sense.

The protagonists of the cause saw it in a very different light, as the statement of the Leeds Defence Committee has illustrated. Of the hundreds of other such assertions, the *Morning Advertiser* offered the most effective when denouncing as the Claimant's enemies 'the monster combination of State and Law, of influence and wealth, of "Society" and "Respectability" '.[35] Such forces, went the refrain, had gathered to crush an innocent man; 'Right against Might' was the cry, the title of a battle song written by the Claimant's backers.

Various features of the legal proceedings encouraged criticism of the Claimant's enemies, not only by his partisans. Coleridge again dominated the story. That a high servant of the Crown should give so much time to a private case was offensive enough. Added to this was his emotional commitment, which was apparent to contemporaries and documented for posterity in his diary. His cross-examination seemed vindictive, and the Claimant's survival a brave triumph in relation to it. Early on, Bovill seemed almost as great a villain as Coleridge. It seems certain that the judge attempted to regulate admission to his court, and in other ways he appeared guilty of bias. The *Spectator,* no friend of the Claimant, rebuked the judge for having said at a public dinner that the problem in the case was deciding between truth and fiction; in the current state of feeling, argued the journal, this endorsement that the Claimant's story was fictitious would lessen respect for the bench—'a national calamity'.[36] The adjournment for a summer vacation provoked more criticism, although its target was not bias but rather negligence.

Feeling reached a much higher pitch with the proceedings for a criminal trial. In calling for a non-suit, Ballantine doubtless hoped to avoid such an outcome; that Bovill nevertheless advised the course appeared all the more malicious. Coleridge as Attorney-General decided that the government should follow this advice: decided, as it seemed, that public funds should continue the family's battle. His opposing bail was yet another propitious touch for the 'Appeal to the British Public'. The *Times* led those who warned that the government was encouraging conspiracy-mongers by itself taking the issue so seriously. Many referred to the contrast between official activity in this matter and refusal to prosecute the Overend, Gurney directors. The government paid no heed. Counsel of high quality and large number were briefed. The Crown moved (so did counsel for the Claimant) that the trial should follow the very unusual course of being 'at bar', that is before three judges—from whose verdict any appeal was the more unlikely to succeed—and a special jury. The case waited until witnesses arrived from South America and Australia. Sooner or later, fairly and unfairly, these items took their place in the charge of conspiracy.

The situation had its echoes in parliament, which were significant in showing the strength not so much of the Tichborne movement as of the attitudes against which it fought. At this stage the cause had two parliamentary supporters, Guildford Onslow and G. H. Whalley. The former had long been one of the powers behind the Claimant; Whalley was less committed, but participated in the 'Appeal' of 1872. Both were Liberals, but highly independent. Neither was involved in the first parliamentary references to the case, which resulted from critics of the Claimant asking Coleridge early in March 1872 about the government's intentions. He replied that the Claimant was to be tried and that 'the arrest of other persons . . . is undergoing careful and anxious consideration'. In April a back-bencher reproached Coleridge for the government's retention of *six* counsel for the prosecution. 'The claim always appeared to me to be an assault on the common sense of mankind', was the Attorney-General's characteristic reply; nevertheless the paperwork demanded much manpower, and all society had an interest in the case.[37] Early in May questioning resumed, again directed against government expenditure. Whalley prompted Chancellor of Exchequer, Robert Lowe, to insist that 'supposing this person to be guilty, it is hardly possible to conceive a case of higher moral turpitude'.[38] Lowe was the most miserly of chancellors but also the most ardent of anti-democrats, and the one trait outweighed the other. Whalley asked the Treasury to aid the Claimant, and so ensure impartial British justice. Rebuffed, he raised the matter in parliament, stressing the public excitement. He professed reluctance to engage in such a movement, but said that the government had left no alternative if justice were to prevail. Heckling was common whenever Whalley spoke, but now it became unusually strident, with H. A. Bruce (Home Secretary) and Henry James (very soon to be Solicitor- and later Attorney-General) in the van. Whalley stood his ground, and often repeated his argument.[39]

Early in 1873 the court of Queen's Bench charged the Claimant and his chief backers with contempt, thus boosting the belief that authority yearned to destroy both man and movement. Whalley and Onslow first came before the court, and Hawkins appeared in his new role of leader of the prosecution. Four judges heard the case, with Alexander Cockburn, Lord Chief-Justice, at their head. If such agitation as the present were allowed, Cockburn told the accused:[40]

we might then . . . have in Political Trials, or in any Trial in which the public felt much excited, an organized agitation carried on throughout the country, sensational meetings held, and the merits of the accusation and the defence openly canvassed by appeals such as you have not hesitated to make to popular prejudice and passion; and thus the course of justice would be interfered with and disturbed.

That men of station like Whalley and Onslow should encourage that situation compounded their wrong. Having regard to their apologies and promises not again to offend, the judges imposed a fine of £100 apiece. Cockburn's final speech warned that should offences continue, penalties would increase. This challenge was at once accepted by another upper-class Tichbornite, G. B. Skip-worth, who had trained in the law and was a justice of the peace in Leicestershire. Ever extravagant in his support of the Claimant, he addressed a meeting at Brighton on the very day, 20 January, of the Whalley-Onslow convictions. The Claimant also spoke and concentrated his attack on the Chief-Justice, alleging—as had his supporters generally over previous months—that Cockburn had expressed bias against him and therefore should not sit on the case. The Claimant said too that the Attorney-General had en-sured that the forthcoming trial should go before a special jury, 'a set of half-bred swells, whom he could nod and wink at'.[41]

Charges followed against both Skipworth and the Claimant, who duly appeared before Queen's Bench on 29 January. Skip-worth came first, irritating the court with his prolixity and ex-tremism. His rodomontade provided a background against which the Claimant appeared a paragon of responsibility. This might have moved the judges. They required him to provide two sureties of £500 for good behaviour—that is, cessation of the campaign—but added no imprisonment. Skipworth had to pay £500 and spend three months in gaol. Not only the Claimant's supporters criticized these cases. The *Law Times* doubted the tact of the prosecutions, and even their legality.[42] It was unfortunate too that the case had not clarified parliamentarians' rights: the *Law Times* believed that the Wilkes case had guaranteed immunity from arrest in all cases save treason, felony, or actual breaking of the peace, and that because parliament had not acted in the current matter, this now was compromised. W. F. Finlason, that detestor of popular influence on the law, came to much the same conclu-sions. So far had the courts offended convention; so far did the Claimant's friends have reason for their cries of conspiracy.

The prosecutions determined the shape of the Tichborne cam-paign in the last months preceding the criminal trial. On the one hand, public meetings and demonstrations dwindled. On the other, parliament received several petitions protesting against public money being spent on the prosecution, against the denial of aid to the Claimant, and against the use of a special jury.[43] Moves strengthened to challenge Cockburn's hearing the case, the plan being to present a mass petition on this point. That Cock-burn long had decided against the Claimant was much more than a Tichborne canard: gossip endorsed the charge, while in his diary for 20 June 1871 Shirley Brooks—of *Punch*—had written of the civil case that 'Sir A. Cockburn wishes he were counsel in it—he "could have doubled the fellow up much quicker" '.[44] Potentially, the anti-Cockburn move was effective strategy. Kenealy's first act as counsel was to rule it out; presumably he hoped thus to gain judicial favour, although this motive scarcely seems strong enough to have outweighed his current animosity towards Cockburn.

The reasons for believing that 'State and Law' were conspiring against the Claimant were thus reasonably concrete. But what of 'influence and wealth, of "Society" and "Respectability" ', as the *Morning Advertiser* further described the machinators? Here the issues were much more amorphous. Yet they were still more important: popular support for the Claimant was part and product of the Tichborne case's being a class matter through and through. Probably the most potent reason for the common people's support of the Claimant was their seeing the issue in class terms. So much is fairly clear; the difficulty comes in analysing the logic of this attitude and finding specific expressions of it.

The movement's propaganda argued a basic difference in the socio-political behaviour of classes and masses. The former were predisposed to act in defence of self-interest, and in devious, conspiratorial ways; the latter upheld truth and justice. This was the assumption behind the class rhetoric that the movement evoked; behind the *Morning Advertiser*'s comment, for example, or the Claimant's sneer at 'half-bred swells' who would comprise a special jury. It explained why the movement's backers responded so readily to working-class support for the Claimant, and stressed it so proudly. Onslow said at an early public meeting that 'The British public were in his favour, and he had never known the British public wrong';[45] cheers responded. Only occasionally did resentment based on class and property become more overt. At another of the Claimant's first meetings a speaker proclaimed himself 'a working man . . . an old soldier . . . an old Australian bushman'. He explained that Sir Roger should have grown so stout because in Australia 'kangaroo tail soup, possums, and other Australian dainties . . . were easily comeatable . . . owing to the absence of the game laws', a hit that also evoked cheers.[46] Even this was oblique, as were most such references. Similarly, there were some, but not many, assertions that the family repudiated the Claimant because he had mixed and intermarried with the lower orders, home and colonial, and so demeaned his own class

and
more
of th
indiv
are e
these
    Th
move
prose
such
'Appe
It bec
Tichb
lengin
'they
Roger
tions b
much
one ca
butche
disqual
Even tl
the glo
nature
    The
class iss
learned
sumably
outset. 1
on that
of the ta
not have
sojourn—
Chancer
humble j
of his wil
further, a
between l
of Punch-
ridge use
Biddulph.

family would disappear. That the Tichbornes were not especially generous benefactors of the church, and that most of the time the Claimant declared himself a loyal Catholic, flawed this argument, perhaps explaining its rare statement but not checking the antagonism itself.

Evidence as to the growth of the anti-Catholic theme is puny. As early as December 1867 solicitor Holmes remarked that 'the opposition are all high Catholics who will stick at nothing to defeat his just rights', and presumably this epitomized very widespread feeling.[50] The accession of G. H. Whalley to the Claimant's camp suggests just how widespread. Anti-Catholicism was the passion of Whalley's life; he and Charles Newdegate were the two Commoners who pursued this subject session after session, enduring jeers from their fellows. Merely by joining the Tichborne cause, Whalley made it a crusade against Rome. The civil case deepened this aspect; Coleridge again was crucial, for his brother was a distinguished Jesuit. The Claimant himself sneered at this relationship during the civil hearing, and at its close the *Morning Advertiser* argued that the interests of the church had provided 'a homogeneity of purpose and action, a common cause and a bonded enthusiasm' for the man's persecutors. In public meetings such argument was common, especially when Whalley took the rostrum. 'Roman Catholic influence was at work in every village, in every town, in the press and elsewhere, joining the hellhounds';[51] the Swansea audience hissed and cheered its agreement. Interestingly, Archbishop Manning did write to Coleridge during the case, endorsing that no priest would have secretly wed Roger and Katherine Doughty.[52]

Critics of any cause, especially one hostile to established authority, like to ascribe it to the neuroses of its protagonists. The charge usually has some truth. Both generalizations stood in this instance. Everyone associated with the case received shoals of letters from individuals who felt prompted to explain how circumstance and conspiracy had cheated them. Bovill disparaged that 'a very large class of persons . . . who had lost relatives, or who had, or fancied they had, claims to property, or had rights, or imaginary rights, and who took upon themselves to write to him'.[53] Others supported the Claimant, one suspects, more to vent their hate of supposed evil than because of the particularities of the case. Skipworth offered one example of this 'cranky' theme. William Cobbett, son of the great radical, similarly used the case to unleash his crochets as to the peril of civil liberty.

A further common charge against popular movements is that at their centre some sinister clique pulls strings and serves its own selfish interest. In this instance, the alleged prize was not political power so much as personal profit. Again the charge had considerable truth. The Claimant's case could not have advanced but for the organization behind it. Often this became ramshackle—the Claimant himself was the least organizable of beings—yet it did keep on and was the work of men who had something to gain by the Claimant's victory. The core of the issue was finance. At every stage the Claimant needed money; he being so great a spender, the problem grew as rapidly and grotesquely as his own girth. The many people who lent him funds staked them on his success. Some pulled out early, but others risked more in hope of retrieving all (and maybe a bonus besides).

The story began at the beginning—Wagga Wagga. Solicitor Gibbes more or less maintained the Claimant through the middle months of 1866; his client gave in return a draft for £500, which would have more than paid his debts had it ever been honoured. A publican, a baker and a commercial traveller were among the country-town plutocrats who helped Tom Castro.[54] Gibbes also talked with the manager of a local bank, and continued the quest for finance in Sydney. Here the Claimant enlarged his spendthrift habits. 'Our suspicious Sydney men would not advance the money he required'. Gibbes told the Dowager, 'and it was only with the greatest difficulty it was at last obtained and then at a most exorbitant rate'.[55] Before she met her 'son', the Dowager received dunning letters 'from an Australian merchant of the name of Lasarus'.[56] Matthew Aaron Worms was another Australian lender whose name echoed the association of Jew and finance.

Holmes played the same role during the early years in England as had his fellow solicitor in Australia, but on a grander scale and stage. His and Norris's papers teem with references to agents, lenders, insurance companies, mortgages, as well as to the demands of earlier creditors. The Dowager and Biddulph helped meet basic expenses, but the Claimant ranged far beyond these. Onslow and Colonel Lushington were probably his most generous creditors, but there were many others. Thus financial ties—but also fellow feeling and probably genuine friendship—linked the Claimant with G. S. Bloxam, wine-merchant and attorney. The literary man and lawyer, G. A. Sala, remembered Bloxam as a friend, but his reputation was dubious both in the legal profession and even within the much-divided Tichborne camp. F. J. Baigent complained of 'Blocky's' intimacy with the Claimant: 'seems to look upon him as the goose that is to lay golden eggs by and by, but the question is if he can manage and provide for him till then and see that he don't stray'.[57] In fact 'Blocky' did stay close to the Claimant. He was probably the most significant, although not the most conspicuous, background figure. In August 1867 Holmes lamented that the Claimant should have become entangled with another financier, G. S. Mackennell: 'If his name was known in connexion with you, people in good position disposed to advance would not do so'.[58] Charles Hingston, a shipping broker, and his brother John also seem to have been dubious characters. Messrs Falcke, Finkinstein and Woolf were among the numerous murky figures in this story.

The upshot of all the effort is impossible to clarify. Estimates of Onslow's loans ranged up to £20 000, and Lushington's to £10 000. Perhaps the rest gave as much again. Interest rates varied from Lushington's five per cent or less, to an agreement to give £6000 in return for an ultimate return of £18 000 with a £1000 commission immediately payable. This deal seems to have firmed, whereas most plans fell down after long traffic. Short-term interest ranged between thirty and fifty per cent. The suspicious men of Sydney set a pattern which their metropolitan peers followed. Yet however careful and importunate, creditors saw little of their money again. Early in 1870 the Claimant filed for bankruptcy, under pressure from the now hostile Holmes who estimated his own debt at over £5000. Court proceedings stated that the Claimant owed over £60 000, but probably this sum excluded loans staked on the outcome of the civil action.

Later in 1870 the Claimant's financial advisers issued 'Tichborne bonds'. These were debentures, for £100 face value, promising five per cent interest pending repayment of that sum. They were sold originally at £65; the Claimant told Coleridge they had realized £2000.[59] Critics alleged that they were distributed as bribes. In November 1871 the *Times* quoted them at £40, in contrast to the nadir of 10s some months earlier, while the *Spectator* said that some reached £50. The 'Appeal to the British Public' wrote a further chapter in the fund-raising story. The *Morning Advertiser* claimed in January 1871 that the public had subscribed £100 000, but probably this exaggerated and the response was sociologically interesting rather than economically overwhelming. Wealthy individuals remained more important.

Of growing weight was Horace Pitt-Rivers, Lord Rivers, who came to rival Onslow and Bloxam as executive officer and financial support.

Every loan to the cause was a wager, but gambling in the more technical sense also contributed to the development of a vested interest in success. 'Betting has probably never run so high upon any event as it does upon the decision of the long-enduring jury', said *Vanity Fair*, in June 1871 when it presented a portrait of 'Sir Roger Doughty Tichborne, Bart.?'. Hats were a frequent wager. The ambiguous result of the civil case provoked many arguments: *Bell's Life*, arbiter among sporting journals, ruled for the cancelling of all bets on a victory for either side. The sporting interest at large had a stake in the Claimant's success. Onslow was very much the sporting gentleman: 'a thorough *bon vivant*', as *Vanity Fair* said, 'always in high spirits, if often in low circumstances'.[60] Of old Whig family, he yet found affinity with the commonest of people, ready to appeal 'to the cab-drivers, the publicans, and the whole race of people who never heard or read but merest scraps of the evidence'.[61] Cab-drivers and publicans were at the heart of the sporting interest, and the support of these groups and of the *Morning Advertiser* belong in this context. Onslow and the Hingston brothers were punters, as well as investors on the Claimant's behalf; Lord Rivers was also a celebrity of the turf. The Claimant transcended all in his fidelity to the sporting type. On the way to his very first public meeting, his carriage passed a racing stable which thereupon 'seemed frantic with delight . . . the trainers and jockey-boys rushing in absolute ecstacy from the stables to the roadside'.[62]

Another interest in the cause became apparent when managers of his meetings took their grievances to court. In August 1872 Mr Abraham Anidjah, cigar merchant, claimed costs under an alleged agreement that promised the Claimant five per cent of gross takings, expenses for a carriage and four, and £10 bonus for each successful meeting. Anidjah lost his action, after charge and counter-charge. The *Times* disapproved: 'the business of organizing Demonstrations appears to be becoming a recognized branch of industry in this country—an innovation on which we think the community is scarcely to be congratulated'.[63] Whalley replied that Anidjah's task had been to regulate popular emotion, not to create it. Some token of the sense of this remark was the employment of a successor to Anidjah, one G. W. Nugent, proprietor of the Royal Cambridge music-hall, Shoreditch. This broke down when the Claimant gave his patronage elsewhere. Again allegations went back and forth, saturating the Claimant's cause in its murkiest light. Meanwhile Anidjah went to law in protection against threats from the Claimant and Edward Napper, pugilist.

If finance was the dominant motif of organization, the gathering of evidence ran it close. The Claimant's side used methods which were at least bizarre and often devious. Particularly reprehensible in the eyes of contemporary critics was Holmes's printing and distribution of favourable affidavits in the early days of the case. There were frowns too for the way in which the Claimant attached some ex-N.C.O.s from the Carabineers to his household, and used them in procuring fresh supporters. That household was indeed a strange one: Coleridge was to sneer at the quarrels and pettiness that its inmates' letters revealed. Baigent, Miss Braine, the Claimant's wife, Bloxam, Hingston—these and others all back-bit and tale-told as they strove to get the Claimant to present his best face to the world. The greatest stir came when Holmes defected and began to force the Claimant into bankruptcy. But Holmes never showed all his papers to the world, as the Claimant's party had feared. After his withdrawal, the record of organization diminishes, but the task continued in much the same spirit. One of the ancillary uses of public meetings, for example, was to attract sympathizers who at some stage had known, or might have known, either Arthur Orton or Roger Tichborne; one or other of the Claimant's closer allies would then vet the candidate in readiness for the criminal trial.

The Claimant's cause thus had many ingredients: self-interest and ruthlessness verging on chicanery, added to belief, righteousness, passion, charisma and romance. The addition of Kenealy's personality to this brew could result only in drama still more thunderous and remarkable.

3

KENEALY RIDES THE WAVE

ON 17 APRIL 1873 KENEALY appeared before the court of Queen's Bench, sitting at Westminster, and argued for either abandonment of the forgery charge against the Claimant or its hearing prior to the perjury issues; he did not want the court to consider the perjuries at length, and then to rush a decision on the forgery, which was felonious. The bench listened, remarking that it could but advise. Its advice went home, and the Crown withdrew the forgery indictment. Probably the law officers wished to avoid keeping the jurymen in confinement and to remove any doubt—which prevailed apropos a felony—that a special jury could sit. Therefore, when the case opened on 23 April, only the two counts of perjury stood. The first listed twenty-three 'assignments', based on the Claimant's examination in the civil case; the first was 'in swearing that he was Roger Tichborne', the fifteenth 'in swearing that he had never gone by the name of Arthur Orton', while the remainder included such highlights as the claim to have seduced Katherine Doughty and denial of having gone to Hobart. The second count drew from the Claimant's affidavit in Chancery in 1868; 'that he was Roger Tichborne' again came first, and the nine following assignments all referred to claims of having acted as did Roger down to April 1854.

The case lasted, with some adjournment but no vacation, until 28 February 1874, 188 sitting days. Alexander Cockburn presided, with Justices Mellor and Lush beside him. Henry Hawkins led the prosecuting counsel; Coleridge did not appear, but his conduct of the civil case was frequently to echo. Kenealy had the assistance of Patrick McMahon, an Irish parliamentarian and a Queen's Counsel who in these years reached the climax of his unremarkable career. Most of the jurymen were substantial trades-people or retailers; two were publicans. Ten months' labour ended with a finding of guilt and a sentence of seven years' imprisonment on both charges. That was the maximum penalty for perjury, but the terms were to be consecutive. In April an appeal protested against certain procedures and alleged bias on the bench; that was abortive, and so too was a subsequent move for a writ of error.[1]

The trial intensified most characteristics of the Tichborne cause. More and more the issue divided masses from classes, common from gentle, residuum (a current term) from respectable. Charge and counter-charge of conspiracy and undue influence grew ever thicker. As earlier, there were both truth in such accusation, and exaggeration of that truth in the consciousness of many involved. The Claimant's friends continued ever more strident and emotional in their convictions.

This was the wave that Kenealy rode. An apostate-critic of Catholicism, a counsel ready to scorn etiquette and to fight against odds, a would-be politician in the popular interest, an aspiring Messiah—here indeed was the man for this situation. During the trial Kenealy became more erratic than earlier, but simply by placing himself so far outside convention he gained yet greater following from the Claimant's sympathizers. He came to share the Claimant's role as focus and surrogate for feelings of protest and outrage. Respectability in general and lawyers in particular spurned Kenealy; in equal measure his popularity grew. This situation reached a climax with his election to the House of Commons by the Stoke-on-Trent electorate on 16 February 1875. For the next few weeks he was the cynosure of the nation. It did not continue long. Seeking to ride the wave beyond its intrinsic force and direction, Kenealy began to sink.

THE PERIOD OF THE TRIAL

To evaluate, even to describe, Kenealy's performance as counsel is very difficult. His belated entry into the case put him literally years behind Hawkins's team, and he never gained much. Various solicitors managed the case, ineffectually; at the beginning of the trial Alfred Hendriks had the job, but in August he withdrew in anger, to be followed by Charles Harcourt. Supplementing and confusing the professionals' task were the Claimant's chief friends. Whalley offered the grossest illustration of the possible dangers: in

July he backed the claim of one Jean Luie to have been steward aboard the *Osprey* when it carried Roger to Melbourne in 1854. Luie appeared, with sensation; but the Crown soon found evidence of his criminality and he too suffered conviction for perjury. Kenealy admitted error in calling him, but the item nourished suspicion of the whole defence case. Meanwhile finance remained a problem. Until September the Claimant still attracted crowds to meetings, theatres, and pigeon-shoots, but expenses always ran far beyond income. A company that was intended to raise £20 000 to fight the cause does not seem to have floated.[2] Kenealy received 500 guineas at the outset and about another 1000 altogether, Lord Rivers being the source. Even that came only after crisis.

The largest problem in assessing Kenealy's performance is to determine relevant criteria. Was his task to strive through technicality and finesse for some break that would save his client? Or was it to fulfil the case's quality as romance, drama, conflict? Neither Kenealy nor anyone else saw those as stark alternatives, but his behaviour is best explained in terms of them. He paid some regard to the former but put more stress on the latter, and in this was true not only to his own temperament and biography but also to the nature of the Tichborne movement.

Kenealy presented the issue as a struggle in which authority and papistry conspired against right. 'Fashion' and 'influence' were terms he used much in his opening remarks. He spoke of press hostility to the Claimant, of the Arundels and the Seymours, of 'the unseen invisible, almost universally permeating influence of Stonyhurst and its associations', and especially of official involvement in the matter. 'I regard it, not as a prosecution by the Crown which it nominally is, and ought to be; but a prosecution by the Tichborne family, supported by the public purse'.[3] By identifying itself with the prosecution, the government had prejudiced his client. In his closing speech five months later Kenealy made much the same points with a rougher edge. Recounting the Claimant's story since his return to Britain, he warned that should the jurymen convict 'they will have his estates for ever'. 'Who are "They"?', asked Cockburn. 'His enemies', came counsel's reply, soon clarified by reference to 'sacerdotal power'.[4] He endorsed Whalley's opinion, given in evidence, that the prosecution was a popish plot.

Against such evil, the people upheld truth: Kenealy was as deliberate as Onslow in asserting this. *'Vox populi, Vox Dei . . .* is

proached the Claimant, offering to sell him information. The Claimant replied in various letters, and Coleridge produced what purported to be this correspondence, intending to show the Claimant's interest in the Orton family. But Coleridge displayed at least some letters that the Claimant had *not* written to Mrs Pittendreigh, and forgery was manifest. The episode had long been in the Claimant's armoury, but Kenealy made it more explosive. Questioning the calligraphic expert, Charles Chabot (whom the prosecution had called), Kenealy learned that before Coleridge produced the Pittendreigh letters in court, Chabot had advised that some of them were forgeries. Kenealy revelled: 'that is a very serious thing; it is one of the most serious and terrible features of this case'.[10] Perhaps it was.

Measure by measure the bench became more angry in response to Kenealy's increasing scorn of court-room etiquette. His charges of corruption and collusion grated particularly. Then Kenealy suggested that the bench itself leagued against him. Cockburn over-reacted. The situation had been very distressing, his summation began, but unavoidable.

When witnesses are misrepresented, when their statements are distorted, when facts are perverted, when dates are set at naught— and all this not for the purpose of argument in the cause, but in order to lay the foundation for foul accusations and unjust imputations against parties and Witnesses—when one unceasing torrent of invective, of dirty, foul, slime is sent forth wherewith to blacken the characters of men whose reputations have hitherto been beyond reproach, it is impossible for Judges to remain silent.[11]

A month's talking left the bile in Cockburn's mouth, and he ended as he began, hate-hymning Kenealy. He, Cockburn, had nothing to fear, went the peroration; he left his reputation and integrity to the care of the bar of England. First the jury and later the profession were to endorse Cockburn's plaint.

A further stock pro-Claimant argument urged by Kenealy was the effect upon 'Roger' of the Australian outback. Many former Australians appeared for the defence. They told of having known Castro *and* Orton, or the Claimant as Castro who spoke of lofty background, or Orton who was not the Claimant; but more generally they built up the picture of a wild romantic life. Kenealy rhapsodized as to how this life would appeal to melan-

cholic, world-weary Roger. 'You have all the Arab independence
of the desert; a beautiful climate, glorious nights of stars and
moonlight such as are never seen in Europe'.[12] The idea accorded
with Kenealy's old longing for some higher level of experience
and exultation. In response Hawkins gibed at Kenealy's more
flowery expressions of the notion, and brought evidence that
Wagga Wagga—for all its remoteness and euphony—had a
mechanics' institute carrying journals from which Tom Castro
could have learned something of the Tichbornes. Cockburn likewise remarked that the mail spread everywhere, but he went
further in combating Kenealy. The judge was maladroit in com-
prehending Australian witnesses: he could not grasp such phrases
as 'to follow the diggings' (to move from one goldfield to another
as news of fresh strikes arose); he even misheard 'horse-stealers' for
'Australia'.[13] Cockburn scorned the idea that Roger would have
forsaken his heritage for such a world. 'Position and affluence are
what all men desire to attain . . . No man throws away affluence,
and ease, and pleasure, and all the advantages, social and intellectual, which those things bring with them, in order to embrace a
life of privation and toil'.[14] This echoed Coleridge's insistence
that no person of gentle birth could have lived as did Castro; now
Cockburn asked how likely it was that Roger Tichborne should
marry Mary Ann Bryant, an illiterate domestic.

In these ways Kenealy's advocacy complemented the Tichborne
cause. What was its relevance to the other criterion suggested
above—that of winning the Claimant's release? There was some:
Kenealy's arguments made their own sense, and Ballantine's
effort warns against easy supposition that a gifted conventional
barrister would have done better. Yet in the end Kenealy's behaviour must be judged as eccentric and unlikely to have achieved
a favourable verdict. Whalley later said that during the trial he
and other leaders in the cause opposed Kenealy, which underlines
both the counsel's difficulties and his oddities. The ill-effect of
Kenealy's defence worked in several directions. To antagonize
Cockburn guaranteed an adverse summing-up. Just as lethal was
irritation of the jury. Even allowing for his difficulties, Kenealy
failed to master detail; his annotations on documents set before
him were cursory and flat.[15] His ignorance allowed bench and
even jury to score points against him, and caused him sometimes
to appear ridiculous. When Hendriks resigned as solicitor he gave
as his reason that Kenealy made unfounded statements. Denigra-

tion of Roger backfired as Kenealy strove to compare him favourably with Orton, who was presented for this purpose as coarse, oafish, ignorant. When Kenealy discounted the Claimant's answers to Coleridge, the bench responded that this supported the man's being a liar. The fantasy about Roger's impotence clashed not only with the Claimant's womanizing but also with Kenealy's own allegations about Roger's lechery. Two points that Kenealy came to rank as first in importance—Chabot's remarks about the Pittendreigh forgery and Gibbes's about the Claimant's physical oddities—arose by accident rather than by systematic enquiry. Many defence witnesses made a bad impression. Legal commentators on the trial have criticized Kenealy's tactics in attempting to prove that the Claimant was Tichborne rather than concentrating on the weaknesses of the Crown's identification of him with Orton. They stress too that Kenealy raised few points of law.[16]

While Kenealy conducted the case in his own strange way, Tichbornites found ample reason for the Claimant's troubles in the alleged misdeeds of authority and Rome. Events gave new fuel for belief in conspiracy and evil at those high, remote levels. Where reality stopped, exaggeration and emotion continued. While the case was *sub judice* these feelings received only limited expression, but that probably intensified them.

In Tichbornite eyes, Cockburn now rivalled Coleridge as chief villain. The pre-trial allegations of his bias foreshadowed this: Kenealy made a rare admission of error when he told Rivers in July 1873 that he regretted having stopped the move against Cockburn's sitting on the case. All the judge's comments and rulings had some justification. Yet his emotions became very deeply involved, even more than had Coleridge's. Hawkins was cool—gibing, correcting, arguing with effect while Cockburn deployed anger and outrage. His summing-up was a long, deliberate and devastating reply to Kenealy. Cockburn surely believed in the Claimant's guilt, and in the ill-faith, even corruption, of those who did not. Hawkins's autobiography claims that the judge applauded his final speech: 'Bravo! Bravo, Hawkins! . . . I have not heard a piece of oratory like that for many a long day!'[17] Tichbornites did not know about that, but they behaved as if they did.

Another grievance was curtailment of discussion and action over the case. In early June Onslow published in two Leeds newspapers a denial that he had forsaken 'Sir Roger'. Rather, his certainty had grown 'in spite of the terrible amount of perjury' on the other side. The Attorney-General secured a rule for contempt against the journal's publishers, who included a parliamentarian, R. M. Carter. All parties, including Onslow, offered apologies, and the matter went no further. The same story applied to publishers of anti-Claimant ephemera; but such restriction fell heavier on the noisier, public-conscious side. Some weeks later Onslow offended by endorsing another appeal for funds to rebut 'one of the most cruel prosecutions that ever defaced the annals of justice'. Again apologies met the situation, but as finances worsened the Claimant resolved on 'starring it again at the Theatres to keep the pot boiling'. Earlier the bench had been non-committal about such appearances, but in mid-September its attitude hardened:

It seems to us that the time has come when what I cannot designate as otherwise than as a great public scandal, should be put a stop to. That a man committed by a learned judge . . . should be paraded about the country preparatory to this Trial, and while the Trial is pending, as a victim and martyr is, in my opinion, an outrage on all public decency and propriety. The effect has been to create a state of agitation and excitement such as has never been known in the history of the administration of justice. There is not a day passes but what the Judges . . . are not assailed with the coarsest, lowest, and most virulent abuse . . . Their lives have been threatened in case this Trial has a certain result, adverse to the Defendant; and the Jury too . . . have been, in like manner, assailed from without and sought to be influenced, or intimidated, as the case may be. We cannot doubt that the effect of all this systematic agitation, carried on throughout the whole country, in every county of it, has the effect, not merely of exciting and stimulating public passion, but of influencing those who are afterwards to be heard here as witnesses . . .[18]

A few days later the editor of the *Cheltenham Chronicle* was fined £150 for saying that the defendant had not been proved to be Arthur Orton. In January 1874 Whalley published a letter affirming his belief in Luie; the court fined him £250 and gaoled him until he paid.

Throughout the previous session of parliament Whalley had attacked the government's conduct in the case. He still called for it to help meet the defence's costs, especially for witnesses from outside London. The authorities refused any guarantee, and this —rather than that some help was offered—was the publicized fact. In alleged contrast were generous payments of up to £1000 for prosecution witnesses from Australia, and general extravagance in fighting the case. One documented item is that the government did pay 'subsistence money' to Charles Orton,[19] a brother of Arthur. Among many other alleged improprieties, the most notable was adjournment of the trial to allow enquiry into Luie's past. The Jesuits had their place in this story too. At the civil hearing one priest of that order, Thomas Meyrick, had supported the Claimant, speaking of acquaintance with Roger at Stonyhurst. He was to have appeared again at Queen's Bench, but in September was confined as a lunatic. The Claimant reported this in a letter to the *Morning Advertiser*: 'How long will England endure this? How long will Stonyhurst politics be allowed to prevail?'[20] But the biggest, best justified grievance was the sentence to consecutive rather than concurrent terms of imprisonment. The judges had the strictest letter of statute on their side, but anger if not malice seemed to be at work.

In stretching the law, in their repugnance at the Claimant's public appearances, and in their abomination of Kenealy, the judges ran with most opinion in the upper-class press. During the trial such feeling was covert, but clear. Kenealy had reason for criticizing 'descriptive' reporting, especially of the *Daily News* and the *Times*. The latter responded with particularly warm approval of the judges' restrictions on the Claimant. 'Those who side with the Defendant have established a regular propaganda', said the *Times*, alleging that it was all the more effective because the inhibition on press criticism left the people ignorant and vulnerable.[21] The verdict released a flood.[22] 'The monstrous record of a a nature so vile' (*Daily Telegraph*), 'monstrous perjurer' (*Echo*), 'the most daring swindler of our times . . . the most audacious rascal that ever devised a scheme to delude a nation' (*Standard*): such were among the epithets. The *Pall Mall Gazette* regretted that the Claimant could not be hanged; *Catholic Opinion* said that the prisoner was an 'atrocious criminal' and his counsel a lunatic; *Cosmopolitan* that this was an unique conspiracy, engineered by the sporting crowd. The *Saturday Review* spoke of the 'credulity and imbecility' of Tichbornites, and the *Birmingham Daily Gazette* concluded that 'a mob verdict is generally on the wrong side'. The *Times* felt that 'the real ground of humiliation is the defect of common-sense and the imperfect education of so large a proportion of the English people'. A *Times* article on 'The Great Imposture' sought further to explain the story in terms of romance, conspiracy, the will to believe 'the improbable and prodigious', and—twisting the argument hitherto used by the other side—the strangeness of colonial conditions which could encourage a man to embark on such a fantasy as had the Claimant.

The press reflected growing strength of opinion among the respectable at large. Kenealy could call fewer upper-class witnesses than did Ballantine, notable absentees being Sir T. C. Constable and various Carabineer officers. Some biographers speak of their subjects relinquishing earlier belief in the Claimant; Hardinge Giffard was one important example. W. E. Gladstone, still Prime Minister, wrote in October 1873 of 'the huge vagabond',[23] complementing Disraeli's earlier verdict and offering the best possible instance of pre-judgement among the ruling class.

Against such judgement and against that class the Tichborne movement still fought. The most significant new stress was the extension to Kenealy of the enthusiasm previously accorded the Claimant alone. Within a few weeks of the trial's outset, crowds in the Westminster precincts began to cheer Kenealy. The barrister had none of his client's massive physique, sporting prowess, geniality or would-be gentle birth. Yet to his credit were 'Dr' and 'Q.C.', books of verse, and a literary knowledge which in the happier moments of the trial enabled him to swap allusions with the judges, sometimes showing him to be better informed than they. These accomplishments added effect to his image as a champion of justice, who transcended his own background and affiliations.

The ephemera that the case continued to spawn incorporated this new element. A ballad issued very early in the new trial caught the theme:

> He's got an Irish lawyer,
>   Who'll do the best he can;
> Dr Kenealy will be there
>   The claimant for to screen,
> And when his Irish blood is up
>   He'll tell them what he means.[24]

Of other songs that referred to Kenealy, perhaps the most expressive concerned Lord Bellew:

> Now in came stuttering Lord Bellew,
> With a got up yarn about tattoo,
> And Lord Bellew, upon my life,
> You know you tattoo'd the captain's wife,
> Upon that lady you did doat,

You did it so nice, for a £5 note,
Your character's got such a shock,
Like Luie, you deserve it hot.
You are a lord of noble race,
But like the rest you're in disgrace,
Thanks to Doctor Kenealy.[25]

One very popular cartoon was 'The Westminster Tragedy'. It showed Cockburn striving to destroy the Claimant while valiant Kenealy defended him. Another of those striking black-and-white comic books presented Kenealy as 'the Claimant's counsel, and makes a gallant fight / For which all must applaud him'. Later the man's critics were to charge that instead of concentrating on the trial he spent time in artists' and sculptors' studios.

Such journals as *Figaro* and *Penny Illustrated Paper* featured Kenealy, and his effigy appeared in Tussaud's galleries. *Vanity Fair* included 'The Claimant's Counsel' in its famous 'Spy' series. Kenealy, it perceived, 'seemed destined to pass an unregarded life and to consume if anything only himself with the fire that burnt within him', until this strange opportunity burst.[26] 'Tichborne and Kenealy' became the cry of the Westminster crowd, which sometimes lifted the counsel into his carriage and followed him to Gray's Inn. Admirers sent paeans of praise, prose and verse. *Reynolds's Newspaper*, still loyal to the Claimant after the verdict, praised the 'bold and brave' Kenealy for his efforts in the defeated cause.

The female element among the Tichbornites possibly increased, or at least became more obvious, in these months. One face among this crowd belonged to Isabella Coombes, needlewoman, who a day or so after the verdict was given broke three danger lamps on the new Hammersmith extension railway. 'It is all through Tichborne', she said in explanation; 'she would lose her life for Tichborne'.[27] The support of the liquor-and-sport crowd also became more explicit. Kenealy's witnesses included professional sportsmen, publicans, and friends of publicans—people, especially from the East End, who had been discovered through bar-room contacts as potentially useful supporters. Some pubs served as cells of the movement. The most distinguished newcomer to the Tichborne leadership, other than Kenealy, was William Quartermaine East, licensee of the Queen's Hotel, St Martin's-le-Grand. Public opinion was well aware of this situation, and to the end rumour said that the publicans on the jury would thwart a 'guilty' verdict.

At one point at least the Claimant's supporters ventured near corruption. During and after the trial, both sides accused each other of attempting bribery of the jury. Early in 1874 some such steps were taken. The mover was Edwin John James, an erstwhile barrister and member of parliament who had suffered professional disgrace in 1861 for various improper practices. Seemingly James urged Onslow to bribe, with himself the mediary; Onslow was tempted, yet finally held back. Of similar provenance and date to the documentation of this story is a note signed H. W. (or so it appears: but who was he?) telling 'Dear Uncle' to 'Bolt!', to Boulogne, where extradition could not catch him. 'It is your last chance'. Were these two sets of correspondence linked?[28]

Behind leaders and pressure groups remained a considerable, if immeasurable, mass sentiment. Lord Rivers told Kenealy in mid-1873 that, 'I think *really* that a conviction against evidence . . . would create a general disturbance', because 'John Bull' had given his money to the Claimant and 'don't like to be rigged out of it'.[29] The *New York Herald* saw in the case a hint of English revolution. Gladstone wrote of 'the huge vagabond' while telling of the belief in him of a foundry worker who spent his leisure in skilful watch-mending. Lord Snell, a Fabian and Co-operator of later years, remembered a blacksmith's shop as the focus of political discussion for the 'village Hampdens' of his youth; he listed the Claimant's trial and sentence first among the subjects of debate.[30] That the bench stopped the Claimant's meetings is sufficient evidence of their effect. His speeches must have become very stale, but the audience could provide some flavour: in their call at a shoot to 'put up the Attorney-General and Hawkins for the next trap' or in suggesting that popular vote, not judicial decision, should decide the case.[31]

New ballads did more than praise Kenealy. The anonymous 'they' was a frequent target:

> Poor old Roger Tichborne now
>   Is on his trial again,
> They will not rest contented,
>   They never will refrain
> From doing everything they can
>   To strike the fatal blow,
> If money can only do it now
>   To prison he must go.[32]

The 'End of the Tichborne Case' was mourned:

> In every town in England,
>   He met with great applause,
> And working men with purse and pen
>   Have tried to help his cause;
> Tho' his witnesses were humble,
>   To him they stoutly swore,
> But the trial's gone against him,
>   And he's done for evermore.
>
> Mr Whalley and Mr Onslow,
>   Have helped him with a will,
> They believed he was Sir Roger,
>   And thousands think so still:
> If that is your opinion,
>   I pray you understand,
> You must not tell them what you think,
>   In this free and happy land.

The loudest voice of public feeling came from the Westminster crowd. It cheered Kenealy; in September 1873 it rioted after the ban on the Claimant's appearance; in January 1874 it heckled Hawkins as he made his final speech. The riot let to seven arrests. Six 'decently attired men' were bound over, but Michael Flynn, labourer, had put his foot on a fallen policeman, calling 'that's the way to serve them', and he got one month's hard labour. In January four men were charged: one was a builder-painter, one a general dealer, and the other two respectively made and sold photographs of Claimant and counsel. They too were bound over. The magistrate accepted that at least two of the defendants were 'respectable', and attributed their behaviour to 'infatuation'.[33]

Usually the crowd's behaviour was less dramatic, but it was resonant enough. Normally 150 police were assigned to controlling it. The task was made more difficult, said the Home Secretary, by the presence of parliamentarians which 'prevents that vigour on the part of the police which they might otherwise display'.[34] In command was Inspector Denning, a tremendously efficient man who cherished the letters he received from his social betters asking for admission to the court. Monday was the day for big crowds as the Saturday break and Sunday gossip whetted interest.[35] The crowds would begin to gather at about 2.30 and would build towards 10 000. Of that number, said the *Morning Advertiser*, only 500 were 'roughs'; and other journals often admitted that the appearance of many was fair enough.

The day of sentence was Saturday, a half-holiday, and the sun shone. These were conditions that might have encouraged some massive demonstration—to seize the Claimant or to attack Cockburn—such as rumour had threatened. Authority had posted even more police than usual, and directed that the prisoner be removed through a little-used tunnel. A handful of people saw him emerge and take a carriage to the gaol. 'He was a good-plucked one, and he will find fourteen years without any bacca a hardish time', remarked a bricklayer. Yet his fellow spectators, and even some in the Westminster crowd, applauded the verdict. A reporter who went to Wapping that night claimed that although every conversation and many street-corner meetings praised both Claimant and Kenealy, no hint of rebellion sounded.[36] Commentators who argued from this that the movement had died were wrong; more likely was it that the Claimant's supporters wanted his freedom less than they wanted confirmation that he was a victim of conspiracy.

BETWEEN TRIAL AND PARLIAMENT

Far from dying, the movement became livelier for a year and more after the Claimant's conviction. One mark of its vigour was its prompting the Queen to reject Disraeli's suggestion that Hawkins win a knighthood for his work in the case: 'it will seem by implication that the Queen's feelings have been biased against the Prisoner throughout, and that she regards the termination as a victory. This Her Majesty thinks would have a very bad effect'.[37] Even without such provocation, the cause found yet new themes and more variants upon old.

The Claimant's supporters saw his imprisonment as torture, preparatory to death. Their hero responded: when removed from Millbank to Dartmoor late in 1874 he wrote to Onslow that he felt the cold greatly and urged vigour in the efforts to save him 'ere its too late'.[38] Another spur to emotion was a remark of Cockburn's that only 'fanatics and fools' would deny that the jurymen had been exemplary. Tichbornites interpreted this as saying that only fanatics and fools believed in the Claimant, and the tag became a boast:

> Us fools and fanatics will all do our best
> That curse to remove we will try . . .

said a doggerel epic on 'Sir Roger Tichborne, or, The Right Man in the Wrong Place', which also vowed God's punishment on the evil-doers, notably 'The Jesuit with all his craft'.[39] Pseudo-science added its testimony with the application of grids and measurement to photographs of Roger and the Claimant: not the first but the most assiduous of pamphleteers in this cause was William Mathews of Bristol. That controversy centred on the Claimant's head, but his more intimate parts continued to receive attention as R. M. Gurnell, writer of endless, unreadable prose on the case, issued a pamphlet, *What did Dr David Wilson Say?*. 'This alone ought to *prove* the prisoner to be Sir R. Tichborne' is a note on the sole copy located.[40]

Whalley kept up an agitation in parliament, where since February the Conservatives had been in power and Onslow no longer sat. Whalley protested at his own imprisonment before both the House and a select committee on privilege, which approved it. He secured returns showing government expenditure on the case, and argued in advance that the sum, £49 615.17.1, was 'entirely fictitious'.[41] He warned that members were being kept in ignorance of popular feeling against this 'gross maladministration of justice'. Members should not have been too ignorant: during the 1874 session the Commons received thirty-two petitions claiming 47 087 signatures and calling for further enquiry. These petitions derived from public meetings which continued in much the same manner as earlier. Tichborne Release Associations often developed in conjunction with these moves. Whalley did not dispute two statutes of 1874 which proved the continuing concern of Britain's rulers with the case: the False Personation Act which provided life servitude for such an offence, and the Tichborne Estates Act which declared the legitimacy of the succession to Roger's nephew.

With the Claimant in gaol, Kenealy's stature in the movement increased. This did not go without dispute: criticism of his conduct of the defence led to some disparagement and rivalry. Nor did Kenealy immediately assert himself. Exhaustion coupled with chronic ill-health might have been the cause of his hesitating before burning all bridges. J. R. Tussaud even said that as Kenealy posed for his model he spoke of himself as a mountebank. However, such self-criticism is notably absent from more direct evidence, and he scoffed at a suggestion that he should temporarily quit England and lecture in the New World.[42] Anyway, equivocation there was. He broke custom by shaking hands with his client after conviction, but was cool in doing so. On 9 March he issued a letter protesting at Cockburn's call to the profession to protect the bench's repute against Kenealy's charges. 'The reign of terror which began when men were fined and imprisoned for advocating the Claimant's cause is now continued against me and my profession, which it is sought to drive into Oriental suppleness and servility', went Kenealy's harangue. But he tried to recall this letter before publication, and on the failure of that he retracted so far as to say that he alleged no bias against the judges' arguments, leaving posterity no doubt that they were substantial.[43]

If Kenealy equivocated his critics did not, and their pressure pushed him further to extremism. Discipline of counsel was then largely the business of the Inns of Court. On 18 March the benchers of Gray's Inn appointed a committee to enquire into Kenealy's conduct as counsel, with regard also to his letter of 9 March. Also on 9 March the Lord Chancellor wrote to the benchers asking what they meant to do about Kenealy: in other words, urging them to do something. The letter did not come to hand, and the Lord Chancellor had to write again. This extraordinary proceeding confirmed Kenealy's thesis that the Claimant's enemies were now seeking to destroy him. On 1 April the Gray's Inn committee reported that Kenealy should answer multiple charges of professional misconduct. Meanwhile the Oxford circuit had been pondering similar matters. One member deplored especially 'that appeals were made to the mob outside'; another 'that after the verdict you shook hands with the convict'. Early in April the circuit mess expelled Kenealy. On 19 April he argued the appeal against the Claimant's conviction, alleging among other things that Cockburn had virtually called him a liar; Cockburn did not now deny the charge.[44]

These moves aroused counter-sympathy. Cockburn's behaviour in the case had always struck many as demonstrative, egotistical, over-committed, and these faults were most obvious in his attack on Kenealy. The jurisdiction of the Inns had long been a matter for liberal complaint, as a relic of mediaeval privilege. The Inns rarely exercised the power in the nineteenth century, and in cases where they did, venal and patent corruption was evident. Kenealy and his supporters gibed too that if he had committed contempt then the courts should charge him; the hint was that they did not dare. Even the respectable and professional press heeded these points, and they fed the enthusiasm of Tichbornites. 'Success to Brave Dr Kenealy' was the title of a ballad of April 1874:

> But his foes they want to deprive him
>   Of his well earned fame and his gown,
> So now they are bravely conniving,
>   At the game kick a man when he's down.

> Then justice let's have for Kenealy
>   He is the champion of fair play we see,
> And good luck to our old friend sir Roger
>   Let's hope we may yet see him free.

Kenealy's response to the crumbling of his professional status was to establish a newspaper, the *Englishman*. The first number appeared on 11 April 1874, price twopence. 'The time has come for the establishment of a Journal which shall be independent of all class influences' ran the prospectus; 'and be actuated solely by the desire to maintain inviolate those rights for which our fore-fathers fought and bled, and which too many persons in the present day regard but lightly, when compared with the acquisition of money, or with selfish success in life'. In following this end the great light would be Junius, who was much quoted. The *Englishman* would thwart 'the further march of Romanism and Jesuitry' and advocate the suffrage for single women having qualifications currently required for male voters. Their virtuous influence 'would help to stem that wave of atheism and communism which is beginning to flow', and their appearance at the polls check electoral corruption. Kenealy called for government expenditure on schools, parks, museums and public recreation. He criticized the lunacy laws and expressed concern over the state of India. 'Every real grievance under which individuals, or communities labour, will find, in THE ENGLISHMAN, an echo of its complaint'.

During the *Englishman*'s early months its message was radical, but erratic.[45] It denounced established interests, 'society', politicians, and especially the House of Commons. 'A concourse which numbers the shoddy men, the squireen mercenaries of Popery, and the trading barristers', went a description of the Commons; 'the railway and shopkeeping interest, which is so largely represented there, tends very much also to lower its tone of thought'. Some articles that praised Cromwell and the execution of Charles I seemed to complement this picture; but the journal applauded the House of Lords as sensitive to public welfare. Bismarck found the editor's good graces, yet the centralization of the British state seemed an abomination. Allegedly this was the work of a despotic Whiggery which—by tying the army to the civil arm, by the poor law, and by extension of government ownership—'will throw the whole power and influence of the country into the hands of the Minister for the time'. Among the victims of this process was the Crown, now unable to act as the guardian of public liberty and welfare. At other times, the Tories were seen as no less evil than their opponents. Again, while ranting against Jesuitry was constant, the same antipathy fell upon the sceptical scientists of the British Association.

The Tichborne issue received considerable attention. All that could be said for the Claimant, and had been said so often, was said again. Efforts for a new trial and for the grant of a writ of error provided more lively, if ultimately negative news. Two Australian witnesses for the prosecution—Mina Jury, who was very important in identifying the Claimant as the Arthur Orton she knew in Hobart in 1853-5, and William Hopgood—provided good fare when they crossed with the police for thieving and bigamy. Reports of public meetings and movements in the Claimant's favour were long and fierce.

Yet Kenealy occupied more space than did the Claimant. Early issues gave much attention to the Kenealy Testimonial Fund, intended to raise £30 000. Petitioners and public meetings were advised to concentrate their attacks on the judges rather than to assert empty hopes for the release of Tichborne. The enormities of Gray's Inn and the Oxford mess loomed very large. Illustrations presented Kenealy in heroic guise: as an armoured St George, for example, killing the dragon of corruption with his sword, the *Englishman*. Horror stories told of attempts to murder Kenealy during the trial.

Critics thought they saw an easy target. One M. A. Orr was an original associate of Kenealy, but very soon quarrelled with him over money matters. He established a little paper, the *True Briton: The Avowed Enemy and Antidote to Dr Kenealy's 'Englishman'*. This promised to reveal the inner secrets of the Tichborne movement, but there emerged little but personal abuse of Kenealy:

> Kind people gather round me, and give me all you can,
> If only thirty thousand for a persecuted man.

Such charges became commonplace, taking their nastiest form in the new year when a pamphlet, *A Thunderbolt for Kenealy! Juggler, Mountebank, and Patriot!!!*, interspersed them with details of the child-beating case of 1850. More damaging was criticism by the *Tichborne Gazette*, the journal which had commenced between the law suits and had revived in May 1874 with the backing of A. J. W. Biddulph.

For the present, the dirt had little effect. The child-beating pamphlet might boom, but so did a hagiography which presented its hero as the victim of Rome.[46] The author also said that the *Englishman* was selling 160 000 copies weekly. The true figure certainly exceeded half that, which was remarkable enough, and its managers might have been right in alleging that W. H. Smith's refusal to handle the paper at railway bookstalls frustrated further demand. The testimonial fund had the same sort of response —less than startling, yet perceptible—as had the Claimant's appeals. More important, public discussion touched not only Kenealy's past but his future destiny. In June 1874 a correspondent to the *Englishman* urged the election to parliament of Kenealy, the Claimant, Onslow, Biddulph and Skipworth. The leader of the vigorous Tichborne movement in Leeds, Edward Foster, suggested in August that Kenealy should stand there at the next election.

For the moment, however, Kenealy's star shone above Leicester. The borough had a long radical tradition, currently upheld in parliament by P. A. Taylor. The Claimant's following there had always been strong. Its leader was T. M. Evans, a merchant of substance and respectability whose service in local government had culminated in his becoming High Bailiff in 1872 and a justice of the peace in 1874. He had himself been approached to contest Leicester in the general election of February 1874, but instead suggested that Kenealy do so. The latter wired his affirmation and policy: 'Independent Principles, Peace, Retrenchment, Economy. Free breakfast table'. But nothing developed.[47] Evans established a local journal, the *Evening News*, devoted to the Claimant's cause, and in August the Leicester 'Tichborne and Kenealy' committee invited Kenealy to launch from there a grand tour of public meetings. 'This is the first step to what we believe will be one of the wonders and glories of the nation for all time' enthused the *Englishman*, 'a spontaneous outburst and protest by THE PEOPLE'.[48] The committee of invitation had discussed its own purpose; one speaker had argued that as people of many opinions had supported the Claimant, any meddling in politics would weaken the cause. A majority, however, foresaw activity in local and national politics, with the hope of electing their own candidates. Committees in other towns followed Leicester's lead in requisitioning Kenealy to address them.

On 29 September Kenealy spoke at Leicester, the first of many such events over the following months. Usually two meetings took place: one at least nominally for members of the local Tichborne Release Association or whatever in-group sponsored the visit, and one for the public. Admission charges applied to both, but were cheaper for the public one. Kenealy dominated proceedings; his long speeches touched politics in general, his own wrongs at the hand of bench and bar, and the Tichborne case. The meetings were generally successful and it was of this period that the picture later painted by Kenealy's daughter had most truth:

He became a popular Idol, the subject sometimes of the most moving and passionate devotion . . . Presents of game, of flowers, of books, of pictures, every description of tribute came from numerous and unknown sympathizers. So too, came letters innumerable, suing for autographs: law-papers with notes imploring opinions on the merits and chances of the suits set forth. Whithersoever he went knots of people recognized and cheered him, and would come up frequently to beg the privilege of a word or of a hand-shake.[49]

A cartoon of the time, 'Dr Kenealy's Flying Trapeze', showed the man swinging from the bar via the press towards the House of Commons; reputedly it sold in thousands at two shillings apiece.[50]

Kenealy's critics kept him clothed in the image of martyrdom so congenial both to his own temperament and to the Tichbornites' view of the world. The benchers of Gray's Inn had continued enquiry into his conduct, but switched their animus to the *Englishman* and dropped charges relating to the trial. For weeks Kenealy fenced with his colleagues. Early in August the benchers resolved to exclude Kenealy from their number and to suspend him from privileges of the Inn. The *Englishman* was said to be libellous and its director unfit to be a bencher. This was not enough to propitiate the furies. In November Coleridge, of all people, felt shock when at a professional dinner Cockburn vented 'a flaming oration, almost bursting with wrath and passion about himself and Kenealy' and denounced the lord chancellor for not having deprived Kenealy of his patent as a Q.C.[51] Almost simultaneously the Lord Chancellor did as Cockburn wished. Cabinet endorsed the deprivation as an alternative to charging Kenealy with criminal libel. Queen Victoria was told that the latter course 'would not be expedient', whereas the former 'though severe' was unavoidable in view of articles in the *Englishman* that impugned the man's sanity.[52] In December the benchers expelled him altogether from Gray's Inn.

Newspaper opinion fluctuated over these moves, especially the replacement of the benchers' original charges with those derived from the *Englishman*. Some agreed with the reasoning. More general, however, was the opinion that by shifting ground the benchers had shown both the weakness of their original charges and the degree to which they felt personal and social detestation of Kenealy rather than professional outrage. This would seem fair comment. The radical *Examiner* and *Reynolds's Newspaper* noticed that for all the talk of libel, the one such action—that in 1874 by Mrs Pittendreigh—had failed.

This dialectic of mass applause and class revenge had its synthesis in Kenealy striving towards political power, much as the 'Flying Trapeze' cartoon suggested. The *Englishman* of 12 December denounced the 'atmosphere of slavery' that pervaded the country. Kenealy's personal experience was one symptom of this; others were the recent Income Tax Act which enabled government to investigate the private concerns of every individual, and the new education system which imposed servility. The Whig and Tory leaders denied power to the Queen and excluded true representatives of the people from parliament. Therefore Kenealy founded the Magna Charta Association of Great Britain. 'Let me have a million subscribers, and within two years I shall . . . return 100 members of the Middle and Operative Class to the House of Commons, and, with these men acting with me, I will destroy the Despotism that now exists'. He hoped that the existing Tichborne committees would sponsor branches of the MCA, but insisted that its nature was 'national and universal. It has nothing to do with the Tichborne case, or with the Kenealy wrong'.

Kenealy was all too ready with more specific aims: a bill of rights, a free press, no income tax, no electoral corruption, triennial parliaments, a stronger Crown and House of Lords, the exclusion of lawyers from parliament, equality of rich and poor before the law, no state interference in education, reduction of national expenditure to £40 million a year, government-subsidized emigration to the colonies, abolition of government patronage—they came pell-mell. The elevation of women would be a constant purpose, while 'compulsory vaccination, Contagious Diseases Acts, Lunacy Laws, Bankruptcy Laws, and all other statutes which enslave, demoralise, or insult the People of England, will be carefully looked after'. The MCA, Kenealy hoped, would fill the need for a third political party, so breaking the system which had forced even such men as Gladstone and Disraeli into submission. His organizational plan was elaborate enough to sustain this destiny. The Pope received a penny a week from every Catholic, so every Englishman should give his penny to MCA.

Various articles of January-February 1875 gave body and colour to this political programme. Centralization and classification were the two great engines of despotism. Workhouses, schools and lunatic asylums all operated on these principles, to the detriment of 'every tie of nature, affection, and duty' and to the enlargement of executive power. 'CENTRALISM *is in political what* ULTRAMONTISM *is in ecclesiastical rule*'. Kenealy also attacked that other great nineteenth-centry principle—industry. 'All the paid newspapers write in one hell-dog howl: "Work! Work! Work!"—Work to heap up gold at the bankers for our great Capitalists; Work to amass wealth that we may spend it in wicked wars, or in abominable profligacy'. The great families had united with the capitalists to suppress the people. They had corrupted parliament, and put into it scoundrels and adulterers. The *Englishman* attacked the railway interest which ignored the needs of the poor and inflicted upon them fearful accidents ('splintered carriages, blood on the lines, passengers writhing, and groaning') ; likewise the shipowners murderously resisted control of their trade.

Kenealy's energy surged along other channels in these manic weeks. Early in February he began publishing an edition of *The Trial at Bar of Sir Roger C. D. Tichborne*. Issued in weekly parts of thirty-two foolscap pages, this was to become one of the minor wonders of Victorian publishing: it was informative, illustrated, indexed. The first issue included directly political matter— Kenealy's dedication of the work to the Queen. This denounced the corruption of the constitution and the shrinking of the Crown's powers; aggression abroad, as represented by 'the Crimean blunder' and 'the Ashantee butchery'; and the condition of England's industrial poor. Therein, suggested Kenealy, lay the vengeance of God. He called upon the Queen to read the trial, to assert her power, and to dismiss her evil ministers. A more purely literary exercise was Kenealy's publishing from January onward the monthly *Englishman's Magazine*. In the early issues Kenealy relived and rehashed by-gone adventures: the continental tour of 1843, his Temperance lecture, his *Montagu* novel. In similar vein, he began republication of his poetry. The first volume gave to Mrs T. M. Evans a dedication of the same ill-fated grandiloquence as earlier had gone to Disraeli and Cockburn.

That dedication was the prize for Evans's master-minding Kenealy's campaign in the Stoke electorate. G. W. Melly announced his retirement early in January, when Kenealy was resting at the Evans home in Leicester. A decision to contest was natural. Kenealy had considered standing there in 1862 and had a long professional association with the district; the electorate was exceptionally popular. In the general election of 1874 a building contractor of proletarian background and sympathy, A. A. Walton, had contested the two-seat electorate against two bourgeois Liberals (including Melly) and a Conservative. The result was that against all odds the Conservative won the second place, with Walton last. The first fruits of Evans's organization were multisigned requisitions for Kenealy to speak at Longton and Hanley.[53] Kenealy answered with equal amplitude: 'We are doing our duty in a Holy Cause, and we shall prosper and win this noble battle'. His meetings there were successful. They caused a stir, said sympathizers, comparable with Garibaldi's visit in 1864. Meetings elsewhere, especially in Manchester, kept Kenealy's name before a wider public, and support came from many centres. An Ipswich memorial, composed 'amid the blaze and din of fires and furnaces of a great Foundry', told Kenealy that if victorious he would be the representative of all working men. The candidate endorsed this theme in his electoral address, saying that he was 'A PEOPLE'S CANDIDATE. I belong to no party, but to England'.

Walton again stood, with official Liberal and trade union support. The *Beehive*, voice of trade union politicalism, rejoiced at this alliance. A Conservative, Davenport, also competed. As at Wednesbury years before, Liberals charged Kenealy with serving Tory purposes by splitting the radical vote. The *Englishman* responded that Walton had no chance anyway: Stoke would never send to the Commons one 'whom the first gentleman that saw him there would probably ask to clean his shoes or brush his coat'. Bourgeois Liberals evidently were no more enthusiastic for Walton now than a year earlier; another circumstance favouring Kenealy was the support of Frank Wedgwood, of the great family.[54] Kenealy's costs were £1755.12.3. They included £270 for the returning officers, £400 for printing, £550 for committee rooms, postage, 'breakages' and voting cards, and £70 for cab hire. Meetings were satisfactory, 'men of every handicraft and none' coming in masses and calling for 'the heroic Dr Kenealy'. Davenport and Walton joined in despising their opponent.

Polling day, 16 February, was foggy and dark in the heart of the Black Country. The gas burned almost throughout. Electoral business ran brisk, Kenealy travelling around with wife and children. Hundreds of soldiers and police stood ready lest Kenealy's defeat provoke riot. There was no need of them, for the poll results were as follows:

Kenealy	6110
Walton	4168
Davenport	3901

Telegrams carried the news to 150 betting stations throughout the country; gambling had been very heavy. Late that night a white-clad Kenealy still harangued the crowds from his hotel window.

HEY-DAY IN THE COMMONS

Presumably Kenealy told his audience what he was soon to say in the *Englishman*: that the Stoke result was the greatest triumph ever won by the British working class, the fore-runner of much electoral success. He pledged himself to serve all members of this class, not just his constituency; he thanked women supporters for their decisive help. The people had freed themselves from the rule of the Carlton and Reform Clubs which hitherto, in collusion in the boroughs with a few big shopkeepers and traders, had imposed their candidates. Echoes of this exultation came from every quarter. 'In Wales, our hearts throbbed in gratitude to Almighty God for your overwhelming triumph over your enemies'; from Thwing, Yorkshire, came ten shillings and report that 'our little place was all alive when news came that you were sent to parliament. Go on, noble Doctor'. Such addresses gave some meaning to Kenealy's claim to represent more than his own electorate.

While Tichbornites cheered, mid-February 1874 sounded like Armageddon to many conservative Britons. Kenealy's election coincided with that of John Mitchel for Tipperary. Mitchel, transported in 1848-9, had escaped from Tasmania while still under sentence. He therefore was a felon, ineligible to sit in the

House of Commons. That only made his success a more insolent sneer at British rule. The link between his victory and Kenealy's is of interest not only because of their mutual activity in 1848, but also because it deepened the portent of their separate roles. On 20 February the *Spectator* offered the most elaborate hostile analysis of Kenealy's victory. At best, electors had the worthy aim of redressing a supposed although mistaken grievance. Alternatively, the motive was sheer love of political extremism. Or the attraction may have been Kenealy's unique character: a man who attacked the most respected names in the land and who spurned the established political parties as he had the protocol of the law courts. The *Spectator* believed that all three motives had played a part. The residuum of Stoke had displayed the temper of a Paris mob during the Terror; it had broken loose from the respectable classes. This behaviour was precisely what many had feared when the suffrage extended in 1867; compounding it had been the secret ballot. At Stoke the constituency had behaved as formerly did the rowdies on nomination day. 'Under the Ballot, the passion which formerly exhaled itself in a sort of half-goodhumoured, half-dangerous carnival, now expresses itself in actual voting; . . . the rowdy element in the electoral body, under the Ballot, can carry seats if it likes; and the perception of that fact will, we fear, be rapidly spread'.

The *Times, Daily Telegraph* and *Daily News* offered a similar verdict, while the *Saturday Review* saw Kenealy's triumph as the product of popular literacy. 'A sort of ranting, irrepressible Robin Hood', he incarnated novelette heroes. *Punch* gave Kenealy and Mitchel a full-page cartoon, showing its estimate of the two at par. The *Graphic* linked the elections with greater foresight, seeing them as likely to destroy the procedures of the House of Commons through filibuster speeches. *Blackwood's Magazine* also spoke of Mitchel and Kenealy in tandem, stressing that the electorates had behaved unpredictably and in contempt of the House of Commons. Kenealy's election, furthermore, had expressed no-confidence in the judicial system, and suggested that mass feeling opposed the movement of power from Crown to Commons, however expertly that power was managed.[55] Even the *Annual Register* forsook neutrality in bemoaning the election of this 'unscrupulous advocate'.

Conservatives were not alone in their repugnance at the election. The *Beehive* naturally felt bitter at Walton's defeat, and grudged any praise to the victor. It countered criticisms of democ-

racy that would stem from the result by arguing that the Claimant
had supporters in many walks of life. P. A. Taylor used the same
derogatory term, 'residuum', to describe Kenealy's supporters as
did the *Times*; and his *Examiner* followed suit. Indeed orthodox
radicals had more to lose by the growth of Kenealyism than had
conservatives.

Some voices warned against taking the election too seriously.
Thomas Carlyle laughed that *he* would have listened to the
Claimant for seven days, and then hanged him.[56] Others recalled
that demagogues had gone to parliament before, and that time or
parliamentary pressure soon suffocated their notoriety; years before Kenealy himself had so argued to Disraeli. History was on
the side of such disparagement, but for the present Kenealy
seemed important to many, and interesting to nearly all. The idol
of masses, he attracted lights of high society to parliament, just
as the Tichborne suits had attracted them to the law courts. No
man could sustain this situation long, but Kenealy lived to his
image pretty well.

The high-spot came at the very outset: Kenealy's introduction
to the House on 18 February.[57] All was dead quiet as the Speaker
called for new members. Kenealy came forward alone. The
Speaker (Sir Henry Brand, later Viscount Hampden) reminded
him that two members should introduce a newcomer. Kenealy
prepared to dispute the point: a splendid addition to his repertoire of rule-breaking. Probably he had pre-determined to defy the
House. On Brand's request, Kenealy withdrew. By earlier arrange-
ment with Brand, Disraeli then moved that the House ignore its
usual procedure; Speaker and Premier wanted to avoid giving
Kenealy a chance for display. The same motive might have
prompted John Bright to offer to join Whalley in sponsoring the
newcomer. Disraeli maintained his resolution, however, and despite some dissent the House agreed. Kenealy scored a victory in
coming forward alone; whatever the truth, he was soon claiming
to have flouted the rules deliberately. He marched up to the
Speaker's table, 'his eyes flashing a quite unnecessary defiance'.
The popular press was to make much of a story that he rested his
umbrella against the mace as he took the oath. A well-known
journalist, H. W. Lucy, later 'admitted' having invented this tale,
but that itself might have been a self-enhancing error. Having
sworn, Kenealy took a seat on the second row of the Opposition
benches, immediately behind Gladstone. 'My first impression of
this man is that he is not going to be so turbulent as many men

suppose', wrote Brand in his diary. 'He has an ungainly appearance and a bad voice, although loud; but he has evidently great
self-assurance'.

Kenealy resumed the limelight on 4 March when he raised a
question of privilege. On 27 February Evelyn Ashley, Liberal
member for Poole and a member of the Oxford circuit, had referred to Kenealy when speaking in his electorate. That district
had much sympathy for the Tichborne cause, and Ashley later
told the Commons that heckling had driven him to extremes.
Kenealy, he had said, 'was where he was not fit to be'. Kenealy
took up the matter with Brand and Disraeli—his notepaper showing the Kenealy crest as always but now in gilt instead of green or
black. Brand believed that Ashley's speech was 'unjustifiable',
and so assented to the matter being raised. 'A very full and excited
House to hear Dr Kenealy', Brand noted on the day. Ashley made
a half-apology, but the doctor pressed forward. Cries of 'order'
thickened. Kenealy responded that he would scorn all personal
aspersions 'as the lion shakes the dewdrops from his mane'. The
timing and manner of delivery touched the members' humour;
how loud they laughed is variously reported, but laugh they did.
From the gallery the Prince of Wales and his cohorts laughed too.
One journalist recollected the episode as killing Kenealy's career,
adding ridicule to the 'Coventry' that he already suffered.[58] This
over-dramatized the incident, but not too grossly. In their laughter, the Commoners expressed their hate-fear of this strange little
man and strove to make him an object of fun, not doom. But
whereas the over-dramatizer judged Kenealy's speech pitiably
broken, Disraeli thought well of it.[59] Still, the Premier insisted
that the matter end at once, with the face-saving formula that
privilege applied only where the alleged derogation concerned
the individual as parliamentarian.

On 15 April Tichborniana again dominated. The House committee on privilege had questioned a petition from Prittlewell
which not merely attacked the Queen's Bench judges, but also
invited the Commons to impeach the Speaker if he continued his
alleged policy of refusing petitions on the case. Disraeli stressed
this attack on the Speaker in moving dismissal of the petition.
However, the debate showed considerable antagonism to any restriction on the right of petition. This did not prevent criticism of
Kenealy. Bright and a trade union member, Alexander Mac-
Donald, taunted him with bad faith in failing to bring on a
motion, promised from his earliest days in parliament, for a royal

commission into the case. Kenealy answered that he would move only when the House had received petitions from the country in support of his plea. Against Disraeli's inclination, the House had the Prittlewell petition read. Then it passed Disraeli's motion, albeit Kenealy and a few others still opposed.

Under this public record lay a more intriguing situation. In fact the Speaker did believe that the House should refuse petitions that used extravagant language. He would have rejected the one from Prittlewell simply because of its charges against the judges, charges which most Tichborne petitions repeated. He advised the Government to this effect. Disraeli had to argue hard before cabinet agreed that the government should object only to the references to the Speaker. Brand was dismayed by the debate's revelation of many members' readiness 'to relax all restraint on the language of petitions', and felt that 'policy' had dictated the government's stand. That was true: Disraeli believed that the Speaker's advice would have led to probable defeat in the House and certain discredit 'in the country'.[60]

The next night Whalley sought to regain some initiative as spokesman for the cause. He argued that, quite apart from Kenealy, the matter had aroused such feeling in the English-speaking world that the House must debate it seriously. Kenealy enlarged on this in his contribution. 'There is a volcano in this Kingdom which may merge it at any moment in utter fire and ruin . . . the morning which follows the rejection of my Motion will carry dismay and rage throughout the United Kingdom'. He spoke of having been treated as a pariah by the House, and alleged that certain members had refused to present petitions. Counter-attack came notably from MacDonald, who denied that popular opinion was such as Kenealy described; while S. D. Waddy dealt personal abuse. The pressure was strong enough for Kenealy to agree to 23 April as the day for his royal commission move.

'House met under much excitement', duly recorded Speaker Brand. Kenealy spoke for three hours, arguing that the case had shown many flaws in the administration of justice. The Liberals had lost the last election partly because of the case; popular feeling had noticed especially the difference in the government's behaviour towards the Claimant and Overend, Gurney. Coleridge had used the Pittendreigh letters knowing them to be forged. Cockburn's bias had denied justice, and the court's use of contempt powers established a rule of terror. So the argument droned, without ever achieving effective climax. In seconding, Whalley denigrated the *Englishman* and spoke of division between Rivers and Kenealy; then he returned to his Jesuit-baiting. Sir Henry James replied with a long defence of judicial independence. Disraeli used a lighter touch. He regretted that 'the people of England . . . —there are people more excitable, but none more enthusiastic—should have their fine and noble sympathies wasted on such a case'. Kenealy he knew to be a scholar; 'some hallucination wilder than has ever influenced a public man' must have possessed him. On division, Kenealy and Whalley could 'tell' but one supporter: the House's funny-man, Major Purcell O'Gorman. Those against numbered 433. 'So the bubble has burst' remarked Brand.

The session was still to hear much about the case, nevertheless. In the House of Lords on 26 April Coleridge (now Baron Coleridge, Chief-Justice of the Common Pleas) denied Kenealy's allegations about the Pittendreigh letters: Chabot had merely suggested *doubts* about *some* of the letters. The Lord Chancellor was effusive in response. In the Commons Whalley kept asking about police expenses, about stories of Arthur Orton still wandering the Antipodes, about treatment of the Claimant in prison. Kenealy was sporadic in such fighting, but scored the best hit.[61] Acting on information from Tasmania, he asked the Home Secretary whether Mina Jury was the Mercevina Caulfield transported thither as a convict in June 1847. R. A. Cross first professed ignorance, and even after some weeks' lapse refused to affirm. Yet Kenealy's proposition was true. On other occasions Whalley and Kenealy joined in a vain attempt to restrict contempt powers, and Whalley drew attention to Cockburn's continuing criticisms of those who disputed the Tichborne verdict. Petitions kept swarming in, generally from public meetings or MCA/Tichborne Release Associations. Altogether in this session some 120 petitions, bearing 280 318 signatures, called for an enquiry. Only the Permissive Prohibitory Liquor Bill, the Contagious Diseases Repeal Bill and the Women's Disabilities Removal Bill scored more support. A further 21 petitions with 44 639 signatures criticized Gray's Inn; two petitions combined these themes.

Apropos non-Tichborne issues in parliament, Kenealy acted as the haphazard radical he was. He tried twice to gain leave to introduce a Triennial Parliaments Bill but met first a count-out and then an adverse vote. He spoke against public money being spent on the Prince of Wales's proposed trip to India and against the naval estimates, yet thought that Ireland should receive its own royal residence as the people there were monarchist at heart.

On the annexation of Fiji, Kenealy joined the small opposing minority: such ventures destroyed 'primitive innocence and simplicity' and led to rum-trading missionaries making wealth while the home government further extended its patronage and power.[62] Kenealy spoke too on the Unseaworthy Ships' Bill, castigating the shipowners. Several times he joined small minorities against civil list grants, especially for the services and colonial administration. He backed the Permissive Prohibitory Bill. Even closer to Kenealy's heart, but no more successful, was a bill exempting incomes of less than £300 from income tax. He supported Scottish universities giving degrees to women; education for the children of agricultural labourers (but not their enforced school attendance); and a royal commission into Irish landownership. These too were lost causes.

Those Stoke-fired hopes of Kenealy's disciples entering parliament shone briefly. Perhaps the man himself was not much interested in this development: co-operation never came easily to him. When possible by-elections offered he found the best candidate in his eldest son, Ahmed—'Jupiter Junior', according to *Punch*. First Norwich seemed the mark, but corruption there led to disfranchisement. Hartlepool came up next, in late July. Ahmed polled badly. Another abortive move of mid-year sought to re-establish Kenealy in respectable society. It appears that Kenealy approached Bright in June, asking if he might mediate to this end.[63] Bright responded that reparation must include apologies to the judges and forsaking the *Englishman* and the Tichborne cause. Kenealy refused such conditions and there the matter rested until 1878 when the two charged each other with initiating the moves.

On 5 August Kenealy returned to form with an attack on Lieutenant-Colonel Valentine Baker, 10th Hussars. Baker had just been convicted of assault, evidently sexual in intent, on a young girl with whom chance had thrown him in a railway carriage.[64] The incident aroused tremendous interest. Baker's trial attracted many spectators, notably a number of his fellow-officers who asserted their sympathy with him. Mr Justice Brett sentenced Baker to one year's imprisonment, and he was removed from the army. In the Commons, Kenealy protested that Baker intended rape; but the judge had decided according to the rank of the prisoner, not the enormity of the offence. So Kenealy acted once more in defiance of custom and status, and also complemented his votes against the armed services. The House was angry. 'He was vulgar and coarse in his reference to the Baker trial', thought

Brand, while Major A. G. Dickson spoke of Kenealy's child-
beating past. Before the House rose Dickson received from
Ahmed a challenge to duel. Brand advised Dickson not to bring
the letter before the House and believed that Kenealy was 'much
disappointed' when no sensation occurred. Whether Ahmed had
his duel is unknown.

When Kenealy determined not to work through Bright towards
reconciliation with society, he showed that his greater interest was
with the mass audience outside parliament. This he addressed
week by week through the *Englishman* (which in September still
sold 70 000 copies weekly) [65] and in another run of public meetings throughout England, Wales and Scotland. The man and his
movement expressed themselves with greater flair and vivacity
through these media than through parliamentary work.

In essence, the themes already suggested were continued, but
there was some perceptible move towards a more militant radicalism—as judged by orthodox criteria. The attacks on wealth
became increasingly comprehensive and violent. Stigmatizing the
rich as 'but idle and disgusting drones' one article continued:

Do we not delve and dig for them in the mines? and do not our
wives and daughters toil for them in the fields and factories? and
are they not torn in pieces for them every year by their unfenced
machinery? and are not our sailors drowned by them in thousands,
so that they may gain gold by their fell insurances? and have they
not parks ten miles long, while the People are confined to dingy
foul-smelling cellars and dungeons; so dear is land made by those
splendid enclosures of our patricians within stone walls? [66]

Kenealy's sympathy for the House of Lords notwithstanding,
other national institutions were found amiss. Anti-clericalism
tended away from the Jesuits to the venality, wealth and sloth of
the Church of England, especially its bishops. Criticism fell on the
whole notion of a standing army, and on imperialism at large and
more especially in India. The Baker case led to calumny not only
of the officer class but of the Prince of Wales, said to be a 'pal' of
the villain.

The Messianic-apocalyptic element in Kenealy's character now
became rather more marked. He cared nothing for worldly life
and fame, said the *Englishman;* he sought immortal glory. The
gold spectacles which long had been his idiosyncrasy had to share
that honour with flashing rings, a Scotch plaid and an elaborate
walking-stick. The last he called his rod of Moses; it had the form

of a staff which his religious writings had described as descending to the twelfth messenger of God from his precursors. His outrage at godlessness pitched ever higher.

Enthusiasm for the man and his movement remained at high pitch throughout spring and summer. The peak came with a demonstration in Hyde Park on Easter Monday, 29 March. Neutral estimates put numbers as high as 200 000; the *Daily News* said it was the biggest crowd ever to gather in London. Some posters hailed Kenealy as the English Garibaldi; others as sitting beside God himself in almighty grandeur.[67] On tour, similar excitement showed itself. At Bradford, railway workers put fog-signals on the rails to provide a salute of welcome to Kenealy's train; at Huddersfield, many women held up their babies to receive his salutation; at Plymouth, hundreds of soldiers attended— at least so said the *Englishman,* which suggested that disaffection was strong in that vital quarter; at Glasgow, Kenealy received his rod of Moses. Rowdies sometimes heckled, but generally audiences were large, enthusiastic and emotional. At Burslem, a Mrs Wade drew tears as she spoke of her own dead son and denied that the Dowager or any woman could ever mistake her progeny. The presence of Mrs Kenealy on these tours varied the feminist theme.

Kenealy put his mail at 250 items a week—one-third of them abusive. The remainder included one letter which told 'our noble and heroic leader' that the Almighty 'has given you already an earnest of what is to come in the confidence and admiration in which you are held by millions of your fellow creatures and will we believe hereafter far more richly reward your honest labour and your heroic fidelity'.[68] Kenealy was asked to preside over eisteddfods at Swansea and Abergavenny, and to be chief speaker at the great annual festival of the Northumberland miners. He refused to address an agricultural labourer's meeting because he opposed its objectives of full manhood suffrage; when the organizer criticized him accordingly, the audience heckled the organizer.[69]

The requisitions that came to Kenealy maintained their interest. Nine thousand names backed a lengthy diatribe from Hull:

For a long time past we have deeply regretted that growing power of Mammon, who today seems to rule everywhere and everything, trampling upon Justice, Truth, and Honour, with impunity; the House of God, the Courts of Justice, the Press, the Merchant's Exchange . . . Our House of Commons is filled with the great *leeches* who suck and grow fat upon the very blood of our toiling millions.[70]

Spirit merchants and publicans ran the country's domestic affairs, while abroad national power forced China to accept opium. The state tore children from their parents to enforce vaccination; charities, established to benefit the poor, flowed to the rich. 'Men can make £10 000 from their works, whilst they will, like the *vile Jew Banker,* grind down their people to the lowest farthing'. Kenealy congratulated these 'exalted sentiments', while admitting he might not accord with all of them.

Popular art and entertainment still fed on the issue. Vast crowds went to Tussaud's at Easter to see Kenealy's model. One of his most active supporters sold Parian marble busts of the leader; they were twenty-eight centimetres high and priced at five shillings. 'All imitations are a piracy' said the advertisement, claiming copyright. In June a London magistrate heard a case wherein a manufacturer of clay pipes protested at the copying of his registered design of a bowl featuring Kenealy. Entrepreneurs of lantern-shows and pantomimes used him as one of their stock figures. The Stoke museum holds a set of three fine jugs, each embossed with his portrait.

The MCA movement provided some institutional counterpart to this story, although less than Kenealy's rhetoric claimed. He described his followers as 'The flower and fruit of the Working Classes of the Empire'; 'they are nearly all allied with the Temperance Societies; they are well-read, thinking, sensible, and religious'.[71] With a million such, and the support of women, he would regenerate the nation and restore to Englishmen their own country, lost since Alfred's day. Notices of MCA meetings filled many *Englishman* columns: fifty-four reports in one issue (29 May) was the peak. Perhaps there were 250 branches altogether, with London having thirty or more. No pattern appears: old towns and new, metropolis and village, industrial centre and rural periphery, all made a showing appropriate to their numbers.

The *Englishman* prescribed an ideal type for each MCA. It should concentrate on political action (only by making the Claimant's release a political issue would it be won), maintain contact with London and channel funds thither, establish contacts throughout the whole working class, and pursue an organization based on the Wesleyan scheme of class leaders, local preachers and superintendents. In reality the situation was such as this:

Some eight or ten, all earnest in the cause, met at our Committee-Room at the 'Earl of Durham', Havelock Street, Islington, kindly lent to us free of all expense by the landlord, a strong friend of the cause. We determined to get two thousand bills printed and circulated (which, by-the-way, were paid for by our good friend, the landlord) . On the following Tuesday, we had a good muster; and though none of us were well qualified to speak to them, we did our best. The result was, 43 members enrolled, and 19s. subscribed . . . The week before the Hyde Park Meeting, we had 120 members and £4.18s. subscribed; by which means we were enabled to join with three other Societies, and march away from North London with a good band, and banners flying.[72]

A penny a week was the normal contribution and, notwithstanding Kenealy's stress on temperance, a public house was the common venue. Political and general discussion did supplement rehashing of the case. Kenealy employed one or two professional organizers and secured a central meeting-place: Doughty Hall in Bedford Row, London. A congress was called for 16 August. Political parties have risen to power from humbler beginnings.

Plenty of problems barred that path, however. Many a sympathizer with the Claimant drew the line at joining an MCA and paying a penny; many who did feel strongly enough for that had misgivings about politicizing the case and attaching it to Kenealy's star. Provincial secretaries were lax about keeping contact with London, especially when it came to sending money. Linking these doubts was the question of Kenealy's own probity. Charges of self-interest became more intense from mid-year when T. M. Evans and the Leicester MCA joined the critics. They alleged of Kenealy that 'he lacks sagacity, caution, and temper; that he is violent and vacillating, irritable under remonstrance, tyrannical and dictatorial, and that his acceptance of the people's pence for so-called Magna Charta purposes in the absence of a responsible treasurer, is discreditable and open to the greatest censure'.[73] The August congress saw physical violence between Kenealyites and their critics principally from Leicester. Earlier in the year Biddulph had publicly attacked Kenealy as a revolutionary, and Whalley added similar charges as antagonism grew between the two parliamentarians.

In the respectable press, hate-fear of Kenealy reached a peak in April; thereafter jeers and sneers became more confident and universal. The *Times* sounded this reaction at its extreme.[74] It took the Easter Monday demonstration seriously, saying that the crowds were larger than ever gathered for other causes. The Irish were absent; the marchers comprised largely 'the lowest class of labourers', with some artisans and tradesmen. The *Times* suggested that the demonstrations threw doubt on the radicals' belief that education was adding constantly to the number of working men who deserved the franchise. In fact 'their gregarious habits, a certain combativeness of temperament, and a deeply-rooted suspicion of the motives of those above them in station' seemed to resist such improvement. The 'gross and palpable fatuity' of the Tichborne movement would prompt a conservative reaction and check any move towards franchise extension. Over the next weeks the *Times* gibed at Kenealy's delay in bringing on his royal commission motion; when he did speak, the journal was contemptuous and critical.

The *Economist* thought the strongest element in the movement was 'the bitter antipathy to Roman Catholicism . . . concealed under the stolidity of the English lower classes', which was just as strong now as in the day of the Gordon riots. Mass democracy threatened the same havoc in Britain as in the United States. The evidence suggested that 'a good many other boroughs' might vote as did Stoke. Kenealyism would destroy first the independence of the bar and second the concept of a permanent civil service. Then 'all the fallacies of an ignorant democracy—and the fallacies of protection amongst them—would soon be upon us'.[75] While this carried to an extreme the attack on Kenealy's public significance, the *Gentleman's Magazine* gave personal abuse its highest polish. The anonymous writer was H. W. Lucy, who afterwards claimed invention of the tale about Kenealy's umbrella. Even the child-bashing got its mention, together with money-grubbing and megalomania. Lucy drew his subject with ugly strokes: 'a short stout man . . . a high red forehead . . . much hair . . . a harsh voice that contains a metallic note singularly repellent . . . a "podgy" red hand'. The House despised Kenealy, said Lucy, because he had outraged 'its love for what is straightforward, manly, and true'.[76]

Various radicals were as hostile to Kenealy. The defeat of Walton and the Parliamentary brush with MacDonald set his relations with the trade union movement. The *Englishman* and the *Beehive* swapped continual abuse. Kenealy, said the *Beehive,* was 'a mischievous demagogue' taking his followers 'along the dusky byeways of history' to the advantage of nobody but himself.[77] Kenealy said much the same about union leaders. Similar relations prevailed with the Irish nationalists, while a still more bitter critic of the Left was Charles Bradlaugh. Responding to criticisms of himself as an atheist and corrupter of morality, Bradlaugh scoffed at

Kenealy's pretensions of gentility and concern for popular wel-fare. 'You now begin to whine because my first blow back has touched you in your only sensitive spot—your pocket'.[78] Brad-laugh, MacDonald, and the Irishman A. M. Sullivan all refused an invitation to the Northumberland miners' festival because Ken-ealy was to have top billing. John Bright offered the best example of a bourgeois radical who strove to clear not only himself but his life-sustaining values from the Tichborne movement. George Dawson of Birmingham, archetype of that city's Victorian pro-gressives, and Samuel Plimsoll, the seamen's friend, were others in this category.[79]

As the months passed, Kenealy's critics found further weak-nesses. They stressed his failure in the Commons, and so his loss of the charisma of February-March. Kenealy's common absence from the House, said his enemies, showed his own sense of this, and also his lack of concern to fight for anything but his own wel-fare. First the 'endorsement' of Ahmed for Hartlepool and then his dismal poll boosted this denigration, and the internal quarrels of the Tichbornites served the purpose further. Comic publica-tions jeered about the umbrella story, the 'dewdrops' speech, the parliamentary rebuffs. 'Why is it called a Cyclopian division?', asked *Judy* of the vote on the motion for an enquiry; 'Why be-cause there was only one aye in it'. A satirical broadsheet pro-claimed 'The Kenealy Dynasty and Magna Charta Parliament' in response to the Hartlepool candidature. *Punch*, evidently learning of the duel, offered a 'Motto for Major Dickson—for Ahmed forewarned'.[80]

Society was having its revenge.

4

KENEALY IN DECLINE

THAT REVENGE SWELLED throughout Kenealy's last years. He remained in parliament until the general election of March-April 1880, and survived defeat at that poll by a bare fortnight. The coincidence suggests that his life had just so much meaning as the intensity of feeling between 1873 and 1875 gave it. The man found no new resources of leadership or belief that could sustain his career. Yet Kenealy never quite forsook his earlier image. As a public figure, he continued to speak in parliament and to lead demonstrations; the *Englishman* and the serial issue of *The Trial at Bar of Sir Roger C. D. Tichborne* added written word to this testimony; Magna Charta Associations survived as cells of Kenealyism. Meanwhile his more private life still served literature and metaphysics.

AS A PUBLIC FIGURE

The debate in parliament over a Newspaper Regulation Bill, 11 April 1877, best illustrated Kenealy's situation in these years. The bill was sponsored by S. D. Waddy, his long-standing enemy, who had been pushing for such a measure since 1875. The debate left no doubt that the *Englishman* was the major object of his attack. Waddy urged that not merely fines but imprisonment should punish any person 'who had deliberately set himself . . . to be a general nuisance to society . . . pandering to the vilest tastes of the lowest, basest, and most offensive of our people'. Kenealy took the challenge and opposed the bill. It was superfluous, he said, for already the judiciary had 'manacled the press' through using contempt powers; and anyway the libel laws were sufficient. A.M. Sullivan, another established Kenealy-hater, made the most dramatic speech. Like Waddy, he avoided mentioning Kenealy by name, but dealt him fierce abuse. The unnamed was a 'coward' who dissembled his editorship (since early 1876 the *Englishman* had carried the by-line 'edited by Kenealy' and his sons had taken at least nominal charge) ; he was a wretch who had beaten his own child. The House 'applauded with much excitement', noted Speaker Brand, who decided not to interfere lest he fit the cap onto Kenealy.

As members divided to defeat the measure, Kenealy called Sullivan a liar. Sullivan reported to Brand, who said the House must know of such insult. Members demanded that Kenealy apologize, and so extended the rule against improper language to cover lobbies as well as the chamber. Kenealy gave his apologies, and had them accepted. Nevertheless he took up that old, recurrent slur about the child-beating of 1850, arguing that justice had then miscarried. The Speaker ruled his questions out of order and the Home Secretary could not find relevant papers. Both dignitaries expressed regret that the issue had arisen, and in doing so gave more subtle colour to the incident. They admitted that Sullivan had behaved as badly as he accused Kenealy of doing. Established powers thus modified the confrontation with Kenealy. The man himself accepted the protocol of apology-and-further-recourse. He remained the wild one of social politics, but was becoming an institution in that role. Other incidents pointed in this direction.

In 1876 Chester cathedral was receiving the final touches of a grand restoration. Authorities had decided that the new corbels should revive the mediaeval practice of depicting public events and persons. The stonemason included a scene of Disraeli defending the Crown from Kenealy's assault. The latter looks fierce and determined, his head growing from some monstrous animal. The carving aroused a stir, but the powers determined that it should stay.[1] Two years later, the *New Monthly Magazine* included Kenealy as number nineteen in a series of 'Personalities of the House of Commons'.[2] The article reflected its subject's ambiguous situation: he 'has been no dummy, and his individuality, if anything, has become more pronounced', since going to parliament; yet, 'the learned Dr has hardly been so successful as his ardent temperament probably led him to expect. He has been listened to, but that is about all'. The first questions of many visitors to the House concerned Kenealy, and should he be speaking there was a thrill such as Daniel O'Connell and W. S. O'Brien had excited in their day. A large head and dark, dishevelled hair gave the little man 'a general leonine appearance'. This fitted his pugnacity but also justified that great laugh of March 1875 when Kenealy shook dew-drops from his mane.

Ridicule continued to beset Kenealy, but perhaps more humour mixed with its malice. Soon after the Sullivan episode, the House laughed again—at Kenealy's assurance that he was speaking from 'the essence of his heart'.[3] Abusive mail arrived in shoals at Kenealy's door: one ploy was to send open postcards, implying— for example—promiscuous paternity.[4] Kenealy's supporters could buy a marble bust of their hero, but his critics a statuette of 'The Lion of Britain' wearing gold-rimmed spectacles, an umbrella, baggy trousers, and his hat scooped out so as to hold matches.[5] A motto ran:

> The tile so oft held out for money,
> With matches now usefully filled.
> The Lion of Britain who roars so,
>   Who roars till he's hoarse,
>   That one man of course,
> Is as good as another—and more so.

Rowdies who disrupted many Kenealy meetings made similar points with less grace.

Kenealy's political rhetoric changed little in this period, its basic themes being his own transcendence as a political leader and the flaws of other aspirants for popular favour. Trade unionists continued to be anathema; George Potter of the *Beehive* retaliated against the *Englishman* with a libel action late in 1875, and his failure strengthened Waddy's belief in statutory regulation of newspapers. Joseph Chamberlain's election to the Commons prompted the *Englishman* to remark that the people would be better to have no franchise than to suffer representation by this scion of 'a bloated, vulgar and low-minded shopocracy'.[6] Revolutionary communists were just as abominable, and a measure of the government's sin was that it encouraged their cause by its class legislation. Among other radicals of the day, only Charles Dilke won praise: in August 1876 the *Englishman* applauded a rumour that he might form a new party. Apart from this, Kenealy reserved acclaim for himself. The *Englishman* presented him as God's gift to working men, although like Christ he faced betrayal by the apathy of most and death at the hands of some. Kenealy seemed anxious for martyrdom, or at least to exaggerate threats that he might achieve that status. Meanwhile he proclaimed his proud descent: twentieth from Edward III.

In these years Kenealy meant less to the Tichborne cause than he had done earlier, and he deliberately diminished its place in his own political image; yet the tie remained and was still a significant phenomenom. Demonstrations and meetings under Kenealy-Tichborne auspices attracted large numbers. On 8 February 1876 Kenealy held a procession in competition with the Queen as she went to open parliament. Among the onlookers was one of the most sensitive of men, novelist Henry James. He saw the scene as a vignette of the two Englands, the Tichborne banners serving as a focus for many social discontents.[7] The *Times* was outraged at Kenealy's impudence, but drew comfort from his supporters having been so diminished as to allay earlier fears that up to twenty electorates might follow Stoke's example. 'The conditions of modern society in England are fatal to the vitality of popular delusions', pontificated the *Times;* the absurdities of Titus Oates and Colonel Gordon had passed forever.[8] But still the crowds kept coming: at least 10 000 to a meeting at Nottingham in 1877; scores of thousands to the rally of Easter Monday, 1878. Bands and uniforms were almost as many as in the hey-day, and the *Englishman* could claim that Tichborne and Kenealy were remembered in ways 'absolutely marvellous in their significance'.[9]

Perhaps the *Englishman* and *The Trial at Bar of Sir Roger C. D. Tichborne* were closer to being 'absolutely marvellous'. The former ran at sixteen pages each weekly issue. It contained some illustrations and advertisements, but a deal of solid prose too. The circulation fell, but probably still exceeded the norm of radical papers, and Kenealy would not have continued a money-losing project. The same might be said of *The Trial,* but with greater wonderment. The last massive volume (number eight, in addition to the Introduction) reached its final 820th, page just as Kenealy's life ended. It proved almost true to the blurb of the *Englishman*:

Probably the most interesting work in the world, in the realm of letters. It is as varied as Shakspere; it presents almost every possible variety of human character. The men and women move before us as in a panorama, or in a pantomime. Every phase of life from high to low is represented. It is a tale of Love, Forgery, Fraud, Intrigue, Romance, Travel, Perjury, Judicial Injustice, Bribery and Corruption, political and social.[10]

The *Englishman* press also found time to produce, and a market to buy, annual Tichborne almanacs and various ephemeral pamphlets about the case.[11]

The *Englishman* and *The Trial* attested to the continuing support and interest of Kenealyites in the Claimant's cause. Documents from Australia occupied a great many column-inches and were all meant to throw doubt on the identification of Orton and the Claimant. They included stories that Arthur Orton was still alive, under the name of William Cresswell,[12] at a lunatic asylum in New South Wales. This emphasis was the more interesting because Kenealy himself doubted the story's truth. Much detail was given about Mina Jury, the crucial Tasmanian witness who had identified Orton and who continued to celebrate her return to Britain by thefts which showed she had skill as a confidence woman, although not enough to avoid detection.

The *Englishman* alleged that Mina had kept a brothel in Hobart. Had the Claimant been Orton he would have known she was an ex-convict and told the police so; therefore his silence proved he was not Orton.[13] This was a nice argument until one realizes that had he spoken thus, he would have admitted his own identity. So the episode gave less proof of the Claimant's innocence than of the superficiality of his supporters' analysis. A further exciting and exotic item was a report in 1876 that another survivor of the *Bella* had been located in Spain. Moves began to bring him to England, but his authenticity crumbled.

Within Britain the most dramatic turn of the tale was the recantation of one of the jurymen, Charles Dunsby. This promised much, but a call that other jurymen follow came to nothing. Equally exciting was a scandal at Scotland Yard in 1876-7 involving detectives who had worked on the Tichborne case. Persistent assertions by Orton's sisters that the Claimant was not their brother offered a stock point of argument, as did evidence that Roger had been malformed and Orton not. Requisitions to public figures to state their opinions on the case, with replies, were common. On one such occasion Cockburn refused 'to lend any countenance to what I believe to be one of the most senseless and idle delusions that ever led the minds of the credulous portion of the public astray'.[14] When a textbook—W. S. Jevons, *Studies in Deductive Logic*—used Tichborne arguments as examples of fallacy, Onslow replied at length in the *Englishman*. Likewise William Mathews argued against the current edition of W. A. Guy and D. Ferrier, *Principles of Forensic Medicine* which, in laying down rules about identification, assumed the guilt of the Claimant.

Bathos and boastfulness saturated most comment on the case and its aftermath. Some articles recounted how patronage and promotion rewarded various people who had helped convict the

Claimant, while others revelled in describing how the 'vengeance of God' had treated the man's enemies.[15] Hawkins and Cockburn probably were the most frequent targets of attack; their lives offered opportunity for tales of adultery and prostitution. A salacious touch was constant. One note said of Cockburn's examination of Lady Radcliffe that 'the foul, gloating, and lustful expression which the Chief exhibited . . . could only be presented by the greatest of painters—by Rubens when he drew a Satyr gibbering over a naked Nymph. The lady cast down her eyes for a second, then raised them up, and gloated back on Cockburn'.[16] The *Englishman* and *The Trial* added to their effect with numerous illustrations. Many of these were formal, stilted, even absurd. Cartoons and portraits of comparatively humble identities in the case win more favour, but the prize goes easily to sketches attributed to the Claimant himself. They have a vitality, ranging from funny to ferocious, that any artist might envy. Tichbornites argued that no butcher could produce such work, but a less class-conscious age might wonder at the absence of evidence suggesting artistic ability in either the young Orton or the young Roger.

The MCA movement was the sickliest of Kenealy off-spring, suffering the conflict between the Tichborne cause and the leader's ambitions. Dissidents wanted democratic organization and put the Claimant first, while Kenealyites insisted on the leader principle and the subordination of the Claimant to the general platform. The *Englishman* denied that should 'Sir Roger' emerge from prison, the MCA would cease; rather, the significance of the Tichborne trial was that it had encouraged general agitation and the expression of grievances. Kenealy's main contribution to these disputes was to assert his own importance. 'If *you* think that any great movement can really be carried on without a Leader in whom faith is to be reposed, and who must be supported against malignant insurgents here and there, you are mistaken',[17] he told a supporter in October 1876, when dissidence was at a peak. Some brave souls tried to mediate, and suffered accordingly. 'There are those who can walk with you in the paradise of beauty and follow you as disciples through the maze of sublimity',[18] wrote one such to Kenealy; this meant not that they were sycophants, but rather that the master should go out of his way to attach their loyalty to him. He did not, and the correspondent was among those to go in the subsequent purges.

The result of this in-fighting was breakaway from the MCA and the establishment of further organizations. Kenealy retained the support of a sizeable fragment of the movement and possession of Doughty Hall, which the rebels claimed their money had bought. Within the depleted movement the Claimant's cause sank to twentieth and last in a list of MCA aims stated in 1877. In December 1879 Kenealy even said that he had abandoned sponsoring the Claimant as a candidate in a forthcoming by-election at the behest of MCA members who were not Tichbornites.[19] He probably dissimulated, but even that the argument could be offered was remarkable.

While becoming less devoted to the Tichborne cause, MCA groups jogged along as clubs of social reformers—something like lodges, something like friendly societies. Almost every week the *Englishman* would report twenty or thirty meetings. Annual congresses were continued, meeting usually at Easter or on Whit Monday. 'I felt proud when I saw our great chieftain and placed my hand in his', reported Mr Seed, a delegate from Bradford in 1876; 'he appeared to speak to and look upon me as one on an equal footing with himself, and when I looked around that hall and saw so many gentlemanly-looking men my heart rejoiced within me, and I felt that I was a member of a great national movement which was being marshalled by such a noble leader as Dr Kenealy'.[20] Every so often attempts would be made at restructuring the movement; they were evidence of both the disappointment and the resilience of an earnest few. Early in 1877 the executive planned to issue 'Magna Charta truncheons' to give physical strength to members against murderous rowdies, while later in that year a 'fund for a million sixpences' sought financial sinew. Bazaars, debates, self-help, excursions, public meetings on the common, private meetings at the pub—such was the normal routine. When elections came round, candidates were approached and sometimes bothered to make complaisant noises; in the earlier years, active MCA members (Ahmed Kenealy still to the fore) offered for local and national government, with small result. Evangelical and masonic ritual influenced MCA proceedings. Hymns and psalms, prayers for Kenealy or the Claimant, were common features. At least the Bristol lodge had a chaplain who read extracts from the *Englishman*. Members there had to swear to God, country and ancient constitution, and declare that 'at the next ensuing elections, the *policy* and the *leading points* of the Association shall take precedence of all others, and independently of *existing party considerations*'.[21] The argument was that only the excitement of elections and political strife had kept, and would keep, the movement alive.

Kenealy always made personal effort to further the Tichborne cause. In spite of his disposition, he occasionally co-operated with other Tichborne groups. Amity with Onslow and the Claimant provided at least vicarious contact with the movement at large. Kenealy's public meetings and rallies—still quite frequent—constantly invoked the cause. In parliament his contributions to general debate often related to the Claimant's story, while occasionally he asked specific questions concerning his client. The most important instance concerned Mina Jury. Enquiries left no doubt that she *was* the Mercevina Caulfield transported from Dublin in 1847, as Kenealy had alleged in 1875 and as R. A. Cross had then refused to affirm. On 5 April 1878 Kenealy sought to ask Cross a question which alleged bad faith in the evasion of the subject three years before. The Speaker ruled the question out of order as it contained argument and allegation. Kenealy responded that this was a matter of privilege and foreshadowed his intention to move a debate accordingly. On 10 May the matter arose; Brand's diary reported 'much excitement' and that the Chancellor of the Exchequer proposed to him that the House be counted-out in rebuff to Kenealy. This happened, against Brand's own inclination. On 24 May Kenealy tried again and argued that the Speaker had no judicial authority over the House. Members assured Brand that he was a good fellow, and the matter did not come to a vote. Nevertheless on 16 July 1879 the Speaker still mildly protested but did not out-rule when Kenealy asked Cross whether he would release the Claimant on the expiration of his first term, or enquire into the new evidence and confirm that the case had cost the country a quarter-of-a-million pounds.

Notwithstanding such incidents, Kenealy did tend overall to discount the cause, perhaps feeling that it impeded fulfilment of his desire to lead a broad-based political movement. Such judgement might have been wrong; that is, the public could have been more interested in the matter than he allowed or wanted. Then, as he deprecated the cause, other protagonists became more closely identified with it, which made him jealous and prone to scorn their efforts. In a draft letter to Onslow, Kenealy wrote that it was 'perfect ruin to Tichborne's cause' to set up other leaders and to foster false rumours. He referred especially to stories about the lunatic, William Cresswell. The Claimant's last words to his wife, stressed Kenealy, were 'you be silent, keep your own counsel',[22] from which the lawyer deduced that 'Tichborne' had participated in Orton's violent death (a view which Ballantine also held). Kenealy and the *Englishman* maintained this scepticism towards repeated hopes of securing the Claimant's freedom by some revelation or legal gambit.

The converse to this down-grading of the cause was the interest of Kenealy, the *Englishman* and the MCA in advocating other reforms and ideas. Circumstances put the administration of justice high among these, and made the passage of the Prisons Bill of 1877 an important occasion for Kenealy the parliamentarian.[23] He even effected amendment of the measure, so as to provide that prison commissioners give annual returns of punishments inflicted under their authority. For the most part, however, he was in minorities voting for amelioration. Kenealy argued that the chaplain and surgeon should be appointed independently of the prison governor so that they might 'counteract the despotic power reposed in the governor, and . . . alleviate the sufferings of the prisoners'. He and Whalley wept over Sir Roger's fate and the consequent anguish of the British people. 'Moral and physical torture' was a commonplace of gaols, Kenealy said, alleging that the Claimant had suffered inspection of his genitals and that often galvanic batteries were applied to convicts' 'delicate parts'.

The prisons debate gave prolonged opportunity for arguing law and its administration, but Kenealy often raised such issues by questions and side-comments. The judiciary was his chief target. 'There are few judges whom any sane man would like to go before', he said on 21 March 1879. He criticized his fellow parliamentarians for excessive deference towards judges; properly, the House should check these, as much as any other, public servants. The case of Edward Habron provided grist for this mill: convicted of murder in 1876, he won freedom and £1000 recompense three years later after the confession of another criminal. Kenealy asked the Home Secretary whether he would legislate for a new trial in all criminal cases where reasonable doubt existed, and for compensation as a matter of right to those who suffered as had Habron. If Habron had been mis-identified, so might have been the Claimant. Cross said he was sympathetic, but not moved to action. Another murder trial to provide ammunition was that of the Reverend H. J. Dodswell: found guilty of killing his wife, Dodswell was declared insane and so spared punishment. Kenealy and the *Englishman* saw this as class law. Their sympathy went to such as Edward Harris, a cabbie whom the police took before a magistrate after he had an accident and was suffering from injuries which killed him. The MCA put reform of the law, to cause it to act irrespective of class, high on its platform.

Moreover, it would have allowed no lawyer to sit in parliament, and Kenealy himself maintained criticism of his ex-brethren. In mid-1876 he disputed in the courts his forced evacuation from Gray's Inn, and counter-claimed £25 000 damages for the 'malicious and torturous and illegal acts' of disbenchment and debarment.[24] Arguing the case he questioned the general rights of the Inns, but the judge refused to listen and determined against him. A subsequent bill concerning bar discipline promised a great opportunity for grievance-mongering, and Kenealy several times urged the government to bring the measure forward, only to be caught out of the House when it suddenly did so in January 1878. When the government dropped the bill, Kenealy alleged it was to avoid the amendments he proposed.

In attacking the law Kenealy was maintaining that onslaught on 'the Establishment' which had characterized his hey-day. The *Englishman* was anathema to the Waddys of the world because it served this purpose with constant zeal. The language used by man and journal, towards every dignitary of the land and every settled institution, was always strong and sometimes foul.

As the stonemason at Chester knew, the Crown itself was an object of this onslaught. There always remained in Kenealyite propaganda a hint that the sovereign somehow might inspire a new era of social justice, but the trend was towards increasing vilification. The most interesting episode, arising from Disraeli's move in 1876 to vest the Queen with the title 'Empress of India', pointed two ways. Kenealy first attacked the measure: the title was despotic, he said, and had particularly repugnant associations in India, where ideas about education and freedom soon might force the Queen to forfeit the new style. Over the next few weeks such hostility spread widely. This might seem to have made the cause peculiarly suitable for Kenealy's polemic purposes, but his contrariness determined otherwise. He refused to support a censure motion and attacked the Liberals as opportunists who never kept their promises. Disraeli approved: 'the speech of Kenealy, which will be read by every rough in Britain and which was well delivered, was apropos'.[25] Royalists would have found less to approve thereafter. Kenealy joined those dissidents in the House, notably Dilke, who were ever ready to dispute the civil list. The *Englishman* made abuse of royalty part of its basic stock. John Brown was a God-send: 'we think a Woman would be a more proper "personal" attendant; but then a Woman no doubt could not serve the Queen equally well'.[26] The last great MCA conference of Kenealy's lifetime—at Nottingham in October 1879—had a strong republican trend, members cheering the hope that their leader would become first president of the United States of Great Britain and Ireland. Coincidentally the *Englishman* published a series of pamphlets on *The Guelphs* (almost certainly by Kenealy), which ladled out scandal.

Antagonism to the Church of England held firm. The *Englishman* was always ready to tell of scandalous pretension from this quarter, and Kenealy several times voted in the same cause. Thus he joined with Opposition and high-churchmen to amend an Appellate Jurisdiction Bill, against the government's wishes, so that bishops lost power to act as 'assessors' in Privy Council cases involving church matters. Even more characteristically, he was with the minority in supporting Osborne Morgan's Burials Bill—which would open parish churchyards to all denominations—and in opposing the extension of bishoprics.

The armed forces were another established enemy. In 1879 Kenealy put down a motion for abolition of the standing army. No seconder offered, but he made his own opportunity to assert that such an army violated the constitution and generated ills at home and abroad. Kenealy was among the smallish minority that pushed for strict delimitation of military flogging; this issue linked his activity over the Prisons Act with his attitudes to class-conflict, for anti-floggers detested that officers should have such power over their men. Valentine Baker returned to prominence when old army friends welcomed him on furlough from his new job with the Ottoman Emperor. The *Englishman* remarked that this delight in profligacy heralded revolution, as in the France of Louis XVI. Conversely, Kenealyites upheld Lieutenant-Colonel W. G. Dawkins of the Coldstream Guards, whose criticism of high command allegedly had led to his being forced from the army. The navy proved less vulnerable; but the *Englishman* cried waste and horror in 1876 when H.M.S. *Thunderer* exploded at Spithead, killing more than forty men. Two years later the sinking of H.M.S. *Eurydice* and the slowness of her salvage encouraged Kenealy to brow-beat the Admiralty. The MCA wanted to exclude service officers, as well as lawyers, from parliament.

Kenealy's opposition to a standing army entailed attack upon empire. Blackbirding in the New Hebrides, the Zulu War, suppression of native peoples in other parts of the British-settled empire, were among his anathemas. Criticism of the new royal style sprang more appropriately from Kenealy than from many, for he always insisted that India had a dignity and worth which Britain must respect; it was monstrous that English dolts should rule her and that she should enjoy less liberty than other parts of the empire. Developing this theme in March 1878 he brushed with his fellow parliamentarian, Sir Henry Havelock, son of the hero of Lucknow, apropos the Indian army. Amid uproar, Havelock declared that he had never felt so proud of his constituents at Sunderland than recently, when they disrupted a Kenealy meeting. Seven months before, Kenealy had spoken of India in different vein. Then he had insisted on the need for Britain to maintain a forward stance in the peninsula, against the aggression of Russia. Were that power to have its way, Britain would lose those Asian markets on which her prosperity depended. How could the Manchester little-Englanders be so blind as not to see this? The argument accorded with Kenealy's antipathy to Liberal shibboleths and with his Russophobia, and did not altogether clash with his anti-imperialism. He could be seen as appealing for the concept of a self-governing empire wide enough to include India as well as the colonies of settlement.

Similar ambivalence appeared in Kenealy's attitude to the Irish issue. His abandoning the Fenian brief in 1867, and his anti-Catholicism, obstructed alliance with the nationalists. A. M. Sullivan's hatred made the point. Yet overall Kenealy remained truer to his principles of 1848 than to the Repeal-baiting of *Fraser's Magazine*. The *Englishman* compared O'Connell and Kenealy, seeing both as the victims of malicious enemies. The journal early hailed C. S. Parnell as the true leader of his people, and compared him too with Kenealy. It remarked that the Irish had a spirit in resisting tyranny which Englishmen lacked. Kenealy put among his political principles, admittedly well down, 'Justice to Ireland in all measures; so that Ireland may be for the Irish, as God intended it should be'.[27] He voted for the new parliamentary procedures that sought to control Irish members' obstruction, but opposed further moves to this end. Kenealy might have cherished some hope of an alliance with the nationalists that would enhance his power in England, but if so this proved but one more chimera.

In contemporary usage, 'imperial' power referred not so much to rule over dependencies as to the influence of the central government within Britain itself; Kenealy remained anti-imperialist in this sense too. Even in welfare matters the theme prevailed. Kenealy thought the church should carry all the costs of poor relief, and he continued to oppose compulsory popular education.

The MCA would have left education exclusively in the hands of religious bodies. Consistency was hard in such matters, and at times Kenealy upheld national education and a national rather than a local (and allegedly uneven) poor rate. Still, his instinct was against centralism, even prompting opposition to some clauses of a factories bill because they violated privacy. Widespread resistance to the Prisons Act concentrated on its transfer of power to the centre, and Kenealy included this charge in his critique. The MCA's plank of abolishing the Local Government Board—grand instrument of centralization—was a similarly forlorn cause.

Hostility to centralism entwined with abhorrence of all-powerful government in general. Income tax was still Kenealy's great bug-bear, although he made his opposition more pertinent to humbler folk, and more interesting to posterity, by developing the notion that taxation could serve social justice. It should fall only on freeholders, or leaseholders, or holders of public or private securities—'capitalists' all who were accumulating wealth while the people starved.[28] Putting words to action, Kenealy paid his tax in 1879 only under protest and after the authorities had threatened punitive action. Years before, the *Englishman* had proposed that government should get its revenue from taxation of great magnates who in the long past had been granted lands from the Crown. In the House, Kenealy often voted against increases in State power. In 1877, for example, he opposed purchase of sites for public offices, government acquisition of the estates of illegitimate intestates, and the extension to Scotland of a Turnpikes Act. He was always in the minority.

The dominant foreign policy issue in these years was, as so often, the eastern question. Its endurance proved its intractability. No one could provide a final answer to where and how Britain should throw its weight in the constant struggle between Russia and Turkey. The ambiguities of the situation lured Kenealy into positions consistent only in their individuality.

In September 1875 the *Englishman*'s chief concern was lest Britain uphold the 'worn-out Despotism' of Turkey. Even at this stage no love went to Russia: the journal argued that when joining in the Crimean War, Napoleon III and Palmerston had aimed merely at squashing the nationalist idea in Poland, and so in Europe at large. However, in June 1876 the *Englishman* proposed that Britain and Russia should now dismember Turkey: the one taking Egypt, the other Constantinople. In the House, Kenealy spoke against any increased hostility to Russia and for the end of support to Turkey. The next switches in the Turkish power-game brought about a change of mind. By mid-July Russia was allegedly conspiring for war, having suborned British publicists to blacken Turkey by bewailing the fate of the Porte's Christian subjects in Bulgaria. For the *Englishman,* these Christians were 'worst of all wretches'. Thus, before the famous outcry against 'the Bulgarian Atrocities' was fully airborne, Kenealy stood against it.

This continued as the issue became a storm-centre of British politics. The *Englishman* told Gladstone, leader of the agitation, that the wrongs suffered by Tichborne surpassed those of the Bulgarian Christians; that British rule, especially in Ireland, was as detestable as Turkish; that he was the tool of Manchester men who wanted to secure stock they held in Russia. Kenealy made such points in the House in two major speeches. He insisted that Britain should not encourage Russia's expansionist ambitions, for that would release 'a very ocean of blood, in which they might all be overwhelmed'.[29] This was said in opposing resolutions moved by Gladstone; Speaker Brand thought Kenealy's a 'wild' speech, but the *New Monthly Magazine* judged that it offered 'shrewd and ingenious observations . . . humorous causticity which the House so invariably relishes'. Gladstone had fled the chamber as the abuse fell upon him. Though Kenealy scored a hit in the House and persuaded many individual MCA members, he probably lost in the country. Broadly speaking, Gladstone's movement attracted types who might have followed the Tichborne cause: little people, hostile to tyranny and power politics, and anti-Catholics, who noted that the Vatican shed no tears for Orthodox Christians under Ottoman rule.[30] Over the next couple of years Kenealyism pursued anti-Russian feeling so far as to assume the 'jingo' colouring of the day. Consequent policies were calls for the abandonment of the Declaration of Paris of 1856—which modified rights of search and privateering, thus curtailing the rule on the seas of that force which the Royal Navy possessed—and for readiness for war with Russia. 'The nation that is ahead in matters of scientific warfare will always have the chances of war in its favour', argued the *Englishman* in calling for naval preparedness.[31]

The allegation about Gladstone being influenced by Russian stock-holders was one example of a fairly insistent critique of capitalism. The *Englishman* analysed the House of Commons to show the strength there of various interests: the services (218 members), aristocracy (160), ministerial (85), magisterial, i.e. major local office-holders (280), law (101), literary-professional-scientific (73), railways (97), money (23), manufacturing-commercial-trading (142).[32] The journal gave stock-exchange swindling its share of abuse, and Kenealy planned, abortively, to ask parliament questions about a scandal-disaster of 1879, the insolvency of the City of Glasgow Bank. By endorsing the Fair Trade movement in 1878, the *Englishman* showed itself quick to criticize free trade, the fundamental dogma of contemporary economic faith. Kenealy's arguments about income tax was one of various summonses to primitive class-war against capitalist evil. The most extreme case was the *Englishman*'s suggestion that all workers should throw themselves on the poor rate, which would become 'so hot' that the capitalists must willy-nilly pay decent wages.[33] The rural labourer's situation encouraged attacks on the land laws—especially those preserving game—and support for Joseph Arch who was alone among unionists to receive this accolade, although but briefly. Kenealy found an especially congenial cause in revealing that while the people were forbidden to play sports in Richmond park, the Duke of Cambridge had game rights over it, and the public purse met the gamekeepers' costs.

Political and parliamentary reform received some attention. As mentioned above, Kenealy kept afloat the ideal of a Crown-and-people alliance, its putative aim being

To restore the authority of the ancient Privy Council of England whereby they and the Sovereign are rendered responsible to the People for all public acts; and to take away from the Prime Minister and his fellows their limitless amount of patronage, which has a tendency to corrupt all classes into servility, and converts the Government into a Despotism; and to give it back to the Sovereign, who should be solely responsible for all public acts and appointments.[34]

By and large, however, the man and his movement pressed for more conventional reforms: outlawing of electoral bribery, triennial parliaments, payment of members, redistribution of seats. Concerning suffrage, the chief aim was that the householder should vote in counties as well as boroughs, but support went towards various other extensions. A minor proposal endorsed by Kenealy was that a full and official record of parliamentary debates replace *Hansard*.

Among more general social reforms the most important for Kenealy, as for so many of his contemporaries, remained temperance. He supported not only Prohibitory Permissive Bills but also Chamberlain's plan whereby local government authorities would buy into the liquor trade. Such an attitude clashed with the backing given the Tichborne cause by liquor interests and with the use of pubs by many branches of the MCA, which appears not to have followed its leader in supporting temperance. Behind temperance came a medley of welfare proposals. Despite Kenealy's antagonism to bureaucratic power, the state was given some role: in sponsoring emigration of the destitute; in providing parks and museums; in enforcing factory acts, industrial arbitration, and Samuel Plimsoll's plans for ships' safety; and even in developing the physical strength of the nation by making hygiene a school subject. Abolition of bankruptcy laws and of payment for debt, together with payment for juries, were planks in the platform of class-impartial law. Railway owners should charge uniform freight-rates and put penny carriages on all trains. Concern for civil liberties showed in steady criticism of the lunacy laws, compulsory vaccination, and the Contagious Diseases Acts. Kenealy supported moves for removal of women's disabilities and against cruelty to animals.

Kenealy had to suffer many jeers that he should have done more. Such was a common theme of his anonymous correspondence, and dissidents at Stoke challenged him to submit for re-election from 1877 onwards. That indolence, perhaps amounting to psychic depression, which appeared as early as the 1840s, may have persisted. He never enjoyed robust health. Kenealy's attendance at parliament was sporadic: in every session his presence at divisions was in the lowest quarter, and in 1879 only thirty-odd members voted less often.[35] But freedom from party discipline would help account for this, and his contributions to debate were more substantial than those of the average back-bencher. Kenealy probably made almost as much of his roles as parliamentarian, demagogue and journalist as the situation allowed. The reasons for decline lie less with him than with the nature of the Tichborne cause.

HIS MORE PRIVATE LIFE

Just as Kenealy's political ideology changed little in the years of decline, so his interests in literature and religion complemented rather than improved those of earlier years. Tenacity and vigour, arrogance and scurrility, remained his imprint. The desire to win fame rather than notoriety ever spurred him. His aspirations in this realm being so high, the failure to achieve them is the more stark.

Perhaps Kenealy's pen scored its highest triumphs in the

columns of the *Englishman*. Just how much he wrote is unknown, as is virtually the whole editorial side of the journal's story. R. M. Gurnell, Kenealy's sons Maurice and Ahmed, and others, presumably wrote much of the material as well as arranging it, but the master's tone still called from the pages. The same applies to *The Trial*. Kenealy always wrote too much and too carelessly, but these defects mattered less in reportage and commentary than in verse and metaphysics. Even the historian is more impressed than bored, and for contemporaries the interest of the subject matter would have further inclined that scale.

The end of Kenealy's venture into literary journalism, the *Englishman's Magazine,* was an early mark of decline, for the last monthly issue was December 1875. Sales had never surpassed 5000 protested the *Englishman,* but even that may have been a gloss. The *Magazine* avoided mention of Tichborne, indeed of all social and political issues. It was literary, polished, civil—in short, a far remove from the *Englishman*. The one failed as positively as the other succeeded. Its sponsor could find no audience among those he saw as something like his peers. The *Magazine* came largely from Kenealy's pen and reflected his life-long interests. Characteristically he published a paean of praise of his own religious thought. It was more interesting than most Kenealy ruminations, especially for its enquiry into his apostrophe to nature: *'thou art not matter/But vital essence'*. The writer suggested what this vital essence might be:

In the structure of glands, it has been observed that the Acini, or ultimate gland cells, have each a nerve-twig passing into them and thus bringing nervous influence into direct association with the functions of the cell. Now, is it not reasonable to infer that nerve-twigs may be supplied to every cell existing in the tissues of the human body, and that the vital principle is directly connected with the nervous system, and may be elaborated by the blood as it becomes oxygenized in the pulmonary capillaries?[36]

Here lay some affinity with the future biology of August Weismann and the philosophy of Henri Bergson.

An article on cricket seems a much less likely Kenealy product, but perhaps suggests that all the while he would have liked to have been a sporting Englishman of public-school caste.[37] The climate of England's green and pleasant land made it a cricketers' paradise, unlike regions of bright sun and hard ground. A charm of country cricket was its transcendence of class boundaries, making it a worthy object of patronage from the local squire—an idea which, more appropriately, G. M. Trevelyan was also to develop. But even this article showed that anti-modernism which made Kenealy hostile to bureaucracy and to Darwin. 'Bowling brought to its modern perfection leaves few opportunities for telling bye-play'. The batsman could do nothing but defend his wicket, the crossing of the fieldsmen was mechanical and regular; the only relief promised when the bowler at last lost his morale.

After the *Englishman's Magazine* ceased, Kenealy still used the *Englishman* for literary purposes. An occasional reminiscence spoke, for example, of his early successes with *Bentley's Miscellany* and *Fraser's Magazine,* or of acquaintance developed there. He dealt with Thackeray and Fraser at one blow in telling how the former as a young man was 'ready to wipe the shoes of that most mean and crawling publisher, who would have sold his soul to anyone for a fifty pound note'.[38] Another echo of the past was the publication first in the *Englishman* and then, in 1880, as a book of *A Blighted Life,* an autobiography by Rosina, Lady Bulwer Lytton. In the steamy literary world of the thirties Edward Bulwer Lytton had been one of William Maginn's great enemies and so a target for abuse in *Fraser's.* Yet in 1846 Kenealy wrote an ode to Lytton, beseeching:

How shall I thank thee for the enchanted hours
Passed with thy spirit o'er thy golden page?[39]

To publish *A Blighted Life* was a very strange answer. The Lyttons' marriage, begun in 1827, was magnificently turbulent. In 1836 the two separated, but their lives continued to tangle and tear together. Rosina wrote the manuscript of *A Blighted Life* in 1864; how it came into Kenealy's possession is unknown. It rampaged with fury and fantasy against wrongs suffered from her husband and her son. To this Kenealy added vicious pen-portraits of the dramatis personae. One result of publication was that Rosina lost a pension from her son, although this returned after a pamphleteer insisted that she had no responsibility in the matter.[40]

To the end, Kenealy was a versifier. The republication of his earlier works continued, the second and third volumes appearing in 1878 and 1879. They received virtually no critical mention, and the set in the British Museum has many pages uncut. Verse of seemingly contemporary, as well as earlier, composition appeared in the *Englishman*. The poet's themes changed remarkably little over the years. Almost obsessional was the many-mooded sea, perhaps signifying the insistence of sex. Brooding over nature at large also recurred, as well as fascination with self, lament for lost youth, yearning for the infinite. Knowledge that the man was approaching life's end encourages appreciation of some of these lines:

> No—no—not in Earth or Sea,
> Let my bones moulder into ashes;
> But in Flame let this pass—
> This, which in its day was Flame.
> Let that which was of clay be blent
> With the fire that purifies the impure;
> And out of the dust let the Eagle Spirit
> Soar in brightness to its God.[41]

Facing death, the writer told much of his living self-image.

While still interested in literature and learning, Kenealy seems to have kept no contact with that world, or with society at large. G. A. Sala had upheld Kenealy at the time of his becoming a bencher but criticized him during the trial; Kenealy responded savagely, and the breach never healed. The relatively kind words of the *New Monthly Magazine* may have echoed the old association with W. H. Ainsworth, who still edited that journal, but no evidence suggests continuing personal friendship. Aldborough Henniker apparently did not use his position as a senior member of Gray's Inn to defend his travelling companion of 1843.

Kenealy became more deeply concerned with religion as he aged, yet in an uneven way. The *Englishman* was no more abusive of the Church of England in these years than earlier; attacks on Jesuitry and Rome diminished. Yet the paper was always ready to invoke divine retribution and to inveigh against such blasphemies as Darwinism and birth-control; while Kenealy appears to have flirted with the idea of fusing his roles as political leader and twelfth messenger. The *Englishman* announced in 1876 that he was ready to hold regular services, perhaps in amalgamation with MCA meetings. About this time Samuel Butler complained to a correspondent that another acquaintance was 'a devoted admirer of Kenealy, and if you want any news of the Dear Doctor or his wife, or any of his twelve children, come to me for it'.[42] To prove his claim Butler summarized the new theology: 'every 600 or 700 years God is made incarnate in man, and at the present moment is incarnate in Kenealy'. An *Englishman* report of a Kenealy meeting late in 1876 told of his displaying a ring 'of the finest gold . . . with twelve precious stones like those mentioned in the Sacred Apocalypse as being placed in the Gates of the New Heaven; and those which the Prince of the Israelites, Moses, the Messenger of God, wore as a breast-plate'.[43] The *Englishman* remarked on the appropriateness of Kenealy's having the ring as well as the 'rod of Moses', that staff presented to him by Glasgow supporters. Such references were few however: the *Englishman* never explicitly hailed him as a Messiah and reported no sermons. Why was this? Was it because the man cared too little about his religion, or too much; or because he feared that publicizing it would destroy his political creditability? The last answer allows the chance that an active inner cell of Kenealyites followed the man as a Messiah rather than as a reformer.

Kenealy's last major publication was *Fo, the Third Messenger of God*, 1878; as with *Book of God* and *Enoch*, his name did not appear on the title-page. The book gave Kenealy's idiosyncratic view of Buddhist history and teaching, particularly in China. Fo far anticipated the Gautama Buddha, bringing his message from Tibet in about 2600 B.C. Who he was in terms of accepted history, and what sources Kenealy used, are even deeper mysteries than the author's other theological works pose. Contradictions and complexities come so thick as to support those who from time to time doubted the man's sanity. Kenealy admitted that his views ran counter to received opinion. 'But popular opinions are not always true; as a rule, they are generally wrong'.[44] Out of this fantasy, and at enormous length, Kenealy's introduction presented a relatively simple message. Buddhism was a religion of love, virtue and happiness, which taught that men could and must overcome their passions. It had achieved global influence, witnessing the one-time universality of religious belief and practice. In China, Buddhism had assisted towards a civilization superior to all others. The secularism of Confucius had dimmed this glory: he was 'the Paul of China'. Buddhist monasticism might have been carried to excess, but by encouraging meditation and altruism it had inhibited 'that fierce and selfish and demoralizing competition which commerce generates'.[45]

The text itself spoke of the world's origin and nature. The earth and other planets had whirled off from the sun. All living matter—plant, beast, man—had once been spirit. Successive breeds had disappeared before modern humanity developed its present form and differentiation. The process had begun in the far north-west of Eurasia, where men had lived in patriarchal tribes and in blessed worship of God-as-nature. That elysium passed, but its lessons continued. Men must seek renunciation, love, charity, obedience to the father. Governments must be moral and serve the welfare of their subjects. Awareness of God should be constant, but avoid anthropomorphism. The verse and prose that told all this were poor stuff; deader than Kenealy's journalism or his meditations.

He did not see things that way. In late summer 1878 Kenealy and his wife nearly drowned while on holiday in Ireland. He wrote to his children, 'I own I did not wish to pass away until I had done something more for mankind and had made some additions to my theological writings—works destined as I hope, to produce a Revolution in Religion all over the earth'.[46] Whatever the calculation with which Kenealy had commenced his theological labours, by now it appeared that he was genuine enough. At death, his papers included work-in-progress towards an edition of Sir William Jones's translation of *Institutes of Hindi Law*. The text merely shortened and clarified Jones's work. The document is a dull, worthy statement of an ethical code. Another work unpublished at Kenealy's death was *The Testament of Jesus*. This presented the Christian gospels in a consecutive, rationalized, yet scarcely original form. The language often merely repeated the authorized translation, while Kenealy's mimicry supplied transitions and addenda in the same style.

Kenealy's health worsened year by year. In December 1879 sickness even prevented his regular visit to the Claimant. Fate would have been kinder had he died straight away. Instead Kenealy lived on until the dissolution of parliament. Throughout his term he had visited the Stoke electorate, and a knot of supporters stayed loyal. However, hecklers had always appeared too, and every sign indicated that he had little chance of re-election. Rumour said that he might switch to Nottingham.

When the challenge came, Kenealy did offer for Stoke.[47] The other candidates were a Conservative and two Liberals, the latter including Henry Broadhurst, who was building his fame as one of the commanding Lib Labs of the late nineteenth century. Kenealy's address to the electorate emphasized destestation of war and of the civil list; it called for separate parliaments in Ireland, Scotland and Wales. The Claimant received a bare mention. While the address attacked the Liberal caucus system, opponents

charged Kenealy with receiving £600 from the Tories; Broadhurst's reminiscences referred matter-of-factly to Kenealy as a
Conservative.[48] The doctor bemoaned his poverty, which evoked
jeers from critical journalists, and they found yet richer pickings
when he told electors that he was a king of men, whom fate had
chosen for greatness. Broadhurst remembered as the major issue
his opponents' attack on the school board system. Kenealy did
inveigh against the boards and received cheers, especially from
women, for doing so. Mrs Kenealy supported him, as in the past.
But Broadhurst claimed that the influence of wives and factory
girls, greater than he had known at any election since, supported
the Liberals overall. The figures were with him:

W. Woodhall (Liberal)	12 130
H. Broadhurst (Liberal)	11 371
R. Heath (Conservative)	5 126
Kenealy	1 091

Kenealy managed the situation with some dignity. 'I shall always
remember the chivalry of 1875', he assured electors at the declaration on 3 April.

Kenealy returned to London, and died there on the 16th. Contemporary sources said that an abcess in his foot had mortified;
his daughter later wrote that he had suffered for many years from
diabetes, while the immediate blow was heart failure. She described a final movement of 'transfiguring, shining beauty' across
his face.[49] On 22 April the coffin was carried first from Kenealy's
home in Tavistock Square to Victoria station. Members of the
MCA attended, and the crowds were large. The cortège went to
the tiny Church of England at Hangleton, Sussex. Notwithstanding the stanzas quoted above, Kenealy had directed that he be
buried there, between the sea and the Downs:

> Yes—by these waters I would fain repose,
> Far from the noise of towns. To me it were
> No gladness in my dying dream to think
> That I should lie amid the rank black dust
> Of old Westminister[50]

The prospect had inspired Kenealy, in those last seven words, to
one of his rare poetic images. The actuality was moving too: a
simple service, magnificent flowers, some two hundred mourners
led by his son Maurice and three daughters.

Obituary writers faced a problem.[51] The *Times* simply told the facts, but most of the great dailies tended rather to exaggerate Kenealy's literary and intellectual abilities so as to bring into relief what they saw as the barren tragi-comedy of his political career. The *Pall Mall Gazette* ground its axe in a different way by suggesting that had he lived another six years, his fame might have returned: 'the rejected of Stoke-upon-Trent might even have found a seat in Midlothian'. At Stoke, news of his death evoked strong feelings for and against his memory. The *Potteries Examiner* differed from the national press both in referring, knowledgeably, to his religious writings and refusing to say anything unless good. The man adopted the tactics of a charlatan and an imposter, declared the *Examiner;* the recent election should warn others who might contemplate 'experiments upon the credulity of mankind'.

Kenealy's will gave only minor hints as to his finances. The personal estate was proved at less than £3000, and the text itself spoke of 'the little that I possess'. However, this might be yet further evidence of the man's money-consciousness, which certainly remained a characteristic. When a solicitor had brought action for costs against him in 1877, it transpired that he had minimized his ostensible assets by distributing them among his family,[52] and the *Englishman* was ever ready to sponsor a fund to meet Kenealy's costs. His home, Stoke House in Tavistock Square, was purchased in 1876, and the retreat at Portslade presumably belonged to him. A reference to Kenealy's being A. C. Swinburne's landlord might be one straw in the wind of considerable property holdings.[53] The *Englishman* continued to deny that he was amassing wealth—£130 000 being one figure alleged—but not altogether convincingly.[54] The will directed that certain books should go to Trinity College and King's Inn, Dublin, but it is doubtful whether this came about. Late in 1881, a sale of Kenealy's effects included 4000 volumes. His papers remained within the family, although the *Englishman* had spoken of them going to the British Museum.

Kenealy was megalomaniac, greedy, bitter, resentful—in all, not a sympathetic character. This was true at least of the public man, although in family life a more benign quality had its play. Even ignoring that, Kenealy must yet command some respect. He was a man of sorrows no less because he sought too much. His pretension ceased to be ridiculous when it prompted one last exercise in that self-analysis which occasionally had glinted through lifelong bombast and conceit:

who would patiently bear the dull monotony of existence upon earth, with its still recurring order of wants, necessities, and inclinations, which are all so opposite to a divine nature; who would pass through toils and troubles for the brief, unsatisfying pleasures which they offer; who would bear the weight of sickness for years, and the sharp agonies of present pain, or the bitter memories which a retrospect of the misused past must awake in all; if he were not ever sustained by this one great thought: that his life here is but a nightmare state, in which all he does is vague and imperfect, but that in a life to come he may expand into a brighter, nobler, and more beautiful form of being? . . . For no man that ever lived on earth was happy, and no man can ever be so, who considers what he has and what he desires, and feels how unworthy of his true nature are all that man can offer, or wealth procure.[55]

Verbosity made this all the more characteristic of Kenealy and so the fitter epitaph.

5

OTHER SUPPORTERS OF THE CAUSE
IN BRITAIN

NOT ONLY IN TERMS of Kenealy's life did interest in Tich-borniana survive. News items about the Claimant's prison life, or his family, or efforts in his behalf, continued to appear throughout the press of the English-speaking world. Photographs of those associated with the story, facsimiles of prison letters, envelopes bearing Tichborne mottoes, were all advertised, and presumably bought. Entrepreneurs could still sell tickets for lectures given by the Claimant's friends—and even by a notorious enemy, Mrs Mina Jury. As with Kenealy's career, the overall graph of this interest showed decline; in both cases the resilience was more extraordinary in final count. Sometimes sustaining this resilience, sometimes attracted by rewards it offered, were continuing supporters of the cause. They fell into those categories—often one person into more than one category—that earlier discussion has suggested: sportsmen, eccentrics, democrats-cum-demagogues, and true believers. They formed many organizations, often fought among themselves, and operated in both hemispheres.

VETERANS WEND THEIR WAYS

Guildford Onslow retained particular standing, being free from the bloodiest quarrels and the grossest self-interest while always exuberant and ruthless in his tactics. He was the most regular of the Claimant's visitors, and ever ready with an appropriate news release. The Claimant's wife, a woman of great caprice and little integrity, appears to have intermittently returned to Onslow's patronage, and he normally accompanied her son, also Roger, when the boy began appearing on his father's behalf in 1875. Onslow put his name to various pamphlets restating the Claimant's case, and published them through the *Englishman*. When Tichborne factions met together in conference he usually took the lead. Southampton, which strongly supported the Claimant, twice saw such meetings. The first was in December 1875 when the Tichborne Vindication Association offered a channel for self-professed respectable men to express their feelings, further differentiating itself from the Magna Charta Association by insisting that Tichborne release stood at the head, not the foot, of its programme. At the second, in April 1877, trustees were appointed to manage funds intended to bring from Spain the alleged survivor of the *Bella* and from Australia witnesses of similar potential value. Characteristically, Onslow fostered hopes of a grand revealing truth coming from an exotic quarter; in this habit, he was considerably less restrained than Kenealy. The two men could co-operate to the end however: as in 1879 when floating the proposal that the Claimant offer for Nottingham in the next election.

Quartermaine East stood with Onslow on all these points. His prestige increased with his election as High Sheriff of London in 1877, itself a mark of the dignity of being licensee of Queen's Hotel St Martin's-le-Grand. East was a little more forthright than Onslow in drawing political morals from the cause. Tichborne's enemies, he bewailed, had forced the people to become rebels. 'The first flood of democracy seems to have set in, and a war of classes to have commenced';[1] willy-nilly, East sympathized with democracy in this conflict and foresaw that the 'hatred and disloyalty' resulting from the case might sponsor 'an Extreme Left party as in France'. In 1883 East settled for the hope that Joseph Chamberlain might lead a vigorous, creative Liberalism. The deaths of Lord Rivers in 1880 and Onslow in 1881 left him the great survivor of the Claimant's sporting patrons.

The relations between East and 'Captain' William Jackson Barry offered an example of how publicans could further the cause. By his own account, Barry had led a life of rare Antipodean adventure since the 1830s as pioneer, stockman, whaler, miner, speculator. He was probably convict and bushranger as well. Barry knew some prosperous days, but by 1872, then in the south island of New Zealand, he was down and out. He recovered by discovering a skill at lecturing, generally on his life story, particularly on minerals and mining. In 1878 Barry returned to Britain and travelled about, intending to lecture on opportunities that New Zealand offered the immigrant. Evidently by chance, he went to East's hotel. Soon his host, Onslow, Rivers and Kenealy became his acquaintances. Rivers and East gave him money and backed the publication, in 1879, of his memoirs, *Up and Down*. The book's final pages boosted Queen's Hotel and East's thoroughbred stud at Epsom. The greater pay-off came in Barry's avowal—in lectures and newsprint, not *Up and Down*—that he had known both Castro and Orton in Victoria during the 1850s, and recognized the Claimant, whom he visited, as the former. Truth did not come first in Barry's priorities. Yet he was not a villain, but rather one of life's yea-sayers who incarnated the theme of Australian romance. His lecture tour over, Barry returned to Australia and then New Zealand where he stood in vain for parliament in 1881. Barry presented himself as a radical and popular candidate, yet boasted his upper-class contacts in Britain.

There was not a single candidate standing, the Captain said, who could do as he had done—land in England with 17s 6d, do the lah-de-dah for twelve months with the nobility of England and the principal men of the world, dine with Beaconsfield at the Mansion House, be honoured by the Queen, &c., &c., and then publish a book and bring back 14,000 copies with him.[2]

Among the features of his rumbustious, ineffectual campaign was opposition to a beer tax and to a gambling law. Before Barry died in 1907, he took the stump again and published another book of memoirs.[3] It told of his association with the Claimant's friends more frankly than had *Up and Down*, but with apparent naivete and innocence. The *Encyclopaedia of New Zealand* honours him as 'undoubtedly New Zealand's greatest literary liar'.

Until his death in 1878, G. H. Whalley continued to use the case in his crusade against Rome. His break with Kenealy attracted more comment than did any other of the Tichborne quarrels. Kenealy's attacks on royalty and on Valentine Baker first prompted Whalley to public criticism; 'his principles are in direct opposition to my own . . . my principle of action is to sustain authority and to promote respect for the administration of the laws'.[4] Whalley argued that Kenealy was a relative late-comer to the Tichborne cause, who pursued it only for professional and personal reasons. The counsel's presentation of Roger Tichborne as 'a monster of vice and dissolution' had appalled the old guard, Whalley said; he had hurried back from an American lecture tour to alter this course, but failed, primarily because the Claimant himself supported Kenealy. Now the latter was continuing his destructive work by joining Tichborne sympathy to the MCA movement and by tainting all with that unscrupulousness which marked his whole career and Irish politics generally. Thus Whalley applied to Kenealy the language that he normally reserved for Jesuitry; the climax was his allegation that 'Romish influence' pervaded the MCA.[5]

Another of the old guard, a man even quicker to denounce Kenealy, was Roger's kinsman, A. J. W. Biddulph. His medium was the revived series of the *Tichborne Gazette,* 1874-5. Its editor was H. B. Harding, who claimed to have been erstwhile secretary to the Claimant. The journal at first concentrated on documentation, avoiding all personal spite, but this policy ended by October 1874. The first attack on Kenealy was for his sensationalism in describing the Claimant's alleged suffering in gaol. In May 1875 Biddulph established a Chief Central Tichborne committee. He disparaged talk of devilish conspiracy either by family or by church. The simpler motives of prejudice and greed had brought his cousin down. It compounded Roger's tragedy that his situation was used to subvert those principles of order that he himself upheld. The new organization had a rocky history, one stress being the closure of the *Gazette,* evidently late in 1875. However, Biddulph persevered: for example, in bringing before Home Secretary Cross affidavits from Orton's siblings—whom Biddulph and others thought Kenealy should have called—and in launching a fund to finance perjury charges against certain witnesses. But when the Claimant's wife acted in precisely this way against Katherine Radcliffe, Biddulph tried to quash the move. While the magistrate refused to issue a summons, recriminations exploded between Biddulph, Onslow and others, especially as to whether or not the Claimant himself had supported the ploy. The central committee evidently broke on this reef.[6]

Biddulph persisted in the hope of saving 'Roger' by true, clean devotion. Late in 1877 he called a meeting of the man's respectable friends, who bemoaned the harm done by Onslow, Kenealy and their motley followers. Onslow's response was to publish a statement allegedly made by the prisoner: 'My cousin makes some allusion to the uneducated classes being with you; if he means the honest, hard-working men, I feel proud to have them with me; and for my cause'. Biddulph answered that this was a fabrication, and so more rifts opened.[7] Thereafter Biddulph stayed in the background. His significance was to offer negative proof that the cause was dynamic only when associated with broader appeals and issues.

This might also be the most meaningful lesson to draw from T. M. Evans's experience. Evans had political ambitions and interests but they concentrated on local Leicester affairs; in sponsoring Kenealy as a national figure he almost certainly sought justice for the Claimant beyond all else. The rupture between the two is therefore the most damning of all criticisms of Kenealy. The form of that criticism was routine: Kenealy used the cause to his own advantage, he threatened to become the English Robespierre or Napoleon III, he was dictatorial vis-a-vis everyone else, and forced his simpleton son Ahmed into a position of false significance. Beyond asserting these charges on one hand and bewailing the Claimant's lot on the other, Evans's *Evening News* had little to say. A smaller paper sponsored by him, the *Flag of Justice,* apparently concentrated still more on Tichborne issues.[8] The *Flag* amalgamated with the *Tichborne Gazette* in mid-1875, and the *Evening News* folded three years later. Since its foundation in 1874, went a final statement, political vitality had shrivelled, while the worsening trade situation led workers to care only for themselves, forgetting the Claimant.

Another old hand at the centre of a fairly distinct group of Tichbornites was Edmund Kimber. A solicitor and erstwhile secretary of the Criminal Law Amendment Society, Kimber led the National Tichborne Release Association which developed immediately on the Claimant's conviction, no doubt building on the defence committees of 1872. Kimber's chief ally was T. E. Powell, who served as secretary of the association right through until 1883; on then resigning he explained that all his energies must go to his trade union.[9] This was a rare combination of interests; appropriately, Powell—and Kimber—had been among those purged from the MCA, early in 1876. Later that year Kimber acted for the Claimant's wife in the move to summons Katherine Radcliffe; so the *Englishman* joined with Biddulph, but against Onslow, in ridiculing that tactic.

Much the same grouping operated in 1879-80 when Kimber moved to have the Claimant released at the end of his first seven years' term. The government granted a writ permitting the case. This probably resulted from Hardinge Giffard—who always had thought the double sentence wrong—then being Solicitor-General, but Tichbornites claimed that the government thus hoped to win favour in the coming elections. The *Times* scorned such rumours and vented its old hate-fear:

To some minds, unfortunately, the Claimant's career is attractive. He has been the discoverer of a whole unsuspected world of vulgar folly and ignorance which an industrious imposter may work for his own ends. The singular success of the butcher's son in deluding people hitherto supposed to be sensible, the number and enthusiasm of his adherents, the durability of the low-typed cult of which he was the object, and his startling demonstration of new possibilities in human folly and credulity, might hereafter tempt imitators if the punishment meted out to him had been small.[10]

The case came before the Court of Appeal in June 1880; giving his adverse judgement, Lord Justice James said that the grant of the writ had been imprudent. The *Law Journal*, among others, believed that the judges' decision itself was questionable, but on appeal the House of Lords upheld it. Tichbornites still had reason to believe in the persecution of their hero.

The Tichborne Release Association attempted to extract favourable pledges from candidates at the 1880 election. The organization kept up some strength until then—presumably much like the MCA—but, lacking any counterpart to the *Englishman*, it was condemned to still darker shades. Kimber himself cherished hopes of a parliamentary career, and his name will appear again.

G. B. Skipworth and William Cobbett long remained the outstanding eccentrics of the Tichborne cause. Skipworth's country-gentleman background gave the sharpest possible contrast to his increasingly raucous denunciations of authority. Edward Walford, compiler of *County Families,* excluded the apostate from his 1874 edition. Skipworth supported every display of Tichborne feeling, but his strongest animus always ran against the administrators of justice. In 1875 he petitioned the House of Commons that it uphold the people's ancient right by listening to all grievances submitted against judges. He publicized cases wherein, he believed, magistrates had uncritically accepted police evidence, and launched a fund to arraign any minister who supported false convictions. Opposed to compulsory vaccination, Skipworth revelled in hate of the punishments given under this law. And always he harked back to the great case: confirming his critics' charges, he urged Tichbornites to refrain from any show of loyalty such as singing the national anthem or cheering the royal family, and to apply passive resistance to the government at every point.[11]

Cobbett strove rather to use the law than to denounce it, spending his last years in litigation meant to destroy the Claimant's persecutors. On the prisoner being gaoled, Cobbett immediately sought a writ of habeas corpus, and the judge had to use all his dignity to enforce a ruling that no layman could appear in the matter. Then Cobbett brought an action against Arthur Griffiths, who was in charge at Millbank prison, where the Claimant stayed throughout most of 1874; Griffiths had refused Cobbett's demand, made in person, for a copy of the warrant for custody of the prisoner. Griffiths later claimed that he had threatened to imprison Cobbett himself, and that this too became a matter of litigation. The charge broke down, however, and both judge and Attorney-General 'laughed heartily at my summary treatment of such an intricate point as that raised by Orton's staunch friends'.[12] Cobbett's next plan was to apply for summonses against Gladstone, Lowe and James Stansfeld, the Lords of the Treasury in April 1872, for alleged conspiracy to indict 'Sir Roger'. So it went on until 12 January 1878 when he died in Westminster, pursuing the cause.[13]

Cobbett's obsession with Tichborne was the last episode of a life given to strange crusades, with such rashness as to cause several terms of gaol. Cobbett used Tichborne journals to present some of these crotchets. One was that everyone should grow maize of a species developed by himself, and so ensure national self-sufficiency in grain. More interesting, at least in its connection with some aspects of Kenealy's thought, was his detestation of responsible government. The French revolutionaries, Cobbett argued, had begun the damnable practice of elected assemblies asserting power over the executive, and William Pitt had followed in Britain. It were better that the Crown be free of all restraint.

From eccentric to scoundrel is a short move. Kenealy, Onslow, Barry all approached the border-line, but Jean Luie crossed it. Charged with perjury (and bigamy) in April 1874, Luie was found guilty on the soundest possible evidence and sentenced to seven years' imprisonment. The press treated his story as an epitome of the Claimant's case. He 'carried out his plans with a curious mixture of cunning and audacity, of impudence and ingenuous simplicity', said the *Daily News*: 'above all, with an amount of histrionic versatility and a truly dramatic instinct, which, had his lot been cast in a revolutionary country, might have raised him to political distinction in the secret service of the state'.[14] Released in August 1880, Luie at once established himself in the Tichborne camp. He and W. J. Barry found affinity, and proved an effective pair on the lecture platform. *The Life, Trial, and Conviction of Jean Luie* sold at a penny apiece. With voice and pen, Luie asserted more or less his original story, the proof of his trial notwithstanding.

While roguery stands at one hand of eccentricity, enthusiasm is at the other. From the multitude who for years kept alive their zeal for the cause, history can know but few. Probably the palm should go to W. A. Frost, who during forty years wrote scores of thousands of words about the case. Frost had some shrewdness: he appreciated, for example, that the crucial evidence against the Claimant derived rather from the South American episode than the Australian, although much more discussion concerned the latter. He was good at pointing out where other commentators were wrong. Still, Frost was scarcely shrewd enough to make a convincing case for the Claimant other than by accepting dubious evidence. He had talent as a song-writer, thus adding to the case's role as popular entertainment; one of his harmonies accompanied a verse by Kenealy, 'Love is a Star'.[15] The two men shared another interest in the life of Bulwer Lytton, concerning whom Frost published a booklet in 1913.[16]

THE 'INDEPENDENT', JOHN DE MORGAN, AND OTHER RADICALS

Leicester and Stoke had been crucial in elevating Kenealy, but Leeds could claim an equal part in the cause generally. Among the earliest local proponents were two druggists, Edward Foster and R. Hogg. The latter became notorious in June 1873 when the bench condemned some pamphlets he had distributed. Thereafter Hogg left the record; Foster, conversely, became more prominent. In mid-1874 he engaged in discussion over the case with one of Leeds's grandest old radicals, F. R. Lees.[17] Lees was the son of a schoolteacher who had admired and associated with the great Cobbett. He himself had supported the charter, and under that banner won a seat on Leeds city council of 1848-9. Between 1846 and 1850 he joined with G. S. Phillips, an upholder of Eastern mysticism, to edit a journal, *The Truth Seeker*. Overall, however, Lees's great cause was temperance, his major publication a *Temperance Bible Commentary*. He stood as a radical for Leeds in the 1874 election. Concerning Tichborne, he argued that workers were mistaken in making the cause a fundamental of action; 'nothing but a *keen* sense of their own supreme interest as *labourers*', aiming at fulfilment of the Charter, should play that role.[18] In response, Foster argued that the case illustrated precisely those evils that reformers must destroy; anyway, the issue already had inspired a political move, and the best tactic was to accept and use the fact.

Effecting his words, in March 1875 Foster established a journal inferior only to the *Englishman* in advocacy of the Tichborne cause. The original full title was *Yorkshire Independent and People's Advocate*, but later it appeared as the *National Independent*, while publishing a Leeds edition under the original title. Foster was editor, with a board consisting of Lees and some other local leftist chieftains. It was a journal of broad, deep radicalism. Franchise extension, law reform, public education, women's rights, cheaper elections, payment of members, lower taxation— these shibboleths received their due. Reduction of expenditure should include cuts in salaries of 'high class officials'. England must concentrate on justice at home rather than venturing abroad to keep up an army led by aristocratic job-seekers. The *Independent* supported labour in the endless struggle with capital, despite the former's tendency to be 'naturally jealous, irritable, defiant, and sometimes unreasonable'. Working men should prepare themselves, through study and virtue, to exercise power. The *Independent* hoped for a new party to emerge from the Liberal Left; obstructing this however was what Lees, a regular contributor, saw as the employers' deliberate corruption of the working class through drink and other means, or what an editorial scorned as the 'dumb docility' of the oppressed. Amidst all these proposals and protests, the Tichborne issue kept its place:

Suppose we got shorter parliaments, and the ratepayers' suffrage, to men and women alike, and yet, notwithstanding, we had an impure administration of justice, should we, as a nation, be much better for these possessions? Suppose the farm labourers and the women had the right to vote, and they sent to parliament the same sort of representatives as are there now, most of whom seem absolutely dead to all sense of equity and right, what would it advantage us? Suppose we were all highly educated, and in possession of our full political rights, what would it profit us if we were unable to receive common justice, and our lives and liberties were at the mercy of such hired perjurers, prostitutes and swindlers as were permitted to swear away the possessions and the liberties of the Tichborne Claimant?[19]

There could be no better expression of how the case stood surrogate for many grievances.

Towards Kenealy, the *Independent* was equivocal. Foster had early backed his parliamentary hopes and saw his election as promising 'political triumphs and social advantages compared with which the achievements of all modern statesmen and philanthropists sink into insignificance';[20] yet the very next week a correspondent deplored Kenealy's Crown-and-Tory aspect. Thereafter criticism pursued the usual line that Kenealy was seeking naught but self-glory. Foster himself became involved in a squabble within the local MCA late in 1875, and the *Independent* took side with the dissidents in the MCA upheaval of late 1876. Apropos 'Bulgarian horrors', the *Independent* took a stand opposite to Kenealy and to its own little-Englandism: Britain should enforce principles of freedom on Turkey, said one editorial in so many words. On other issues the *Independent* spoke much as did the *Englishman*. It questioned that education and virtue went together. 'Have we not . . . men literally crammed with education, and at the same time steeped up to the very necks in corruption and wickedness! While, on the other hand, we have millions of men of limited education, but whose natural sense of right and justice is so strong'.[21] The *Independent* criticized school boards on points such as their teaching of military drill, allegedly a technique whereby the ruling class prepared the masses to serve as cannon fodder. The journal was steady in its abuse of the Church of England, and at times turned on the monarchy itself, and also on Roman Catholicism. Disraeli's imperialism abroad was seen as complementary to his centralization of government at home, and both were detested. Many editorials criticized the administration of justice.

The *Independent*'s greatest distinction was hostility to established medical practice. The attitude spread wide at this time: its most common expressions, hostility to compulsory vaccination and to the contagious diseases acts, already have obtruded. The *Independent* gave much space to both these questions. Many columns came from the couple who fostered the anti-vaccination movement, William and Mary Hume-Rothery (the wife's father was yet another old radical, Joseph Hume) . Their main theme was often ramified:

for every instance of active complicity or passive acquiescence in national crimes and atrocities, such as the wholesale murder called war, the unutterably infamous Contagious Diseases Acts, the brutalizing opium traffic, the cruel and tyrannical Compulsory Vaccination Laws, the selfish and oppressive Game and Land Laws, and too many others that cannot be enumerated here, will every member of every political party or government have to face judgement hereafter . . .[22]

True to Joseph Hume's heritage, the Hume-Rotherys disliked all trends towards positive government, while among their other crusades were women's suffrage, the end of capital punishment, and the Tichborne cause.

A common development from specific hates like vaccination or contagious diseases legislation was accusation of the medical profession establishing monopoly and power. Foster's own calling as a druggist predisposed him thus. Not only did he produce patent remedies, but the *Independent* publicized the British Medical Reform Association, and extolled homoeopathy, hydropathy, eclectopathy, and botanoeopathy against the conservative allopaths. It delighted in publishing Herbert Spencer's account of the medical profession's 'unmistakable wish to establish an organized, tax-supported class charged with the health of men's bodies, as the clergy are charged with the health of their souls'.[23] A contributor alleged that the profession sought to vest medicine with mystery and esoteric vocabulary—but any intelligent layman should be able to see through the facade thus raised. The *Independent* deprecated legislation for the registration of doctors, and felt that even sanitary reformers sought power for themselves as much as health for the people. Offering a policy that might inspire a new radical party, the *Independent* nominated as point six 'that a stop shall be put to the insidious encroachments of the medical profession, which under the plea of preserving the national health is creating a powerful vested interest and invading the liberty of the subject to an alarming extent'.[24]

Still higher on that platform, was a call for unlocking the land —a foretaste of the *Independent*'s second great cause. 'In the minds of the people of the United Kingdom there is a deep and widespread discontent on the subject of the whole land system of this country', said the journal in January 1880; 'They are beginning to awake up to the fact that a free people should possess a free soil'. This generalization arose from such concerns as unlocking the land, hostility to the game laws, sympathy for Joseph Arch, scorn for the landed interest. Above all, it proceeded from emphasis on the people's right and need to claim commons land. Agitation and triumph at this point, declared one editorial of December 1877, promised to 'split up the block of the territorial ascendancy in this country'. Those were the sentiments of John De Morgan, who for many months had been the *Independent*'s driving force and who became second only to Kenealy in the story of Tichborne politics.

By his own account Morgan had supported total abstinence and other social reforms from childhood.[25] He first mounted the platform in 1868 in Belfast to urge republicanism and disestablishment of the Church of Ireland. Consequently dismissed from his job, he began to give lectures and readings. Morgan's repertoire was large, with stress on men and issues of radical trend; denunciations of British imperialism in India and Ireland were among his favourite pieces. Especially interesting in view of Morgan's later tie with the *Independent* was his advocacy of hydropathic treatment as against 'Medical Science, a delusion and a farce'. Fenianism was another of his causes. He crossed to Manchester in 1869 and became one of Bradlaugh's associates, but a quarrel soon drove him back to Ireland, allegedly under a cloud of dishonesty. Moving next to Cork, Morgan took up the cudgels against compulsory vaccination and contagious diseases acts, and established a section of the International Working Men's Association. From Cork, he contributed to the *Republican* and then to the *International Herald,* both of London, showing that he had ease with pen as well as voice. At hectic meetings Morgan spoke of the International as 'destined to bring about a glorious future of peace and contentment, of harmony and justice' and called on 'Democrats of England and Nationalists of Ireland' to join under this banner. The townsfolk became most disturbed and victimized the radical in their midst. Sympathizers in Britain raised money in support. Frederick Engels was among those impressed.[26]

Returned to England in July, Morgan remained active in the International's politics. Within the British section he supported the Marx-Engels line against reformists. Engels and he corresponded. Dubbing himself 'Professor of Elocution and Oratory', Morgan toured the north and the midlands, and then settled in London. There he became a regular spokesman for radical republicanism. The Royal Parks and Gardens Act, restricting public meetings in Hyde Park and elsewhere, offered an immediate cause. Late in 1872, Morgan and about a dozen others—including the renowned George Odger—found fame and notoriety when they broke the regulations pertaining to Hyde Park; defending himself in a consequent police action, Morgan won permanent adjournment of his case and later claimed thus to have helped smash the prohibition. Critics alleged that he had stolen a fund subscribed to defend the others as well as himself.

At a congress of the British International in June 1873 Morgan represented the National Reform League, founded by Bronterre O'Brien in 1850 and 'the only society in Britain to maintain, in the period between the decline of Chartism and the socialist revival of the 1880s, a consistent propaganda in favour of Socialism'.[27] The congress carried Morgan's motion urging use of national credit for co-operatives. A few weeks later Morgan was fishing for support as a parliamentary candidate at Northampton; his platform upheld most points of the charter, most of the causes mentioned above, and nationalization of land. He was a republican, went the message, but no atheist. Northampton was the preserve of Bradlaugh, and so his *National Reformer* told of earlier scandals concerning this rival. Morgan replied, but Northampton encouraged him little. In early 1874 Morgan worked for the short-lived *Republican Herald,* which in contrast to Bradlaugh's journal did applaud Kenealy's defence of the Claimant. Then, too, he lectured in London on the true meaning of Christianity. C. M. Davies, chronicler of *Unorthodox London,* found the speaker 'suave', 'very juvenile', and 'rather good-looking'.[28]

Henceforward Morgan added the Tichborne cause to his armoury. In July 1875 appeared a new Tichborne paper, the *People's Advocate and National Vindicator of Right v. Wrong,* backed by Kimber and East but dominated by Morgan both as manager-editor and as news-item. The *Advocate* gave space to labour and trade union news and beat the drum of class war. 'The Monarch amasses wealth, the Royal Princes in their greedy longing, extract all they can . . . rich criminals by bubble companies extract the last sovereign from the pocket of the poor widow and orphan; capitalists, like ogres, grind down the wages of the workers to the lowest point'.[29] Morgan looked forward to the election of at least a hundred working men to the House of Commons; even then, he said, the people would not have their proper representation. A variant of his concern for medical reform was the provision of vegetarian recipes. The *Advocate* followed a common pattern by first supporting Kenealy and then finding him increasingly at fault. Morgan was among the leader's critics at the MCA congress in August 1875. 'If . . . he should feel unequal to the great task of welding all parties', said the *Advocate* of Kenealy at this time, 'the Magna Charta Association is not likely to allow the great cause to flag, but will be able to pick out someone whose leadership all can follow'. The *Advocate* suspended publication from 2 October 1875 until 15 April 1876; it then alleged irregularities and fraud in Morgan's management. The charges may have arisen from either truth or spleen, for at about this time Morgan joined the *Independent*.

Between late 1875 and 1878 Morgan strove to transform the commons question into an issue of mass anger. In recent years commons' preservation had aroused some concern, but chiefly among the high bourgeoisie. The leader and historian of this conservationist group, G. Shaw Lefevre, explained that its inspiration was twofold: to provide 'oases of nature' for the mass population of the new England, and to protect the agricultural labour from hardships that enclosure always imposed.[30] Lefevre and his peers—J. S. Mill, Henry Fawcett, Octavia Hill, Charles Dilke were the best-known names—formed and supported the Commons Preservation Society. The Metropolitan Commons Act of 1866 was an early victory, allowing for regulation of land within London. Over the next decade, battle waged back and forth, fought law-suit by law-suit. Gladstone attempted further legislation, most notably in 1871, but the House of Lords thwarted him

Morgan brought physical force into play, first at Hackney Downs, where enclosure of the common currently proceeded. On 11 December 1875 he addressed a multitude there, repeating his speech five times so as to reach all his auditors, 'the last time on a platform sustained by the joined hands of the people'.[31] At his signal, the crowd advanced on the railings, uprooted them, and twisted them 'into every variety of shape'. The enclosure halted while the matter went to law, and Morgan established his own Commons Protection League, supported by Kimber and T. E. Powell. In the next session, the government introduced a further commons bill, enforcing more stringent conditions for enclosure. The Home Secretary remarked that public opinion, concerned with health and welfare, called for such action. He may have had Morgan in mind—as was later claimed—but doubtless the Preservation Society and the agricultural labourers were more important. Lefevre and Fawcett felt the measure was not radical enough, but overall it was a victory for their movement. To the bill's opponents in parliament, defenders of popular rights over the commons appeared to advocate 'the confiscation of the property of one set of men . . . in order to give it without compensation to another class',[32] in the manner of extremists of the French Revolution.

While the bill went through, Morgan struck again, this time at Plumstead, Kent. The provost and scholars of Queen's College Oxford, Lords of the Manor, had been leasing and selling Plum-

stead land since 1859.³³ Locals responded with spirit, and with
backing from the Preservation Society. Litigation, continuing to
1871, favoured the commoners, although some small pieces were
sold thereafter. Giving Morgan his chance was the lords' leasing
the common to the War Office for purposes of drill (albeit the
actual practice of drill there dated back to 1740). That many
local residents worked at Woolwich arsenal might have spiced
their feeling against the military-government-Oxford complex.
Battle commenced on 1 July 1876 with much the same pattern as
at Hackney: bands, placards, speeches, rousing a crowd to angry
enthusiasm and physical force. Morgan finished his oration with
verse:

> No, we dare erect to stand
> Freeman—in our native land.
> Fooled no more with vain pretences,
> Down shall go the robbers' fences.
> Hearts, and hands, and wills unite
> Battling for our sacred right.³⁴

Succeeding nights saw repeats of the performance.

As turbulence continued, the Preservation Society dissociated
itself from the Protection League—and Lefevre's history of the
former gave the latter not a word. Kimber wrote in length and
anger to the *Independent* and to Gladstone, whose response was
at least polite. Simultaneously Morgan boosted his prestige by
successfully arguing a case concerning Hackney before the Master
of the Rolls; the judge's deprecation of his tactics if anything
enlarged the triumph. On 8 August Dilke raised the question in
parliament, alleging that the War Office still threatened 'this
monstrous step' of compulsory acquisition of the land. In late July
three commoners sought from Chancery an injunction against the
Secretary for War. Told that they must petition the Crown direct,
they did so, and early in September received an injunction thence.
Morgan had been haranguing almost every evening, and now he
led a massive celebration of at least 10 000 people.

To maintain this pitch was difficult, but Morgan tried. He kept
on talking at Plumstead and other places where commons were in
danger, until in mid-October he went to prison on charges dating
back from July. The *Morning Advertiser* sympathized, and the
Observer felt that as a moral protest his action made sense. From
Maidstone gaol the prisoner addressed 'The People of England'
through the *Independent*: 'I am reminded that Wat Tyler made

Jean Luie

These and other illustrations reflect the quality and impact of *The Trial*
[E. V. H. Kenealy, *The Trial at Bar of Sir Roger C. D. Tichborne*]

'Captain' W. J. Barry

John De Morgan
The rustic romanticism of the decoration accords with Morgan's style
[*De Morgan's Monthly*]

'The Wallaby Track'
The Tichborne vision of romantic Australia
[E. V. H. Kenealy, *The Trial at Bar of Sir Roger C. D. Tichborne*]

'One of the "Sympathizers"'
Jeames: 'I'm afraid, me Lady, I'll require to Leave you.' *Lady*: 'Why?'
Jeames: 'Well, me lady, I can't agree with Master's suckasms against that
poor persecuted Sir Roger.'
Class-division is apparent not only in the dialogue but also in the
publisher's contemptuous caption   [*Punch*, April 1872]

the very prison I am incarcerated in his headquarters . . . A greater revolution than Wat Tyler's will be originated at Maidstone now, if the people be but in earnest'.[35] On 6 November a massive meeting at Woolwich welcomed Morgan to freedom. However, the royal injunction halted the army but briefly, for in the new year the courts sanctioned drilling of soldiers. Demonstrations resumed and the *Independent* remarked that the French Revolution had begun with dispute over commons, inferring that Plumstead could have such significance for Britain. On 20 January Morgan led another physical force action. Questioned in the Commons, the government insisted on the suitability of the land for its purposes and declined to justify itself further; Julian Goldsmith, a parliamentarian sympathetic with the Preservation Society and associated with Plumstead, remarked of Morgan that 'though a spirited, he was a misguided individual, and the persons who acted with him were not commoners at all'.[36] Morgan used violence again in June, and briefly went to prison in consequence. An election for Plumstead vestry gave victory to commons-righters. At last, the Metropolitan Board of Works purchased manorial rights from Queen's College, and the War Office agreed that it should use but part of the land.

The intensity at Plumstead remained unique, yet Morgan continued to give comparable incidents his dynamic care. The two most important were at Selston, Nottinghamshire, and Hunslet Moor, Leeds. The Selston case reached its climax with a riot on 11 September 1877 and Morgan's subsequent imprisonment for contempt. While under sentence he took his case to appeal; the judge ruled against him and lamented 'to see a gentleman of education and ability' inciting riot.[37] At Hunslet Moor, the Lords of the Manor had encouraged use of the land for coal-mining and a tramway, illustrating the frequent clash between the commons movement and the railway interest. Morgan began agitation and Leeds Corporation decided that it would treat with the lords. The result was agreement that the corporation should pay £4000 while the lords retained mineral rights and the tramway stayed. Morgan denounced these terms. At a public meeting, his viewpoint carried the vote. The corporation then decided to put the agreement to a referendum, which 19 160 votes supported against 16 498.

All this while, Morgan spoke and wrote and agitated for the Tichborne cause. The highlight was a march on the House of Commons on 17 April 1877. He called for 100 000 supporters to gather; the number fell short of that, but nevertheless the scene

was excited, with hawkers of Tichborne songs and Morgan
biography selling their wares, and police present in very large
numbers. Morgan gave one of his usual orations, threatening that
if this demonstration did not force Tichborne's release, revolution
would follow. Then he, Skipworth, and some others, followed by
the crowd, entered the precincts of parliament. Whalley met
them, with bad news: he had meant to present a petition to the
Commons whereby Morgan claimed as of right to address the
House, but it had not come to hand. The next day Home Secretary Cross met the deputation. Morgan argued that his own
leadership was restraining Tichbornites from desperate action,
but Cross gave no ground. Early in June Whalley did bring the
matter before the House, but still to no effect. Meanwhile Morgan
tried to establish in terms of the Tichborne cause the sort of permanent agitation that had prevailed at Plumstead. Skipworth,
young Roger and the apostate juryman Charles Dunsby, all gave
their support, and Morgan floated a Tichborne Propaganda
Union. Skipworth saw Morgan as a Messiah, and Kenealy saw him
as a threat. The *Englishman* declared Morgan a red-republican adventurer, and recalled Bradlaugh's charges against him. 'To set up
Morgan and others as leaders against me', was an important part
of the 'perfect ruin to Tichborne's cause', which Kenealy alleged
might result from Onslow's mishandling of the situation.[38]

Synthesizing and capping his work on commons and Tichborne,
Morgan sought to establish himself as a likely parliamentary
leader of the people. One venture to this end was the establishment in September 1876 of *De Morgan's Monthly*. The first issue
featured a letter from Garibaldi approving the Hackney Downs
episode. Land reform was the chief theme of the paper throughout
its eight-month history, Morgan sounding his usual threat-hope of
revolution unless action were taken. The *Monthly* also documented Morgan's aspirations to win support from Leicester as a
parliamentary candidate. Throughout the year Morgan visited
that city, speaking on both Tichborne and commons; the *Evening
News* gave him some space, but concluded that, like Kenealy, he
sought to use the cause for his own ambition. A shadow organization, the People's Political Union, offered itself as a band wagon
for Morgan's admirers to push.

The Social Democratic Club (International and English section) praised Morgan in these months, but the response from
Leicester evidently was so poor as to prompt him to try Leeds
instead. His address in August 1878 was much as in Leicester.

Over the next few months the candidate kept up his frenetic activity—trying still to thwart the Hunslet Moor purchase, winning a seat on the Leeds School Board, urging the Durham miners to strike, acting as agent for the Texas Freehold Farm and Emigration Union Limited. In February 1880 appeared his campaign propaganda-sheet, *De Morgan's Weekly*. The electorate failed Morgan yet again. He withdrew before polling day, although keeping the *Weekly* alive long enough to answer revived charges concerning his erstwhile behaviour, and to memorialize Kenealy as a 'truly honest man'.

Thus crumbled the hopes of another democrat-Messiah. His relations with the *Independent* appear to have been worsening since mid-1879, and the process sharpened when F. R. Lees became proprietor-editor early in 1880. On 4 March 1881 the journal published a report that Morgan, now resident in New York, had criticized the new management. The *Independent's* response was that its critic had twenty years ago cheated a temperance society of £100, and that he had fled to New York owing money to the *Independent* itself. Morgan still hoped for a comeback: he continued to issue pamphlets oriented towards British radicals,[39] and in 1885 wrote to the *Independent* urging that Tichbornites force the cause into the coming election campaign and fishing for money to enable himself to stand for Hunslet. With that, the record ends. Morgan probably had greater political force than Kenealy, and charisma too, but his faults were more patent and his opportunities smaller.

Among lesser men to whom the cause offered scope, the most interesting was E. W. Bailey. He had come into Kenealy's circle during the Wednesbury election of 1868, when a Methodist lay-preacher of humble status—Kenealy claimed to have taken him from the forge, but probably that exaggerated.[40] Their relationship continued and Kenealy brought Bailey to London to help manage the MCA. Bailey's admirers claimed that, following his appointment as executive secretary in June 1876, the organization became much more effective. He appears to have had his own share of charisma: 'Mr Bailey is an excellent organizer, an orator, and a perfect master of logic and of language, honest, brave and conscientious in all his undertakings'.[41] Bailey soon pushed his power to its test. The schism of September-October 1876 was the result.

Thereafter Bailey formed his own National Magna Charta Association. Among its leaders was S. C. E. Goss who, in attempting to avoid a split had offered to accompany Kenealy through the maze of sublimity, but alleged that after the quarrel he spurned Kenealy's offer of conciliation. The *Englishman* described Bailey's group as conspirators who, in the hope of selling Tichborne Bonds, broadcast 'most daring and mendacious tales', especially as to the discovery of Orton in Australia.[42] Soon the new body experienced that tell-tale of weakness, a change of title: it became The People's Social and Political Reform Association. It argued for Tichborne justice, franchise extension, law reforms, temperance, abolition of primogeniture and game laws, commons preservation, a reduced Civil List. It called too for 'periodical investigation of monastic and conventual institutions, lunatic asylums, and unions'; both Bailey and Goss were scourgers of Romanism. Probably because of this, their association said bitter words about the Biddulph group of Tichbornites. Otherwise, it did nothing but decay. The Eastern question then took much of Goss's political energy: he hated Russia even more than did Kenealy, and would have been happy for Britain to go to war against 'that insatiable Beast of Nations'.[43] Bailey concentrated rather on the next world, becoming a full-time gospeller from 1877.

After Morgan had left the *People's Advocate* and it had resumed publication in April 1876, the editor was Maltman Barry. In the early seventies Barry had been very active in the International. Controversial and disliked, he yet became an ally of Marx and Engels in their squabbles with Bakuninists to the Left and trade unionists to the Right. Barry vainly sought working class endorsement at the 1874 elections. He carried the *Advocate* to the Leftmost point of the Tichborne cause. Nationalization of religion, education, land and the instruments of production; abolition of the monarchy and the House of Lords; international federation of workers—these were the leading, although far from the only, ideals. Barry found fault with Kenealy's excessive respect for the constitution; 'neither he nor anybody else can guarantee the temper and the patience of his followers',[44] went one statement which surely threatened a take-over from the Left. 'A Plea for Revolution' headed an editorial which bemoaned that while eschewing violence, the British ruling class was just as determined and effectual as any other in suppressing protest. The only extant *Advocate* file ceases with new series number five, although expansion was then planned.

Barry next took up, in 1876-7, the Manhood Suffrage League, a chartist old-boy group. Then he became another enthusiast for Disraeli's tough line against Russia: in late 1877 and early 1878 he helped organize the London meetings which sang 'Rule, Britannia' and other works of music-hall patriotism. 'Jingo' entered the language. Some MCA groups supported Barry in this activity; Marx also approved, despite doubt as to the man's sincerity. In 1885 Barry became more widely known for his involvement in the Conservative 'corruption' of the Social Democrats by providing them with electoral costs. He survived, to play an important role in the foundation of the Independent Labour Party, evidently seeking to establish it as a constituent partner of Tory democracy. That he openly proclaimed his coincident membership of the Conservative Party might indicate good faith, if also irrational thought; however, he long suffered the same sort of charge of treason to the Left as did Kenealy.[45]

Meanwhile, the *Advocate* had come under the editorship of Frederick Longman, a veteran supporter of the cause. Presumably he used the journal as an instrument in his rather simple-minded crusade against all evil and oppression. In 1900 Longman returned briefly to battle, and three issues of a renewed *Advocate* assaulted vaccination, vivisection and the law.

Another curious apostle of Tichborne radicalism was M. A. Orr. Orr worked for Kenealy on the *Englishman* in its early days, but was among the first defectors from the leader. The *True Briton: The Avowed Enemy and Antidote to Dr Kenealy's 'Englishman'*, which he launched in May 1874, concentrated on vilifying Kenealy, but abused the whole management of the Claimant's cause, alleging that swindlers and rogues managed it from the outset. Nor was the Claimant himself spared: since 1870, the *True Briton* said, he had lived in adultery with an erstwhile actress, at times visiting his wife in Kentish Town. Yet Orr evidently still saw himself as a Tichbornite, and continued as a reformer. In November 1877 the Medical Defence Association charged him with possessing birth-control literature. The *Englishman* remarked that he was now an associate of the big trade-union leaders—Broadhurst, Potter and company.[46]

NEW VARIANTS IN THE 1880s

The early eighties saw the cause at low ebb. Kenealy's death, Morgan's migration, the failure of the writ of error, all combined towards this end. Yet even then a few Tichbornites remained active. The most interesting elements of the story centred on the MCA-*Englishman* nexus, which survived until 1886, chiefly through Maurice Kenealy's effort.

The *Englishman* remained radical, sometimes more extreme yet usually more conventional in its extremism than it had been. Through 1880–1 it presented reports and notices from a scatter of anarchist, Marxist and other such groups: in one issue the Dutch section of the Social Democratic League, Eleusis Club, Guild of St Matthew, Ladies Land League, Lambeth Democratic Association, Manhood Suffrage League, National Land League of Great Britain, Peckham Liberal club, Somerville club, Social Democratic club, proposed Socialist conference to re-establish the International, Willesden Radical Association, Walworth Free-Thought Institute, and a dozen MCA groups. Editorial policy reflected these interests. The establishment of English land leagues analogous to those in Ireland, aiming at nationalization and led by an English Parnell, was one ideal especially stressed. Education in general and school boards in particular had an esteem which Kenealy himself would never have granted.

The peak of this new wave was for the MCA to play a significant part in the birth of H. M. Hyndman's Democratic Federation in spring 1881.[47] Leaders of the MCA were active in the preliminary discussions and especially at the founding conference on 8 June. The first executive included the three then most active MCA leaders—Maurice Kenealy, Finlay Finlayson, and William Morrison. At this time, Hyndman was still moving from Toryism to Marxist socialism and the federation did not become 'social-democratic' until 1884. In doctrine, then, the new body accorded with the MCA. Amalgamation was proposed, and Hyndman spoke to a special MCA conference. Proceedings began bumpily as Jean Luie made an unwelcome appearance. Hyndman failed to persuade his listeners to forsake MCA autonomy. For the next few months federation business occupied much *Englishman* space, but a rupture evidently took place in September.

This did not reflect any change in *Englishman* policy. The final editorial for 1881 insisted that the old, compromising Whig-Liberal party must soon disappear: 'now-a-days the State consists of two parties, Conservative and Democratic; or, to put it still more plainly, Royalists and Republicans'. The United States pointed the way to republican social justice; this, although not communism, must be England's aim too. The most interesting variant of concern for land reform was appreciation for Henry

George. In international affairs, the *Englishman* still upheld isolation. Joseph Chamberlain, Joseph Cowen and R. M. Pankhurst all appeared as possible leaders of a new order. From 1880 the *Englishman* published a slight (although durable) journal, *Modern Society*; it gossiped about the upper classes, sport and the theatre, but also argued for social justice in such matters as law administration and tax policy.

Older loyalties still won homage. For a while, Kenealy's name and works bulked almost as large after his death as before. The reluctance of the MCA to amalgamate with the Democratic Federation further testified to the memories of earlier days. Tichborniana always retained its place both in MCA discussions and in the *Englishman*. A highlight was the confession in 1884 by a detective involved in the Tichborne case that he had assisted in ensuring that jurymen enrolled in the criminal trial were favourable to the prosecution; a special leaflet broadcast this item.[48] Reports from Australia, conferences of supporters in Britain, the essays of Frost and Gurnell, all continued their cycles. Luie may have been unwelcome at the MCA conference of mid-1881, but the *Englishman* published his letters and reminiscences.

Yet the old cause found new advocates, even within the *Englishman*-MCA stronghold. Pre-eminent among these was Mrs Georgina Weldon, a splendid Victorian eccentric.[49] Born in 1837, the lady had fortune, beauty and musical talent. From the late sixties, her life became turbulent indeed. Her soprano voice won considerable reputation; she began publicizing her reformist ideas on music and its teaching; friendships, and presumably sexual liaison, with Charles Gounod and a conductor, J. P. Rivière, led to her outpouring of scandal about both men; spiritualism engrossed more and more of her attention. The Weldons separated in the mid-seventies and in 1878 the husband determined to have his wife put under restraint as a lunatic. She escaped, and there began a maelstrom of litigation. This centred on libel actions deriving from her extra-marital adventures, on proceedings against her husband and doctors respecting the attempt at restraint, and on the distribution of property between herself and her husband. She typically spoke in court on her own behalf, with much energy. The British Museum holds eight items from her pen, dealing with belief and biography; five were published in 1882.

The association between Mrs Weldon and the *Englishman* appears to have been spontaneous. Lunacy reform and women's

rights had long been in the *Englishman*'s repertoire. Even more
compelling was the lady's joust with the legal system. Early in
1880 she suffered imprisonment for libelling Rivière. The *Englishman* and MCA took up her cause, Maurice Kenealy leading. Mrs
Weldon wrote regularly for the *Englishman* thereafter, and in
May 1883 became vice-president of the MCA. Also in that year
she launched a radical paper, *Social Salvation*, and organized a
series of Tichborne Release concerts, she being the star. In July
1884 she won her greatest victory, £1000 damages against one of
the doctors who had declared her a lunatic; both the judge and
the *Times* remarked that the case clinched the need for new
legislation.

Less flamboyant and talented than Mrs Weldon but still interesting was W. Parker Snow. He was the author of several books
telling mainly of travels in the Arctic and off South America, but
dabbling also in theological and social matters. His first contributions to the *Englishman* had been in July 1874, but only in the
eighties did they flourish. Some issues came largely from his pen.
On the one hand Snow denounced all manner of worldly evils,
on the other he told his adventures. The two interests often came
together, most notably in his advocacy of British annexation of
New Guinea and colonization of the Pacific islands. Like W. J.
Barry and the Claimant himself, Snow represented the tie between
exotic romance and the Tichborne cause.

Now the time approached when the Claimant himself could
resume the fight. Not that he had ever been completely absent
from it: reports on his prison life, the audience of supporters with
him, the statements he supposedly made, had all proved useful
propaganda. Its temper changed little during his year at Millbank, three years on Dartmoor, and six years at Portsea, near
Plymouth. The Claimant continued to assert that he was Roger,
and to influence those around him. Griffiths, his gaoler at Millbank, remarked that his manner was courteous yet demanded
respect; he asked for books that bespoke an educated, French, and
Catholic background. 'Many of our warders firmly believed in
him'.[50] The Fenian Michael Davitt gave a similar account of Dartmoor, declaring that 'Sir Roger' was a 'lion' among the prisoners,
who respected his rank and his opinion on whatever subject it
might be given. Virtually all believed in him, said Davitt, linking
this with most criminals' self-persuasion that they too were victims
of an unjust law.[51] The Claimant later criticized Davitt's account,
pointing to some factual errors.

Tension began to build during the summer of 1884.[52] Asked what were his plans, the Claimant reportedly said that he would not allow himself to be made a show, but would speak to the people in assertion of his rights. Some hopefuls considered nominating him as a parliamentary candidate for Leeds. Quartermaine East bought a house near Southampton intending that there the Claimant should live. The *Manchester Evening News* reported in September that the Claimant had become 'the photographic hero of the hour', and Madame Tussaud's prepared a new model. The *Englishman* alleged that details of the release were concealed so as to thwart demonstrations. But at last, on 20 October, the Claimant emerged, holding a ticket-of-leave.

For a few weeks, the stars shone brightly. His first political move was to issue a manifesto which claimed that the government, while persecuting him and spurning the people's will, had yet admitted his case by establishing a court of criminal appeal. A meeting at St James hall, late in October, brought out crowds. East was in the chair; Maurice Kenealy, Mrs Weldon, W. P. Snow all sat on the platform. The Claimant declared that God had sustained him, that he would sin no more, that he would fight for his children. He went north to more lectures, more enthusiasm, greater militance in protesting his wrongs and the evil of government. His manner was slightly awkward, but some commentators found that impressive and authentic. Much thinner, hair greying and face lined, the man was more prepossessing than before. An aspiring candidate in the west country found plenty of electors who asked his views on the case,[53] and the *Western Mail* said that the 'vast majority' of Welshmen still believed in the Claimant. Respectability's hate-fear echoed. The *Times* bemoaned that a man on ticket-of-leave should be allowed so to behave.[54] The *Standard* ground its axe against the 1884 Reform Act by arguing that should, 'as is by no means impossible', the Claimant recreate the popular movement in his favour, men like Gladstone and Chamberlain would have to abide by their recent professions of faith in popular judgement. The *Pall Mall Gazette* ran a poll which declared the Claimant to be the greatest living humbug.[55]

The moment of glory was short, giving way to new division in the Tichborne camp. East wanted the Claimant to abstain from politics and demonstrations, while Kimber hoped to use him in the service of his own intended candidature for Woolwich. Kimber won this round, but soon found fresh troubles. As early as November 1884 the Claimant found it convenient to appear at music-halls and variety concerts: they paid more money and allowed scope for liquor and lechery. Although using these appearances to state his case, and interspersing them with straight public meetings, the Claimant's role as variety star lost him standing, presumably among the public and certainly before his faithful rank-and-file. Even by the end of 1884 the Stoke MCA criticized him on this score. Kimber and Biddulph both supported the Claimant, and early in 1885 the MCA made him nominal president. But he did nothing for the organization, and meanwhile failed to fulfil his promise to subsidize the *Independent*. Nor would he maintain his wife, chiefly because of her promiscuity, and this scandal might have further disgraced him.[56] Thus the Claimant's release did more to kill the cause than had his imprisonment. That was the theme of a letter published in the last issue of the *Englishman*, 22 May 1886. Sir Roger's indifference simply proved what always had been known about his character, remarked the writer, but still it was sad that he should so treat the *Englishman* and his other followers. Yet the fight should continue:

If Sir Roger does not care to encourage the movement—nor help a demonstration, I would say—let us have one in spite of him, and if he never gives a token of gratitude, God will smile upon us in proportion to our labours to advance truth, justice, and fair play. When we pass away from this sphere of toil and injustice, cant and fraud, our love of truth will be imprinted on our souls in another realm, where we must know *no heaven* unless we earn it here and carry it with us.

This was an appropriate obituary for the journal.

The Claimant still lived. As early as January 1885 he wrote to Morgan suggesting that the latter might be his agent in arranging an American tour under Barnum auspices. Sixteen months later the Claimant did go to the United States; failing as a star, he became a bar-tender. One saloon to employ him was Cassidy's Shades near New York's Bowery. A report told of him 'in an elevated condition', confidently forecasting a return to his domain.[57] Instead his move back to Britain led to quicker descent. Failure to raise a deposit quashed plans to stand for a Stoke by-election in 1890. Next he aspired to 'get the management of some hotel or sporting house', but had to be content with a tobacco shop, music-hall appearances, and sitting around pubs as an attraction for (and guest of) drinkers. 'He became a sort of Prince

Charley of the tap-room and contented in his condition'.[58] In 1895 the Claimant published a confession.[59] He declared himself to be Orton, and that his imposture began as a lark in Wagga Wagga. Maurice Kenealy and W. A. Frost were to argue that this account was full of errors; no doubt the author's purpose was to raise money rather than to tell the truth, but in fact his story is accurate about many matters that can be checked, especially Orton's Tasmanian life. Thus the confession virtually proves its author's guilt. The essay once sold, the Claimant went back to insisting that he was Roger.

The final account of the Claimant is that of J. Churton Collins, a littérateur interested in the case. His reports tell that the Claimant's dignity stayed to the end—and also, one infers, enough sex to keep a young 'wife' happy. 'He praised Kenealy very highly', when talking to Collins on 5 August 1897.[60] Death came on the following All Fools' Day. Five thousand mourners went to the funeral. His elder daughter, Agnes, that child of Wagga Wagga, maintained the cause. She did not particularly revere her father, but insisted that his very weakness proved him incapable of maintaining an imposture. Like Ballantine and Kenealy, Agnes believed that her father had killed Orton in Australia.[61] Her tactics became increasingly odd, the most dramatic being an attempt in 1912 to assassinate the current Tichborne heir. She died in 1939, thirteen years after her mother, with whom she had had no contact for decades.

The *Independent* outlived the *Englishman*—but not the Claimant—continuing until 1889. As Morgan protested, its general character did change a little: suspicion of Irish nationalists and fervent support for free trade were the chief evidences. F. R. Lees's interests tended to push other matters aside. Medical matters and land reform (Henry George won the *Independent*'s favour, too, and he expressed his gratitude accordingly) [62] kept a place, but to nothing like the extent of the Morgan-Foster regime. The real interest of the later *Independent* was its reporting Tichborne news from Australia. It had always been more confident than the *Englishman* that thence might come a coup for the Claimant. This disposition became much stronger from about 1883 when Miss Georgiana Baring began contributing regularly. Miss Baring, the second daughter of William Baring of the great financier family, had supported the cause at least from 1879. At first her interest centred on England, but soon she took her place at the head of those who looked to Australia for the final solution.

6

THE TICHBORNE CASE AND CAUSE
IN AUSTRALIA

HE CASE ORIGINATED in Australia and Tichbornites ever
hoped that thence might come the key to its mystery and
to the Claimant's cell. The fundamental points have
already come to the fore. Those that will now be advanced are
less than fundamental: bizarre, incoherent, obscure are better
adjectives. The significance of this chapter may lie in how little
it has to tell rather than how much, confirming that the cause in
Britain derived its force from the particular social context there.

William Gibbes, the solicitor at Wagga Wagga who 'discovered'
the Claimant, remains one of the most fascinating people connected with the case. The further one traces the record, the more
positive would appear his initial role. In a statement of mid-1869,
Gibbes stressed that he personally had first said in so many words
that his client was Tichborne, rather than waiting for the man
himself to do so. The butcher, said Gibbes, had 'seemed offended
and annoyed at anyone presuming to doubt him or desiring the
slightest information . . . he always appeared so thoroughly confident of being recognized and *immediately* acknowledged'.[1] Gibbes
might have been lying, but his words always bore the impress of
truth. Very likely, the hope of becoming agent for a wealthy
baronet prompted him to rashness in 1865–6, but he never compounded that slip, and merely accepted one more disappointment
in a humdrum life. Of the Claimant's various other backers in
Australia probably the most significant was Arthur Cubitt,
through whom Lady Tichborne advertised in the Australian press
in 1865. Hope of riches excited him, too, and he might have been

less honest than was Gibbes. The nature of Cubitt's service to the cause after the Claimant left for Britain is not clear. His name is linked with potentially the most extreme villainy of the whole narrative. That link is conjectural; however Cubitt seemingly did continue to gather evidence in support of the cause as late as 1871 or 1872.

When John Holmes sought an Australian solicitor he selected the Melbourne firm, Sedgefield and Allport, because of his personal friendship with S. W. Sedgefield. Sedgefield and Allport were quick to discover the link between Castro and Orton, and they traced Mina Jury, who was to identify the Claimant as Orton, the Tasmanian immigrant of 1852–3. They at first assumed that 'Sir Roger' originally had taken the name of Orton; when the Claimant denied this, and any connection with Tasmania, they were left in a desperate position. The family's agent, John Mackenzie, had only to harvest this data to do his job. He did it well, and was assiduous in spreading reports of the Orton-Claimant identification. He missed only one important point: a contemporary newspaper report that Orton departed from Hobart, Tasmania, for Gippsland on 17 November 1855. Meanwhile Sedgefield and Allport struggled along as best they could and acted for the Claimant before the commission that gathered evidence in Australia from April to November 1869.[2] Their witnesses offered only a little: that there had been a Frenchman in Gippsland in the later fifties; that old Hampshire acquaintances in Sydney appeared to accept the Claimant in 1866; that Mackenzie had been careful to win over local journalists to his view of the matter. More interesting in retrospect was the apparently incidental remark of William Fearne, a travelling photographer, that in November 1864 Castro had suggested that he, Fearne, guard a packet to be opened should Castro die. This was a ploy reminiscent of Roger's depositing confidential papers as he left England in 1853. Another potential gain was a comment by Michael Guilfoyle, one-time Tichborne gardener who first welcomed the Claimant in Sydney but then repudiated him, that he had long ago heard of Roger having some peculiarity, by which Guilfoyle might have meant the genital malformation.

During the 1871 recess of the civil case, representatives of both parties visited Australia. The Claimant's agent was Francis Jeune, a junior counsel to Ballantine; the family's man, H. F. Purcell, had already been active in finding anti-Claimant evidence in Chile. Now Purcell located at Wagga Wagga a pocket-book which

allegedly had belonged to the Claimant and which bore notes
apparently indicative of his preparing the imposture. A law clerk
employed by a firm that Jeune called into co-operation, wrote in
October 1871 that his district, crucial in Castro's movements, 'has
teemed with detectives and lawyers and witnesses'.[3] All this
activity added little usable evidence for the Claimant—or at least
used evidence, for various would-be witnesses were to insist that
they had offered their views and news to Jeune without effect. One
clue that he did follow related to that lunatic in an asylum near
Sydney, William Cresswell.[4] For years preceding his confinement,
Cresswell had lived around Wagga Wagga. He had used various
names, most importantly Smith, perhaps Orton too, and had been
a very close mate of Tom Castro. The above-mentioned law clerk
claimed to have first traced him to the asylum on the supposition
that he was the true Arthur Orton whom the Claimant had said
was still living around Wagga Wagga in 1865–6. Jeune visited the
lunatic, but with negative results. Purcell also followed this line
of enquiry, and to a similar dead-end.

During neither case did the Claimant's lawyers import any witnesses from Australia, implying that they thought nothing would
result. In the criminal trial various old Australian hands added
touches to Kenealy's picture of the Australian wilderness; Gibbes,
although called by the prosecution, maintained his fathomless
doubt. This sum was much less than that put into the opposing
scale by Mina Jury and other Australians, especially Mrs Matthew
Macalister of Gippsland. Mrs Macalister recognized the Claimant
as Orton, an employee of her erstwhile husband, William Foster,
in the late fifties; her current spouse had told the commission
that he had been the first to make the crucial identification based
on a portrait of the Claimant sent from Britain.

Just as the civil proceedings ended, early in March 1872, there
occurred in Sydney a double murder, which possibly arose from
the case. Such was the burthen of a message received by a news-
paperman, Leicester Cotton, as he prepared a book on the episode
in the early 1960s.[5] Following this lead, Cotton argued that the
murders might have resulted from an attempt to identify Cresswell not as Orton but as Roger. Although some of his facts were
wrong, Cotton certainly discovered many details to support this
hypothesis. He suggested too that Arthur Cubitt, who had at
least a remote connection with the story, might have been the
ultimate master-mind, hoping to offset the likelihood of the
Claimant's failure by exploiting this alternative source of wealth
and fame.

Perhaps linking these murders with the case merely indicates that Australian interest in Tichborne affairs allowed any wild conjecture. The case always attracted much local attention. 'I assure you this sad history makes a great stir in this place', wrote a Hobart woman back to Hampshire in October 1867 of 'Sir Roger's' plebeian life in Australia.[6] John Mackenzie was able to spread propaganda on behalf of the family because Australian journals were avid for any relevant news. Gibbes complained that in 1870–1 he found 'Tichborne, Tichborne, Tichborne, everywhere wherever I went, that I hated the very name of the thing'.[7] Residents of Launceston, Tasmania, could buy terracotta figures of the Claimant, the lawyers and so on, each enclosing a scent bottle. Free of censorship, Sydney's major theatre advertised a skit on the case in June 1872: 'the greatest success achieved by any Colonial Writer . . . the fact is now admitted that it is needless to import second-hand burlesques when such sparkling travesties as the TICHBORNE BURLESQUE can be produced in the colonies'. A railway stop in central New South Wales still bears the title 'Tichborne', which derived from the nickname of a miner who found gold thereabouts—a massive man, nearly two metres tall and 120 kilograms in weight.[8]

Despite such evidence, of which there is much more, colonial attitudes to the case appear to have differed from those in Britain. There was not the same intensity of concern, either for or against the Claimant. The case amused very much more than it aroused.

The most comprehensive view of Australian attitudes was that given by Anthony Trollope in *Australia and New Zealand*, the account of his travels there in 1871–2. In his manuscript, modified before publication in 1873, Trollope wrote:

throughout the colonies generally I found that the opinions of men and women ran very much in favour of the Claimant;—not in any way because he was an Australian, for no colonist was fond of him, but apparently because there was a pleasurable excitement in the idea that the lowest blackguard that had ever returned home from the wild, reckless life of the Australian bush [should] turn out to be an English baronet. I discussed the question with an Australian judge, who is perhaps second in reputation as a lawyer to no English lawyer out of England, inferior to very few if any at home,—and I found him to be strongly in favour of the butcher. The evidence, in his mind, was all but conclusive in the butcher's favour. Had he heard the case with his wig on, I do not doubt but that he would have thought differently. As it was the romance touched even him.[9]

Trollope thus gave a new twist to the concepts of romance and Australian mystery. Hs was probably right in suggesting that the theme of return from Antipodean poverty to metropolitan grandeur struck a note in Australian breasts: this must have been the stock of many a colonial day-dream. Local novels took up the theme, just as did those of Dickens, Reade and others at home. Examples of the former were Trollope's own *John Caldigate* and, more importantly, the nineteenth-century Australian classic, Marcus Clarke's *For the Term of His Natural Life*. Written during the early seventies, the latter was but one illustration of Clarke's fascination with the case. The theme was a fact of colonial life itself. The more such critics of the Claimant as the *Times,* Coleridge and Cockburn scorned him as a colonial, the more one might expect colonists to rally in wounded self-esteem, even to express a sub-nationalist affinity with him.

Trollope himself denied that, and evidence is scant even for what the novelist did say about Australian sympathy. An American adventurer remarked of the Claimant that 'the people of Wagga Wagga thoroughly believed in his cause and were indignant at his treatment', without offering much support for his verdict.[10] Generally speaking, newspaper comment did not show the disposition Trollope suggested. One provincial sheet, the *Geelong Advertiser,* published a few items sympathetic to the Claimant; the doyen of Australian newspapers, the *Sydney Morning Herald,* rebuked the English press for its animus against him before he was found guilty; the Hobart *Mercury,* in one of the few editorial comments provoked by the end of the criminal trial, remarked that a baronet's forsaking his past to live in the bush was no stranger than many a true incident. But that editorial itself went on to judge the evidence as supporting the Claimant's guilt, and nowhere during the seventies appeared any mass movement in favour of the man.

More remarkable, indeed, was some criticism from Australia directed against the Claimant; it might have represented a minority view, but its edge was sharp. Some journals published from Tom Castro's home district seemed especially willing to publish Mackenzie's propaganda against him and to scorn his claim.[11] 'Castro never came within the range of probability as the lost heir', declared the Deniliquin *Pastoral Times* on 7 March 1868, while granting that many locals still held otherwise and later admitting some further doubt.[12] This journal specifically denied any prejudice against Castro on the grounds of his humble occupation, but some colonists showed themselves as class-conscious as

WE'LL NOT FORGET
Poor ROGER now.

itons all, come pay attention,
    And list awhile to my sad song,
And when you've heard some facts I'll mention,
    You'll say they've proved that right is wrong;
That the claimant is the right man,
    To many people it is quite clear,
But the jury found him guilty,
    His sentence it is fourteen years.

Tho' in prison they have cast him,
    To speak one word they'd not allow,
Our friendship for him still is lasting,
    We'll not forget poor Roger now.

As the case it was proceeding,
    From the day it did begin,
It was clear to all by reading,
    They never meant that he should win
If he dared to ask a question,
    Like a dog he was put down,
While the other side indulged in—
    Jokes, more fitting for a clown.

The witnesses against poor Roger,
    I think it is a shocking thing,
Dragged up from the back slums of Wapping,
    To take their words it was a sin,
While among the friends of Roger,
    Were soldiers who in battle cool,
Had nobly fought for England's glories,
    They were put down as rogues or fools.

A deal of sympathy and humbug,
    Was got up for Cousin Kate,
You may abuse the lower classes,
    But mind you do not touch the great,
That they are angels dropped from heaven,
    Divorce court trials will prove to you,
But then of course we must excuse them,
    Because they've nothing else to do.

If there's any mothers standing round me,
    I ask you truely, every one,
If you think that you could ever—
    Once forget a long lost son,
And so his mother recognised him,
    Which filled the family with dismay,
But suddenly she died, poor lady,
    Or a different tale they would tell to day.

Then jolly good luck to brave Kenealy,
    Their threats he did not care a jot,
Thought he had five to one against him,
    His voice was heard above the lot,
They may call the Claimant an impostor,
    A lump of fat—the counsel bawl,
But it is the universal feeling,
    That he is the right man after all

Disley, Printer, London.

A Ballad Incorporating Many Themes of the Tichborne Cause

Arabella Kenealy
[A. Kenealy, *Memoirs of Edward Vaughan Kenealy LL.D.*]

Alex Kenealy
[From a study of 1912, evidently designed to present him as a model of the New Journalist]

Coleridge or Cockburn. From Wagga Wagga came in 1871 the crudest of all attacks: *The Butcher-Baronet; or the Wagga Wagga Mystery: A New and Original Musical Burletta in Three Acts* by Frank Hutchinson, a journalist. A major theme of Hutchinson's humour was the incongruity of Mary Ann Bryant, former laundress, aspiring to wealth and title; generally the claim was presented as blatant conspiracy. The Melbourne *Herald* abandoned satire when, in May 1872, it reported an interview with Mary Ann's one-time employer at Wagga Wagga. She told, with convincing detail, of the girl giving birth to a bastard child. 'Curiosity was beginning to wane, when the propriety of the village was startled by the announcement that Tom Castro was going to wed Mary Anne'. The article pictured Castro as a low and surly cheat.[13]

Very soon the case became if not Australian folk-lore, at least material for local-colour story. By the end of the seventies there was already vigorous debate in Wagga Wagga as to just where the Claimant's hut had stood: probably the site was that currently filled by the Tichborne Buildings but a photographer had dressed a nearby shed with the sign 'T. Castro, Butcher' and sold authentic-looking prints.[14] An *Australian Reader* published in 1882 included Gibbes's early interview with the Claimant among its 'memorable historic events'.[15] Reminiscences have followed down the years. Especially notable were those of James Gormley, an important man around Wagga Wagga who had been Castro's employer and had, in vain, warned his fellow townsmen from the outset against investing in him.[16] In 1967 Dame Mabel Brookes, a leader of Melbourne society, told in her history-memoirs of Sir Roger having met violent death at a gold town, West Wyalong.[17]

While overall the case evoked less intense concern in Australia than in Britain, some individuals found it absorbing enough. One was Sir Alfred Stephen, Chief Justice of New South Wales from 1844 to 1873. In a letter to the *Sydney Morning Herald* on 28 August 1874, Stephen repudiated all doubts he had once expressed and so hinted that he was the judge whom Trollope had cited as the Claimant's sympathizer. At length, Stephen bared 'the monstrous imposture' and quoted witnesses of his own discovery whose evidence supported that view. Another Australian enthusiast was J. D. D. Jackson, interesting as an ostensibly convincing 'witness' who was in fact wrong. Jackson claimed that in 1855 in Launceston one Edward Souper had been introduced to him as Roger Tichborne, and that the same town then housed Arthur Orton and his sister, licensee of the Royal Oak public house. Jackson told this story as early as 1874 and was still doing so in 1900, although official investigation in Tasmania during the 1870s proved its falsity.[18] The licensee of the Royal Oak for a while was Mary Ann Hedger, whereas one of Orton's sisters was Mary Ann Tredgett: from such a base did fantasies like Jackson's derive. Another crank or joker in 1882 published a booklet purporting to reveal from personal knowledge the machinations of the Claimant, Gibbes, and other plotters at Wagga Wagga in the mid-sixties. His story included such improbabilities as that the director of the campaign was the Claimant's mother-in-law; that Castro was then known to have used the name of Orton; and that he told of having met in Tasmania a co-survivor with Tichborne from the *Bella*.[19]

The Tichborne cause did have some overt support from Australia. The *Englishman* and the *Independent*, be it remembered, filled many a column with purported revelations from the Antipodes. Some of these were obviously absurd, but others appear convincing. Woodruff discusses two such: the first concerned a woman who had known Roger in 1847–8 and claimed to have met him in Victoria in 1855, and the second a man who went to school with Orton and said that he knew both him and Tichborne in Australia. One or two others may be even more impressive. There was for example, an affidavit purportedly from Mrs McMillan, widow of a notable pioneer of Gippsland; the statement insisted that a Frenchman of breeding lived in that district in the late 1850s.[20] All the circumstantial detail is correct, save that the woman's first name is given as Mary, whereas Mrs McMillan's was Christina. Still, the affidavit might have had the same authority as did a letter from A. B. Jones, a respected public servant in Hobart, who broke to Kenealy that Mina Jury was an erstwhile convict. Even Jones was awry in some particular assertions: especially that Mina could not have communicated with Orton in Hobart, this being contraverted by Orton's homeward letters.

To pursue the intricacies of these scores of Australian statements would render little profit. Not only are most beyond checking, but anyway their importance was limited. They helped fill the *Englishman* and *Independent*, and no doubt strengthened Tichbornites in their resolve, but Jones's information was unique in that it provided ammunition capable of immediate effective use. The more significant aspect of the Tichborne cause in Australia was a series of attempts to establish and exploit the lunatic Cresswell as key figure in the great puzzle.

In the mid-seventies this area was occupied primarily by Guildford Onslow. His Australian instrument was William Henry Lock
of Melbourne, an agent to the insolvency court there. Lock himself claimed to have known Orton and Castro as separate individuals in the 1850s, and to have offered this evidence to Jeune
in 1871. How he and Onslow contacted each other is not recorded.
Anyway, in September 1876 Lock visited the asylum at Parramatta, outside Sydney, which then housed Cresswell, and soon the
false story spread that the two had left for England. 'The Australians themselves have been at work, and have responded to the
sympathetic call from this country', enthused the *Independent*.[21]
Next, Orton's sister, Elizabeth Jury, came to Australia. She and
Lock went to the asylum early in 1877; declaring that the lunatic
had neither tattoo nor pierced ears as did her brother, Mrs Jury
failed the cause. Yet in September, Lock asked for permission that
Cresswell return to England. W. B. Dalley, the Attorney-General
of New South Wales, refused.[22] Dalley was a Roman Catholic, and
as such became a hate-object for Tichbornites.

The episode set various pressures operating. The possibility
that the lunatic was Sir Roger himself received an airing, but to
no great effect. J. D. D. Jackson and Sir Alfred Stephen both
protested against any leniency towards Lock, suggesting that his
party would misuse the lunatic. Stephen found an ally in Charles
Taylor, medical superintendent at Parramatta. Taylor spoke of
having deflated several would-be identifiers by inviting them to
pick 'Orton' from among his patients, in which task they always
failed. He argued too that bodily marks and the evidence of an
old Cresswell family friend proved that the lunatic went under
his proper name. Meanwhile in England Onslow sought to persuade the Colonial Office to call for the lunatic's release. This in
turn provoked H. B. Harding to object, claiming that he had
located Cresswell's relatives in Britain, found their evidence to
exclude the possibility of the lunatic being Orton, and offered to
reveal this evidence to Onslow, East and Kimber. They had side-
stepped, said Harding, showing that they cared not for the truth
but only for opportunity to provide 'a platform for demagogues
and revolutionists'.

When Lock next moved, visiting Cresswell in January 1878, he
was joined by Joseph Eckford, member of the New South Wales
Legislative Assembly. Again, the record does not explain how
Eckford entered the cause. Born and bred in the country outside
Sydney, he had entered politics in 1860 as a supporter of John

Robertson, a moderate reformer. A publican and a mason, Eckford fitted well into the Tichborne context. Insolvency in 1870
had interrupted his career but briefly. By 1878 his political chief
was Henry Parkes, most remarkable and effective of all New South
Wales politicians in the latter nineteenth centry. Eckford supplied
his leader with both gossip and loans, commodities on which
Parkes depended heavily.[23] Parkes himself, according to one
dubious report, had visited Cresswell in the early seventies. Eckford's speeches to the House usually invoked reform and
moralism. Thus in October 1881 he supported a licensing act
amendment, proclaiming that no honest publican should fear the
police; 'the honourable member knew very well', retorted a fellow
licensee, 'that while he remained a member of parliament, and was
a knot in the tail of the government, no constable would have
the temerity to break down his door'.[24]

Following their visit to the lunatic, Lock and Eckford applied
for his release. The new application was rejected in March, and
next month Eckford raised the matter in parliament (as, simultaneously, did Whalley in the Commons, to be told the matter
was not within imperial responsibility). In mid-year, Eckford saw
Cresswell again, and at about this time won supporting affidavits
from the lunatic's wife and from a shipmate of Orton on the
voyage to Tasmania in 1852-3. In October he called for the publication of papers relevant to the counsel's enquiries of 1871 and to
the more recent applications.[25] As to Cresswell's identity, the
papers suggested that in 1871 the lunatic had called himself
Orton, and confirmed that he still spoke of the Tichborne case.
Letters of 1870–1 to the lunatic from Cresswell siblings in
England confirmed that their brother had known the Claimant in
the bush, and spoke of the Cresswell family having hopes of inheritance. One might infer that Cresswell was an extreme case
among those who substituted the Claimant's troubles for their
own. The papers also included letters from a Frank O'Brien, who
claimed to have been the fount of Eckford's knowledge, but now
disclosed a grudge against him. On 15 October 1878 O'Brien advertised in the *Sydney Morning Herald,* warning 'agents and
others' in the Tichborne case against further use of data secured
through him.

Eckford next moved late in 1879. He now acted for Thomas
Cresswell, the lunatic's putative brother, thus meeting the terms
of a recent lunacy act. The procedure implied an admission that
the lunatic was not Orton, but evidently all concerned were ready
to blink at this anomaly. On 10 December 1879 Henry Parkes—

who had become Premier in December 1878—minuted that a
deed should be prepared, stating conditions under which Eckford
might take Cresswell to Britain. Early in the new year a judge
confirmed this agreement, which among other things required
payment of a £500 bond. The whole episode was so quick and
smooth that suspicion of improper influence arises: later Eckford
wrote to Parkes concerning 'when you assisted me in getting the
lunatic's release'.[26] As the six months allowed by the deed neared
completion, Parkes reminded Eckford; but the latter received no
funds from Britain, and so ended the best chance of a coup from
this quarter. Years passed before Georgiana Baring's money revived the issue. Evidently she operated, through Edmund Kimber,
at two levels: by arousing Eckford, and by sending from Britain
Charles Orton and a watchdog-companion, Daniel Smith. 'I
expect the Tichborne Commission every hour', wrote Eckford to
Parkes on 18 December 1882; 'I told you long since . . . I had a
large sum due to me for the great expense and trouble I had been
put to in working up the Case and I must still try and get it'.
Eckford went on to bemoan his defeat in the recent general elections, attributable, he said, to Catholic priests advising a vote
against him—alas for hemispheric continuity, he did not link this
with the cause. A still worse augury for the current move was that
Parkes left office in January 1883.

The membership of the 'Tichborne Commission' was odd.
Charles Orton was the most barefaced rogue in the whole Tichborne story: he took bribes from the Claimant in 1867-8, informed against him when the money dried up, and took money
from the Crown during the criminal trial. After the Claimant's
conviction, he 'admitted' that the prisoner was indeed his brother,
recanting this in 1877. Smith was a Clerkenwell whitesmith, long
active in the Tichborne Realease Association. At a meeting on
Clerkenwell Green late in 1877 he orated and

exhibited throughout the meeting, a specimen of his improved
torch, and the result was all that could be desired. Clear, brilliant,
and durable, nothing could be better for the purposes of a demonstration. Their construction is simple—a pound of rushes from
twenty to twenty-two inches [fifty-one to fifty-six centimetres] long,
and a couple of rushlights placed in the centre, end to end, and
the whole bound round with a piece of glued paper . . . They can
be further improved by being encased in a brass tube.[27]

The total cost was about a shilling, and Smith would make to
order, without profit. A Tichborne museum was another of his

projects. He had spoken of going to Australia to retrieve the lunatic as early as mid-1880, but doubtless indigence cramped his aims.

Eckford reopened the matter very quickly, visiting the lunatic and asking for a renewal of the bond before the end of 1882, and making a formal application again in March 1883. Over the same period, one Walter Fossey began writing to the New South Wales authorities, as he had already to Onslow and Kimber, telling his views on how Arthur Orton had met Roger Tichborne—concerning whose arrival in Melbourne Fossey was most specific—and then found his way to New Zealand where he still was. The government instituted yet more enquiries. These seemed to confirm remarkable similarities between Cresswell and the Claimant: both were butchers and sportsmen, and had the habit of grimacing as they talked. The police discovered Cresswell's original employer in Australia, whose evidence strengthened his identity with the lunatic. Dalley, again Attorney-General, blocked Eckford's new application, which meanwhile had alienated Smith. One report said that the latter believed it wrong to accept the fiction that the lunatic was Cresswell, but probably the dispute concerned Miss Baring's money.

Smith took a more direct line than Eckford. He went up-country seeking evidence, but by April 1883 was back in Sydney to build a popular movement in his own support. At a meeting in the Protestant hall, his appeal for Australians to support their victimized 'chum' fell flat,[28] but a more congenial audience awaited him at the Domain, Sydney's counterpart to Clerkenwell Green. A public meeting there on 15 April moved that as Charles Orton had recognized the lunatic as his brother, release should follow. The response of authority was to bring Smith before a magistrate for distributing the pamphlet wherein Dr Wilson described the Claimant's malformation. To the crowded court, Smith bellowed forth his Tichborne beliefs. 'You have considered in one hour a trial which took 188 days to decide', he told the magistrate on his sentence to fourteen days' imprisonment or a £10 fine; 'remove that obscene old man' was the answer.[29] At home the Tichborne Release Association suspected evil: that the pamphlet 'should under the wider and more liberal laws of an almost republican Colony, have been regarded as an improper and obscene publication appears too extraordinary and too singular to admit ordinary interpretation'. The *Independent* believed that Catholic and governmental influence, local and British, were conspiring; it was confident however that Smith and the people would win. 'Rough and ready as Mr Smith's utterances are, they are more likely to influence the people of the colony than they did those of Clerkenwell Green'.[30]

Rifts within the cause widened in May when Smith sued Eckford for a half of the £82.9.6 he had brought to the colony. Smith's conduct of proceedings won laughs, but no prizes. His position weakened as Charles Orton refused to support him. Quarrels grew hotter, but Smith continued his efforts. In July he asked what conditions he must fulfil to return the lunatic to Britain. Dalley reiterated that the government would heed only the relatives of William Cresswell. Yet Smith did make a move towards litigation at this time, only to withdraw in August. Then there arrived in Sydney Jean Luie, who had come from England to strengthen the identification of the lunatic as Arthur Orton. If anyone were less equipped, in commonsense terms, than Charles Orton for this role, it was Luie: his claim, however perjurious, had been to know Roger Tichborne. Luie joined with Smith in arousing feeling on the Domain. In November-December Smith brought the issue to court, but Charles Orton and Eckford opposed him (alleging that he wanted to use the lunatic for mob display), while the Crown again resisted. The judge ruled that Smith, being neither friend nor relative, had no standing.

Smith and Luie resumed lecturing. Drought conditions had brought a concentration of unemployed workers to Sydney, many of them recent immigrants; and so, a contemporary remarked of Smith, 'the orator found a sympathetic audience when he spoke of the *cause célèbre*'.[31] The culmination of this effort was the presentation to parliament in February 1884 of a petition, bearing 10 500 signatures, for an enquiry into the case. At last Australia had echoed the feeling in Britain. The petition was presented by A. G. Taylor, a rumbustious and even lunatic man, scornful of protocol, who was soon to become editor of *Truth*, a smut-and-libel sheet which documented the many 'scandals of Sydney Town' in the century's last decades.[32]

The parliamentarian who inherited Eckford's mantle in the House of Assembly was J. N. Brunker. Born in New South Wales in 1832, Brunker achieved distinction in that vital role of Australian rural life, 'stock and station agent'. He too had close links with Henry Parkes. Interested in philanthropic, social and church organizations, temperance especially, Brunker entered parliament in 1880 and duly became something of an elder statesman. He first struck for the Tichborne cause on 13 February 1884, when he asked for the printing of further papers concerning Cresswell. The papers included a letter from Sir Alfred Stephen showing that this veteran and esteemed judge had accepted J. D. D. Jackson's fantasies; and a statement of Mrs Deborah Simpson, Mary Ann Bryant's employer at Wagga Wagga. Mrs Simpson had identified Cresswell at the asylum, being one of scores to visit the institution in relation to the matter.

The issue came to court again early in May 1884. The applicants for custody of the lunatic were Charles Orton and his brother Edmund, who now at last emerged to participate in the case. Georgiana Baring paid the voyage to Australia of Thomas Cresswell, hopefully to deny that the lunatic was his brother. Leading counsel for the Ortons was Edmund Barton, who in 1901 became first Prime Minister of the Commonwealth of Australia; on the bench was the eminent Sir William Manning, while the government opposed release through William Owen Q.C. Opening his case, Owen declared the Crown's belief that 'it had a very high duty to perform in order to prevent this unfortunate man from being taken out upon a sham identification, merely for the purpose of having a man released who was very properly in prison'; the judge responded that this was extraneous, while Barton sneered that opposing counsel behaved 'as if they were briefed by the Tichborne family'. So each contender took his stance. The most surprising as well as the most important was Manning's: he proved sceptical of evidence identifying the lunatic as Cresswell, even suspecting that some of it had been 'got up very cleverly . . . romanticized'. Eckford and Brunker won a good hearing as they accused Dalley of having formerly deceived them as to procedures necessary for making their case. The irony was that Miss Baring did too much: the court adjourned from late May until mid-September to await Thomas Cresswell's arrival, upon which he recognized the lunatic as his brother. Even so, the case was not shattered. Among further witnesses were W. J. Barry, still continuing his travels and exercising his charm, at this stage over Manning; and one Horace Brown. In judgement, Manning declared that the Ortons impressed him more than did Thomas Cresswell; the lunatic's own remarks to the court had by themselves induced him to decide that the evidence was not quite strong enough for release. The judge defended Miss Baring. Nevertheless, the verdict was defeat, and in November Eckford's death compounded it. He died in Melbourne, while returning from Hobart in search of new evidence. His daughter later said that on his deathbed Eckford enjoined Brunker to uphold the cause.[33]

Meanwhile, Daniel Smith had gone his demagogic way towards leading Sydney's unemployed into revolution. The period was busy with political activity, more or less radical-proletarian. The trade-union movement was becoming more articulate, its first intercolonial congress having met in 1879. A common policy of radicals and unionists was to oppose government expenditure on immigration, a policy interpreted as subsidizing the employer at the cost of wage-earners. When the government determined in January 1884 that again that year it would spend £150 000 on migration, over 7000 protestors signed a petition to parliament. Like the simultaneous 'Cresswell enquiry' petition, this was presented by A. G. Taylor; very probably many names appeared on both. Out of this agitation emerged the Democratic Alliance, led by E. W. O'Sullivan who was president of the Trades and Labour Council and also confronting a handsome political future. The alliance urged protection and opposed immigration; nationalization of the land was another plank, and generally the alliance aimed at becoming a working-man's political party. 'Most of the themes of the reforming agitations of the next two decades had an early statement in this programme', writes O'Sullivan's biographer.[34] The alliance news-sheet had Taylor among its contributors; Spencer, Mill, George and Blanc were its heroes, and O'Sullivan preached his gospel of an Anglo-American federal republic. The body only lasted a few months, to be followed in 1885 by the Land and Industrial Alliance, a worker-and-farmer coalition.

Smith operated at the Leftmost edge of the Democratic Alliance. From preaching to the unemployed about Tichborne, he came to spearhead the men's protest at their situation; immigrants were still among his most responsive listeners, as they felt their own grievance against being brought into a drought-depressed society. The discontented met in almost continual session, 23 April being a key date in the accession to leadership of Smith and other extremists. Moderates scorned 'reference to the necessity of resorting to bombs and dynamite', and reminded the rank-and-file that 'when the cauldron boils, the scum rises to the surface, and it would appear to be the same in times of political excitement'.[35] Talk of dynamite probably echoed newspaper reports concerning Fenians and nihilists; nevertheless the local unemployed were militant, refusing government assistance as contemptible charity.

Moreover, 'the perleece knows yer when yer goes there, and then drops on yer for bein' vagrants'.[36] When an immigrant ship arrived late in May, a government spokesman addressed the new-comers:

There are a few discontented people here who do all they possibly can to pump out of you all the self-reliance and resolution you have. I say to you pay no attention to the tales you may hear from these people who are but demagogues . . .[37]

With this accent, colonial respectability answered Smith and his fellows. In mid-year the drought broke, and the dissidents' moment passed. The government did cut its immigration vote, however, and the working class remained hostile to all such ex-penditure. The Trades and Labour Council sent John Norton to Britain so that he might warn potential immigrants. Norton was later the wildest of 'the wild men of Sydney'—a colonial Horatio Bottomley, but worse. Himself a recent immigrant of 1884, Norton is said to have been active in the Democratic Federation before leaving England, and so might have had some Magna Charta connection.[38]

The end of the depression did not quite finish Smith. Eckford had tried to do that: first alleging that he was embezzling funds subscribed for the unemployed, and then bringing an action against him for costs arising from Smith's earlier claim for a share of Miss Baring's money. Smith went to prison, but public meetings supported him and attacked Eckford. On release Smith found redoubled audiences and returned to Tichborne as his major theme; coincidentally, W. J. Barry was lecturing on the Domain, and early in August Smith's supporters mobbed him when he criticized their hero concerning the unemployment fund. These partisans subscribed to discharge Smith's debts and pay his return fare to England. Late in 1885 he sailed from Sydney, declaiming that his spells in gaol resulted from government conspiracy and that in Britain he would thwart further migration.

Miss Baring had now found a new Australian agent, that Horace Brown who gave evidence before Sir William Manning. Brown then identified the lunatic as Arthur Orton, whom he had tended in Hobart late in 1853 for a gash on the back of his left hand. Probably inspired by his contact with Eckford, Brown sub-sequently wrote to Miss Baring. He told that he had denied the identification of Orton with the Claimant ever since the first en-quiries in Hobart, that he had reported his evidence to Kenealy, and to Onslow several times, but no-one had listened to him; he did not tell of his own convict origins. Brown's revelations first appeared in the Tasmanian press in October 1873, the report then saying that the injury was to the palm of the hand. The matter received publicity and Kenealy heard of it in January 1874, too late for use. In 1872 Brown had adduced evidence to an examining board in Tasmania 'of having been engaged for a sufficient period in learning the business of a druggist and also as to his moral character',[39] but was refused a licence to sell medicines because of his ignorance in Latin and chemistry. Nevertheless it was as a pharmacist, resident in Melbourne, that he wrote to Miss Baring in 1884. The correspondence flourished, Brown providing wads of fresh affidavits which Miss Baring rearranged for publication in the *Independent*, to a lesser extent in the *Englishman*, and in a pamphlet of 1886, *Twenty-Three Letters . . . Proving on Medical Evidence that the Parramatta Lunatic is Arthur Orton*. Brown's documents rehashed the ambiguities and counter-reports concerning Castro, Orton and Tichborne. The chief emphasis concerned bodily marks and the alleged arrival of the *Osprey* in Melbourne. He spiced his letters with scandal: that anonymous villains had offered a bribe for him to abandon his efforts, that the Foster-Macalister clan was corrupt. Brown's work fortified Miss Baring's contributions to the *Independent* until its close in 1889.

That journal told a little more about the Australian aspects of the cause in the late 1880s. It published in April 1887 a letter from Jean Luie to Miss Baring which referred to the forthcoming visit to Britain of Robert Wisdom, another New South Wales politician, a successful land speculator, and a supporter of Henry Parkes. Luie spoke of Wisdom as having conspired with Eckford to defraud Miss Baring, but she disparaged the letter. Late in 1888 Luie came before a Sydney court, himself charged with conspiracy. He had encouraged a man to advertise for a companion, a woman had responded, and then Luie had prompted her to blackmail the man for breach of promise, himself sharing the pay-off. Luie's sentence was five year's gaol. Meanwhile, Miss Baring reported that Quartermaine East was to go to Australia to enquire about the *Osprey*.

The early nineties were a lull before a final storm. No doubt scrutiny of the press would find regular items concerning the case. Thus, a Catholic paper in Tasmania reported in January 1895 that one of the oldest priests in the colonies had revealed that Sir

Roger died years ago in a benevolent asylum at Geelong, Victoria.[40] The very same issue reported new moves involving Cresswell—moves which were to strengthen over the next five or six years. One point differentiated them from previous events: since 1871 the possibility that the lunatic was Tichborne had hovered and titillated, now it became dominant. Thereby the issue ceased to be logically germane to 'the Tichborne cause'. But, as ever, logic played little part. Proponents of this theme fought with much the same style and spirit as had those who identified Roger as the Claimant. Illustrating this best was Lord Clifton, seventh Earl of Darnley, 1896–1900. Clifton had long supported the orthodox cause, especially as a financial backer of the *People's Advocate* when edited by Frederick Longman. From November 1895 Clifton wrote several letters to the New South Wales government; he alleged truckling to Catholicism, and that 'the detention of missing heirs by false names and under collusive identification in Parramatta Asylum had been for some time a regular business of your Government'.[41] This tone permeated the man's public activity: he refused to sit in the House of Lords, and collided with the law enforcing compulsory vaccination.

Australia provided earlier and leading advocates of the lunatic-Roger identification. The initiative seemingly belonged to Mrs Kate Mary Jenkins. Her name first appeared in this connection late in 1894, but ten years earlier her husband, himself the son of a pioneer of southern New South Wales, had supplied information to the government concerning Cresswell. Most detail about Mrs Jenkins's activity comes from a petition she presented to the Governor-General of Australia in 1903, and a similar statement of July 1914 in which she claimed *'Patent Rights'* over the discovery of Tichborne, and told of saving the lunatic from the plots of Luie, Miss Baring and others. When the Governor's secretary of the day first heard her revelations, he 'said I was a second "Joan of Arc" '. But then, Mrs Jenkins alleged, one Edward Priestman stole her ideas and evidence.[42]

Priestman, an accountant, took over from the lady in the mid-nineties. He probably caused Luie to 'confess' that the *Osprey* had indeed plied to Melbourne, but with Orton aboard; the real Tichborne, said Luie (but how did he claim to know?) , was indeed Cresswell. Priestman began pestering the authorities for an interview with the lunatic. Rebuffed, he found parliamentarians who asked questions in the House. They included J. C. L. Fitzpatrick, future senior minister, and W. M. Hughes, currently a member of the young but burgeoning Labor Party and Prime Minister of Australia from 1915 to 1923. The minister to whom they protested was none but J. N. Brunker, whose leader was G. H. Reid. Despite Brunker's answers that any disturbance was unfair to the lunatic, Priestman evidently did win an interview. When he sought to arrange a full medical examination, authority again obstructed. Fitzpatrick put more questions and then presented a motion criticizing this hindrance. In the debate on 11 August 1896, he alleged that the movers in earlier actions had always known that the lunatic was Tichborne, but did not care to say so until they returned him to Britain. One debater said that Fitzpatrick and William Affleck, another member from southern New South Wales, had been working on the case for years; Brunker remarked that Eckford had spent thousands of pounds on the matter. The motion failed.

Priestman went to law. An application was made to the Lunacy Court late in November 1897. Two doctors examined the lunatic, reporting that he did not show Roger's bodily marks. The judge scorned the application. The matter bounced back to parliament, Fitzpatrick moving for an enquiry on 4 October 1898. He got much support, notably from Labor members, but the motion lost, twenty-nine votes to thirty. In June 1899 Priestman published a booklet, *The Tichborne Mystery*. It gave various documents on the case, endorsing J. D. D. Jackson's claim to have met Roger in Launceston and identifying the latter with the French 'swell' said to have been in Gippsland in the late fifties. Orton, so Priestman alleged, had known Tichborne and stolen his diaries, thus laying the basis for his claim. He produced an affidavit from one C. H. Petterson who said that the *Bella* changed its name in mid-passage from Rio de Janeiro to become the *Osprey* at Melbourne.

In September 1899 the Reid-Brunker ministry resigned, to be followed by a more radical group under the leadership of W. J. Lyne; O'Sullivan was Secretary of Public Works, while another minister was W. P. Crick, one-time colleague of O'Sullivan in various 'enterprises and escapades in radical politics'.[43] Later, Crick was central in the grandest of all 'scandals of Sydney Town', arising from his behaviour as Minister for Lands. Of immediate significance was the new government's comparative acquiescence to Cresswell agitation. On 7 November 1899 J. C. L. Fitzpatrick moved the appointment of a select committee of enquiry: the motion was carried, with Brunker among the minority. Fitzpatrick himself was appointed chairman. The committee, transformed into a royal commission in 1900, echoed every stage of the fantasy.[44] Priestman was the major witness, concentrating on medical evidence and denying the efficacy of the examination in late 1897. One point to emerge was that the lunatic had no genital abnormality. Among the witnesses were J. D. D. Jackson, who poured forth more of his 'evidence'; Mrs Smithers, daughter of Eckford, who said that her father had always believed the lunatic to be Tichborne; and a Mrs Wines who remembered a self-claimed nobleman having pledged his troth to her in the bush in 1869, and last having seen him in Sydney three years ago. The commission reported that the lunatic truly was Cresswell, but that his mental condition justified release.

One member, R. D. Meagher, dissented from the commission's decision on the ground that the lunatic would be used in a cause which his identity as Cresswell made false. A lawyer and partner of W. P. Crick, Meagher had won Kenealyesque fame-notoriety in the mid-nineties for his defence of one George Dean for attempted wife-murder. A jury found Dean guilty, but conviction provoked agitation in his favour; as this gathered strength, Dean confessed his guilt to Meagher; Meagher said nothing and—in company with Crick and John Norton—supported the agitation; a royal commission sat and, in accord with its report, the government released Dean. But then Dean's confession became known, and so he went back to gaol and Meagher off the professional roll. He did not return there until a special act of 1920 so determined. In the meantime Meagher had joined the Labor Party and enjoyed success as Lord Mayor of Sydney: the municipal politics of that city had been the stamping-ground of homespun unrespectability since their beginning in the 1840s.

The Lyne-O'Sullivan government balked at the recommendation for Cresswell's release. Fitzpatrick accordingly moved, on 9 August 1900, that it so act. Most debaters spoke in support. Alfred Edden—Labor parliamentarian and Methodist lay-preacher who was born in Stafford in 1849 and was a miner from childhood through to his emigration in 1879—reacted to a jeer that Priestman was seeking to become another Kenealy. 'I think Dr Kenealy, now dead in his grave, was badly used by the powers in England at the time . . . he was a man to be admired'; only after talking to James Gormley—Castro's erstwhile employer, now also a parliamentarian—did he cease to believe that the Claimant was Tichborne. Another Labor man, Richard Sleath, alleged that Brunker had received £10 000 from Miss Baring to investigate the case, but had put it all into his own pocket. The royal commission should have investigated this scandal but had not, probably because there were 'wheels within wheels, swindles within swindles'. On 14 August Brunker responded—'in every part of the world there will be found bands of ruffians who use every effort at their command to debase society'—and the House roared. Fitzpatrick's motion passed without division. Still the government did nothing. On 12 September 1901 Fitzpatrick and fellows again objected, alleging Tichborne family influence on the Crown Law Department. They thought it monstrous that the bureaucracy should thwart the will of parliament, and denied that the matter should again go to court. 'I say that the supreme court of the realm is this House, not the District court, or the Banco court, or the Full court', said Mr Daniel O'Connor. Meagher offered a diversion with the hypothesis that Cresswell was the bastard child of Roger's father; that he and Orton had been privy to Tichborne's violent death in the bush; that the two planned that Cresswell should claim the baronetcy, but that when his mind slipped, Orton decided to go it alone.

Meagher's theory might have approached the truth. If some dark event in the Australian bush linked Orton and/or Tichborne and/or Cresswell, it was probably such as he suggested rather than that Tichborne had murdered Orton, the hypothesis of many of the Claimant's semi-supporters. The Meagher argument accords with the fairly substantial evidence that a well-bred Frenchman lived in Gippsland in the fifties. It could also harmonize with the report that James Moorhouse, Bishop of Melbourne from 1876 to 1886, learned from Mrs Macalister, whose identification of the Claimant with Orton counted heavily at the criminal trial, that she had not been allowed to tell all she knew. She believed that Orton and a man named Smith (Cresswell's favourite alias) had stolen papers from 'Gentleman Jim', another of her ex-husband's employees. Moorhouse presumed that 'Gentleman Jim' was Tichborne, and referred to corroborative evidence as to his murder by Orton.[45] The murder accomplished, one might speculate, Cresswell and Orton went to ground, the latter changing his name in the hope of covering this particular misdeed. Reunited in the Wagga Wagga district, learning of the Dowager's advertisement, pressured by Gibbes, they embarked on the grand design.

The Assembly spared no time in such speculation. The debate ended, and Cresswell remained in charge. A last question on 18 September 1902 met the answer that only the courts could release

Cresswell. In fact, death did that, in 1904. Some reverberations continued, most notably Mrs Jenkins's allegations against Priestman, from whom she called for protection in 1914, reminding the government that her work justified the punishment of the Claimant.

The case had some part in the history of New South Wales. It had touched three politicians—Parkes, Barton and Hughes—whose eminence and fame excelled any others in their time and place. Smith, O'Sullivan, Crick and Meagher all represented significant themes in the social radicalism of their day. Australian populism will have a small place in the next, the key chapter of this study.

7

THE POPULIST FACTOR

POPULISM IS EVEN MORE difficult to define than most ideology movements. A few years ago the term normally referred to surges of socio-political protest in the late nineteenth-century, on the one hand among the farmers of the United States and on the other among Russian peasants and their intellectual would-be leaders. Recently historians have found it useful to apply the term to movements much more widespread in time and space. Such diffusion inexorably takes the meaning out of any word, making it more and more difficult to use without restructuring to meet a particular case. An observer might well feel that in the restructuring the intrinsic validity of the term disappears. That objection could apply here: 'populism' is inflated so that it embraces the primitive (after the meaning of E. J. Hobsbawm, *Primitive Rebels*), the chiliastic, the libertarian, and even the absurd. He who finds these traits irrelevant to populism, or who believes the term appropriate only for rural communities, will find much to criticize.

It might be safer to speak merely of 'popular politics' as does Henry Pelling in his *Popular Politics and Society in Late Victorian Britain*, which treats subject matter akin to that of this chapter. Other comparisons suggest that a better label for such phenomena as Tichborne politics could be 'expressive'. J. R. Gusfield uses this term in his study of the American temperance movement, positing it as the antithesis of 'instrumental'.[1] Expressive politics are those in which the real aim of proponents is ulterior or incidental to the professed aim; instrumental politics those in which the two coincide. The concept has meaning, but poses as many problems as does that of populism. Indicative of this is Gusfield's use of alternative adjectives for the political style of which he writes: symbolic, status, dramatistic, goal-less. Each of these variants suggests ideas relevant to the present discussion. Nevertheless, populism is retained, with the intent that it comprehend these ideas as well as primitive, libertarian, chiliast and absurd elements.

All this both reveals and relies upon the fact that there exists no perfect, accepted definition of populism. Speakers at a symposium at the London School of Economics in May 1967 strove towards one, and the resultant book—G. Ionescu and E. Gellner, editors, *Populism*—must be the base for further efforts. The following paragraphs do work from that base, although not every point made by the contributors to *Populism* comes within the definition now offered. Conversely, awarness of the Tichborne story has influenced the shaping of this definition, but hopefully a theoretician of populism could accept it, irrespective of such circumstances.

Populism is social protest that asserts the welfare and capacity of the people at large against those of society's ruling elites. It sees the people at large as the repository of society's virtue; therefore popular benefit outrides all other considerations, and popular judgement is always correct. Conversely, elites establish and maintain their power by conspiratorial cunning. One alleged elitist technique is to impose notions of social hierarchy and conformist behaviour; the populist accordingly rejects these notions. He believes further that the most important bastions that elites occupy are political office and the public service. As a result, servants and instrumentalities of the state are likely to be corrupt and ruthless, although at some more abstract remove the state itself might not necessarily be so, and may recover grace if the non-political classes assert themselves to extirpate the bureaucrats and politicians. In some golden past this happiness had prevailed.

Reactionary attitudes of this type occur time and again, imbuing populism with many elements that by latter-day standards appear Right rather than Left. The populist suspects economic as well as other forms of change, and idealizes small-scale enterprise, especially on the land. There is a tendency to emphasize particular causes rather than to embrace programmes, to attack symptoms rather than roots. The populist cherishes traditional groups and loyalties, and grieves at their disruption; he wants a society of simple structure and little specialization, and often hates modernity and outsiders. By Marxist criteria his sense of class loyalty is naive and indiscriminate, and his reading of history awry.

The populist is ill at ease in his world, tending to become desperate, even hysterical. Consonant with this he backs causes that veer towards doom and destruction; populist movements are fated to fail. By the same token, leaders of these movements are often ill-equipped to win victory in the day-to-day political world. Rather they are oddities and adventurers, close to the bounds of the law or even beyond them. Yet the doom of their causes and the failings of their leaders do not much bother populists. The reason for this, and probably the key to the phenomenon generally, is that the aim is not so much to right wrongs as to provide release which palliates the suffering imposed by those wrongs. The tone of populist discourse is emotional and religious rather than intellectual and scientific. Indeed (and again the reactionary note obtrudes), populism is generally averse to logic and learning. It is, in short, hostile to liberal beliefs and style. When this tendency becomes extreme there develops 'the apocalyptic fantasy world, full of sadistic elements, holocausts, and retributive punishments'.[2] This anger of the soul has its counterpart in physical force: 'populism . . . is capable of violence. But this violence is inefficient and short-winded . . . not glorified or erected into a principle'.[3] The apocalypse and the fantasies need not end in woe, however; alternatively, sometimes simultaneously, the populist finds solace in a dream of perfection, which no worldly society has ever won, and which in terms of hard cause-and-effect he is doing little to bring nearer.

This yearning for perfection creates a major contradiction within populism. It encourages an ultra-moralism, consistent with the religious and emotional tone of populist discourse, and with contempt of commonsense norms. But simultaneously, populism rejects the attempts of society's rulers to impose a conformist creed. Thus Victorian populists were hostile to Smilesian respectability and the work ethic, yet insistent that the ruling classes were debased and that common folk could transcend all impurity.

This is about the sum of meaning in populism as an abstract. It is not very great; all sorts of men and movements could come within it. But Kenealy and the Tichborne cause did much more than that. They gave such generalities depth and colour and life. This movement was a paradigm of populism.

THE STORY SO FAR AS A PARADIGM OF POPULISM

'Just think . . . of the flood of human idiotism that spent a couple of years or so of its life in writing, printing and reading the Tichborne trial', went one among several of John Ruskin's harangues on this subject; 'the whole of that vital energy and time being not only a direct loss, but loss in loathsome thoughts and vulgar inquisitiveness'.[4] Archpriest of all that was most removed from populism in the British radical tradition, Ruskin offered negative proof of the paradigmatic argument. So did all those upholders of respectability—conservative, liberal, radical, trade unionist—who anathematized the Tichborne cause. The preceding narrative shows that positive evidence is yet more abundant.

The Tichborne cause was of the people in two separate although mutually-enhancing ways: objectively, in that ordinary men provided an increasing bulk of the Claimant's supporters; subjectively, in that the leadership embellished this fact. Without the former the movement could not have been populist, but the latter clinched the matter. Fundamental were those assertions that the very fact of popular backing indicated the Claimant's authenticity. The Claimant's (or his press agent's) pride in the support accorded him by workers told the same message. Kenealy and the other demagogue leaders were all to take the same line: the people had determined, and the people must be right.

The class element strengthened when the identity of the Claimant became a question of whether anyone could cross status barriers as he claimed to have done. Coleridge's insistence in the civil hearing that no gentleman could forget the code of class behaviour, and Cockburn's in the criminal trial that wealth and position were delights never relinquished voluntarily, were the supreme denials of this possibility. Faith in the Claimant repudiated these standards; it affirmed that a baronet could turn to butchering in the colonial outback, absorb proletarian customs and language, marry a servant-girl—and be happy. Thus the movement protested against the rigidities of caste and behaviour so strongly upheld by the elites of mid-Victorian Britain. The point becomes sharper if truth is allowed to the gibe that Tichbornites supported the Claimant because at heart they believed him one of their own class who was tilting at established wealth and property. More tangible evidence, colouring the same general picture, was the sympathy for the Claimant offered by family servants. Deference and dependence bred all the greater eagerness that masters should feel unease.

That liquor-and-sport interests strengthened the cause further defined its populist aspect. At least in modern English-speaking societies, publicans and sportsmen have been patrons of the average working man, and especially of groups beyond respectability. Ex-convicts in colonial Australia, Negroes in the southern United States, European immigrants in the northern United States—all were to enjoy this benevolence. However self-interested the patrons may have been, they strengthened their clients' resistance to the ethic of work-thrift-sobriety-subordination. This was exactly the case in the Tichborne instance.

Tichbornites became angriest when alleging that the ruling class and the state united to destroy their hero. Here they saw conspiracy and its instrument, corruption. Some commentators would see a lust for discovering conspiracy and corruption as the key characteristic of populism; certainly it marks a direct antithesis to the liberal belief that the grand causes of all things are rational and discoverable. Lacking such faith, the believer in conspiracy and corruption is open to fear, despair, hate—in short, the populist syndrome. Certain that the administration of the state is malign, the populist will bewail its every aspect rather than attempting gradual reform. Thus Tichbornites scorned both the established parties. That the Whig-Liberal government of 1868–74 should be the Claimant's persecutor showed how empty were its claims to care for reform. Likewise Kenealyites may have been representative in abominating the Broadhursts and Mac-Donalds who sought a trade-union alliance with the Liberals. At a further extreme, Kenealy's sporadic support for the Queen, the Lords, the Privy Council and the unreformed parliament, while genuinely populist (compare the Russian veneration for the Tsar as father of all his people) were personal whims rather than the views of the movement generally. Even so, they were the whims of the leader.

For Tichbornites, the first evil of the state was its corruption and capture by the powerful; a consequent bane was illegitimate extension of its power. Thence resulted both protest at public resources being used to uphold the Tichborne family, and affront that the state should have intervened between the Dowager and he whom she recognized as her son. This underlay the bathetic yet sincere invocations of motherhood, its rights and its emotions, that suffused the Tichborne movement. The populist assertion of intimate blood loyalties also came into play, rousing antipathy to the state ever higher.

The Tichborne case concentrated this hostility on the law and its minions. That Coleridge, Solicitor- and Attorney-General, and

Cockburn, Lord Chief-Justice, were enemies of the movement symbolized this situation. Against them was pitted hatred of the laws themselves, the legal profession, and the administration of justice. Here, Tichbornites asserted, the ruling class had its citadel of power; mystique enwrapped the laws and only a fortunate few knew how to operate them. Lawyers were the identifiable group among the 'they' who ballads presented as Roger's conspiratorial persecutors; in the courts, venality was most open and scandalous. So operated populist animus against both elites and intellect. Women especially put store on the Dowager's recognition and resented the law's denial of that recognition; perhaps they were more hostile to intellect—and so to its elites—than were men. That Kenealy and other Tichborne leaders upheld feminism both complemented this situation and accorded with the populist tendency to invoke groups outside conventional politics.

The case involved lawyers alone, but Tichbornites attacked other elites of intellect and power. Priests and doctors were both accused of wishing to form an establishment that would tyrannize the people by means of a false claim to special wisdom. Likewise the armed services were seen as engaging in conspiracy to enhance their power by embroiling the nation in imperialism and war. In this way the fairly consistent Little Englandism of Tichbornites accorded with the populist theme and hinted at the xenophobia that was also part of the syndrome.

The Tichbornites' attack upon law made sense, yet had some oddities. The courts were indeed a bastion of the powerful, but a post-Marxist age must see this as a symptom of economic structure and historical development. These fundamentals received little analysis, even by those who tried to build a broader political movement around the case. The outrages of capitalism were blazoned; the railway, that most powerful engine of the new society, had somewhat the same evil quality for the *Englishman* as it did for American farmers; there were yearnings for a pre-capitalist agricultural society—but that was about the sum. Such a response to the problems then confronting the 'people' seems inadequate and inappropriate. That this protest should find its flashpoint in a claim to a baronetcy certainly was bizarre. If the Claimant truly was Roger then the law was being operated against a member of the ruling orders, so modifying the case as an instance of class war; if he was not Roger, then justice insisted that he lose the case. This analysis simplifies too much, but even so the uproar was illogical. Tichbornites should have used their energy to other effect if they wanted to secure justice and welfare for all. The cause perfectly represents the populist model in its concern for episodes rather than programmes, for symptoms rather than roots. Likewise, and consequently, the movement followed the model by running into failure and futility. Probably most Tichbornites did not especially hope for or expect their champion to win; they wanted a man of sorrows rather than a conqueror. To deprecate the movement because it failed is meaningless. Both by its own nature and as an exemplar of populism, failure was a necessary, or at least an appropriate, attribute.

Complementing this disregard for reason and purpose was stress on emotion and religiosity, immutable right and eternal judgement. Sport-and-liquor people may have spurned the Protestant ethic, yet they were as enthusiastic as any in denouncing Roman Catholic influence. And so they expressed not only populist-type xenophobia, anti-elitism and conspiracy-fear, but also a backhanded affirmation of pure personal religion. Kenealy alone presented himself as a Messiah, but the movement at large responded to images and vocabulary drawn from Christianity. John De Morgan switched easily from weekday speeches to Sunday sermons, and E. W. Bailey progressed from lay-preaching to Tichbornism to the professional ministry. Women were said to have been 'idolatrously' fond of the Claimant, while the *Graphic* jested:

Tichbornism . . . has almost assumed the dimensions of a new religion. Its worshippers have a Grand Lama, who, upon the breezy heights of Dartmoor, dwells in the same sort of mysterious seclusion which the Mikado of Japan affected before he was Occidentalized. The Grand Lama has his College of Priests, the arch ecclesiastics among whom are Monseigneurs Onslow, Whalley, and Kenealy . . .[5]

Sentimentality about motherhood and exaggeration of the Claimant's sufferings in gaol were secular variants of the wish for total emotional immersion. Banners, bands, ceremony, mass meetings—all built up this atmosphere.

The final stand in this argument must be the reassertion that logic and evidence pointed to the Claimant being an imposter, while belief in the Claimant was a matter more of faith and instinct. George Dawson of Birmingham said that the case was 'a battle between the educated and uneducated men of the country . . . it was not a question of rank but of training'.[6] Just as Tichbornites spurned intellectual elites, the ruling-class ethic and Whig-Liberalism, so they rejected the accepted norms of common-sense and consequence. Acceptance of the label offered by Cockburn, 'fools and fanatics', represented their stance. They were proud to appear fools by the standards of such a man; proud to express themselves with reckless fervour. Thus, to remark that the case was entertainment does not imply its political irrelevance so much as relate it to the populist preference for expression rather than effect. The display of grievance was more necessary, perhaps even more satisfying, than removal of its cause. Tichborne crowds were violent in their disgust of Hawkins and praise of Kenealy, but they did not attempt to rescue the convicted Claimant; Wapping was excited rather than outraged on the night of the verdict. The populist pattern stayed firm.

That leadership mattered much to the cause itself might be part of the populist paradigm. 'Unusually much is demanded of leaders in respect of their dress, manner and way of life', argued one analyst at the London symposium; 'Populism tends to throw up great leaders in mystical contact with the masses'.[7] Certainly the great men of the movement, while differing much among themselves, all had populist traits.

The Claimant himself must take first place in this story. His appeal is most meaningful in terms of the rejection of the work-thrift-sobriety ethic. If ever an individual lived by the antitheses of that ethic, it was he. 'Old Jolly Roger', applauded the balladists, hinting at the exultation roused by the hero's swashbuckling. The Claimant's bulk, that stigma of his martyrdom to pleasure, gave him further prerequisites for popular leadership: recognizability and idiosyncrasy. Skill with a gun and easy adoption of the demagogue's chores contributed to this image, while his out-facing of Coleridge in cross-examination was an exemplar of how Everyman would have liked to defy the law.

In so far as Tichbornites supported the Claimant because they saw him as an ordinary man seeking to acquire wealth and standing, his story accords with Hobsbawm's study of the bandit-hero at the head of 'primitive rebels'. Hobsbawm develops in a sophisticated way the truism that rascals have often been popular heroes. He may be over-disposed to see such figures as the particular product of Latin peasant societies; perhaps the greater truth is that the 'primitive' attitude that makes such heroes can exist in virtually any society. Audacity, nerve, bombast, flamboyance—

these were all bandit-traits that the Claimant showed. Even more relevant is Hobsbawm's verdict that

one of the chief attractions of the bandit was, and is, that he is the poor boy who has made good, a surrogate for the failure of the mass to lift itself out of its own poverty, helplessness and meekness. Paradoxically therefore the conspicuous expenditure of the bandit, like the gold-plated Cadillacs and diamond-inlaid teeth of the slum-boy who has become world-boxing champion, serves to link him to his admirers and not to separate him from them . . .[8]

Even those who genuinely believed that the Claimant was a baronet, and only a sojourner among the proletariat, could see some of this glamour in him.

That the *Saturday Review* once spoke of Kenealy as a Robin Hood suggests that he too had something of the bandit's charisma. Although the Claimant and his counsel were opposites in many ways, there were affinities, symbolized by their continuing amity. To decide which was the truer prototype of populist leader is a nice puzzle. The Claimant was the more thorough bandit, but Kenealy otherwise illustrated more of the populist syndrome. Placards that hailed him as 'the English Garibaldi' made a point relevant to contemporaries and pregnant for posterity, especially in light of Hobsbawm's analysis. Garibaldi, Hobsbawm argues, was the supreme figure among leaders of modern urban primitives. He was the man who first carried adoring city mobs away from their erstwhile support of church and king towards more positive aspirations. Hitherto the mob 'was traditionalist only for want of something better, and this is what the new movements, Jacobin, national, Socialist, seemed, however vaguely, to provide'.[9] Kenealyism was very much in the spirit of these 'new movements'.

Norman Cohn's picture of those prophets who throughout mediaeval Europe led 'the pursuit of the millennium' is yet more relevant to Kenealy. Such men

would construct their apocalyptic lore out of the most varied materials—the Book of Daniel, the Book of Revelation, the Sibylline Oracles, the speculations of Joachim of Fiore, the doctrine of the Egalitarian State of Nature—all of them elaborated and reinterpreted and vulgarized. That lore would be purveyed to the masses—and the result would be something which was at once a revolutionary movement and an outburst of quasi-religious salvationism.

Those *prophetae* who had the necessary personal magnetism did more than build up a revolutionary ideology—they set themselves up as divinely appointed leaders in the Last Days: heralds of Parousia, Last Emperors, even reincarnated Christs. No doubt some of these people were megalomaniacs and others were impostors and many were both at once—but to all of them one thing is common: each claimed to be charged with the unique mission of bringing history to its preordained consummation.[10]

Kenealy, then, belonged to a very long tradition. Whether that tradition pertains exclusively to populism might be debated, but the debate would reveal that Kenealy showed certain paradigmatic traits: flamboyance, emotion, religiosity, unreason. In all this he is linked not only with past Messiahs but also with fascist and near-fascist leaders of the twentieth century. One tell-tale mark of this was his deliberate peculiarity of apparel: gold spectacles, Scotch plaid, rod of Moses, bejewelled rings.

This argument tends to the conclusion that the characteristic populist leader is a rogue and a robber. That is only a little too blunt. At least, this leader will have traits of rogue-robbery, which will appear as such to his critics. The point parallels that earlier made about failure being natural to populism. It is meaningless to speculate about the result had the Tichborne movement found noble, self-sacrificing, intelligent leaders. The movement did not want such men, as Evans and Biddulph found, and in this it was true to populism. Likewise, Kenealy's use of his family appeared to his critics as evidence of greed and corruption, but it too meshed with the populist pattern: thereby he displayed characteristic reliance on intimate loyalties. The development of a party-type machine, bound by conventions of office-holding and shared responsibility, was beyond his conception.

This attitude was part of a hostility to modernism, which overall was probably the most telling sign that Kenealy was a true populist. It showed not only in his occasional loyalty to Crown, Lords and Privy Council, but also in his endorsing that the Norman yoke had destroyed old England's liberty. In contemporary politics this attitude prompted scorn of the Whig-Liberal claim to care for reform and popular welfare; Kenealy fits R. T. Shannon's hypothesis that many opponents of the 'Bulgarian horrors' agitation spurned the fundamentals of Victorian liberalism.[11] The theme of Kenealy's religious works—that civilization bred vice and evil—was pertinent, while his ludicrous incapacity to understand Overend, Gurney affairs measured his distance from modern capitalism. That Darwin and the British Association spread infidelity; that professionalism erased charm from cricket; that the gospel of work was a sham—through all such arguments Kenealy disdained specialization and sophistication. He treated similarly the protocol of class and the conventions of law. That these were particular hate-objects and that law was a field in which Kenealy had distinction must have made his actions all the more appealing for populist Englishmen of the day.

Populist traits were strong too among the lesser leaders. Morgan had the airs both of a gentleman who had repudiated his class and of a demagogue; the evidence suggests that if not a bandit, he was at least an adventurer. Onslow was of the perfect type of sporting gentry, Whalley an anti-Catholic ranter. William Cobbett's antipathy towards responsible government and hopes for national self-sufficiency in grain both accorded with the populist pattern, but as his father's son he was especially appropriate. One speaker at the London symposium described the senior Cobbett as 'a very complete case'.[12] The *Daily News* description of Luie as one who would have won fame in the secret service of a revolutionary state is relevant, and so too Mrs Weldon's campaign for law reform. Maltman Barry transcended distinctions of Left and Right as did no other Briton of his time.

A final pertinent quality of the Tichborne movement was its connection with other populist causes. Dominant among these were commons' preservation and state medicine. These are best discussed, however, in terms of a broader survey of British populism. This will place the Tichborne movement in the populist tradition and show how significant that tradition was. It was significant simultaneously for British history and for the Tichborne movement, because the movement's populist quality interacted with the populist tradition and presumably became all the stronger as a result.

THE POPULIST CONTEXT

Modern Britain owes its form to the decades of the mid-seventeenth century more directly than to any other period, and populist attitudes were strong within the ferment that then brewed. Agrarian Utopias, Messianic apocalypses and cataclysms of class all had their many prophets and disciples. Donald Veall's study of *The Popular Movement for Law Reform: 1640–1660* (1970) shows that point after point made by nineteenth-century protestors were

at least two centuries old. The cost and intricacy of law, its defence
of vested interests, and the alleged venality of the profession, were
chief among these; even a trivial issue like the Magna Charta
Association's proposal to ban lawyers from parliament had been
aired. The outstanding populist demonstration of Britain's next
hundred years came in opposition to the change of calendars. The
idea that 'they' thereby filched eleven days from the people
appeared absurd to the educated, but disturbed the common
people, very much as the Tichborne case was to do a century later.
The works of G. F. E. Rudé and E. P. Thompson provide very
rich materials concerning the subsequent two generations. Complete identification of 'the crowd' with populism would be false,
especially if one accepts Rudé's emphasis on the purposefulness of
his subject's behaviour and the sensitivity to economic forces,
especially to grain prices.[13] Nevertheless strong affinities remain:
the idolization of John Wilkes, with his scandalous history and
scathing pen; the execration of Catholicism in the Gordon riots;
the delight in mob uproar. Rudé studied the pre-industrial crowd,
but maybe the difference between its members and the Tichbornites is less rather than more remarkable—just as between the latter
and Hobsbawm's primitives.

In *The Making of the English Working Class,* Thompson
asserts his aim to reinterpret certain aspects of the half-century
around 1800:

I am seeking to rescue the poor stockinger, the Luddite cropper,
the 'obsolete' hand-loom weaver, the 'utopian' artisan, and even
the deluded follower of Joanna Southcott, from the enormous
condescension of posterity. Their hostility to the new industrialism may have been backward-looking. Their communitarian
ideals may have been fantasies. Their insurrectionary conspiracies
may have been foolhardy. But they lived through these times of
acute social disturbance, and we did not. Their aspirations were
valid in terms of their own experience; and, if they were casualties
of history, they remain, condemned in their own lives, as
casualties.[14]

Thompson does not apply 'populist' to the movements of which
he writes, but it would seem legitimate to do so. Inasmuch as he
tells the truth about his subject, there disappears any mystery as
to why the Tichborne cause or any other such issue should be
potent—tradition was all for it. A consensus on Thompson's
validity has yet to form. Certainly he exaggerates. Much of the
new working class accepted industrialism and obedience to its

ethical requirements: many of those who sought to improve their condition eschewed anything like chiliasm or the violence of despair. But Thompson has told part of the truth, and it is that part which belongs to this context. William Cobbett senior's central place in Thompson's concluding pages illustrates the point.

Thompson gives too little attention to the agitation surrounding Queen Caroline's divorce in 1820. This issue aroused massive contention very like that of the Tichborne case. That it concerned the King and Queen made it more of a public question, and so somewhat more relevant to commonsense politics—yet the episode remains strange enough. Francis Place, contemporary incarnation of all that was opposite to populism, grudgingly admitted the episode's importance as 'a step toward democracy which can never be retraced'.[15] Very recently H. J. Perkin has agreed that the divorce agitation ranked with Peterloo in crystallizing the working-class consciouness of modern Britain.[16]

The turmoil of the 1830s and 1840s had a strong populist tinge. It was present even in the agitation surrounding the Reform Act, but the aftermath of the new poor law was more significant. The law epitomized the utilitarianism of Jeremy Bentham and Edwin Chadwick, and was the foundation of nineteenth-century 'welfareism'. From those whom it aimed to benefit and improve, the response often was hate. The law defied those blood loyalties so dear to populist man; it interfered between parents and children much as the state was seen to do in the Tichborne case. Around it, moreover, developed a bureaucracy, loathsome for its power and centralizing. Pelling puts opposition to the law first among signs and causes of opposition to the early welfare state.[17] He stresses too that this reaction contributed much to chartism. Within that movement in turn, the populist note was clear, although not always dominant. The traditional distinction between the physical-force faction, led by Fergus O'Connor, and that of moral force, led by William Lovett, makes the argument. O'Connor, with his land schemes and demagogic charlatanry, belongs to populism. The movement had its chiliast strain too, and in becoming linked with Irish nationalism acquired a further affinity with populism. Kenealy's involvement with these extremist and Irish elements in chartism was a portent.

The impact of the Crimean War, as analysed by Olive Anderson in *A Liberal State at War* (1967), belonged to this story. The stresses of the war strengthened belief in the ancient constitution and in the feeling that it had been perverted in recent times.

Springing from this idea were others that Tichbornites, Kenealy especially, were to expound: the evil of centralization; the desirability of abolishing cabinet and re-establishing the Privy Council, with direct ministerial responsibility (and liability to impeachment); the corruption of parliamentarians by party and influence. Nor was this reaction apparent only among the intelligentsia. From 1854 David Urquhart, already a veteran publicist, expounded these and associated ideas to working-class audiences throughout the country. In response there developed a National Movement of considerable strength especially in northern England. Affection for Turkey and hatred of Russia were the great dynamics of Urquhart's life, but he combined these with an incoherent radicalism—anticipating Kenealy at almost every point. Urquhart exploited working-class xenophobia in presenting the aristocracy and monarchy as corrupted by German influences—a theme of Kenealy's last writings on *The Guelphs*—and argued too that the aristocracy had enslaved the common people by engrossment of the land. The *Morning Advertiser* was foremost among national journals that echoed his opinions. The *Englishman* was to honour him after his death in 1877, and to appeal for back files of his *Free Press*. In attacking the Declaration of Paris it upheld a cause particularly dear to Urquhart. Hugh Cunningham, one of the very few academics to notice the MCA's existence, has remarked that its followers and Urquhart's alike 'were essentially backward-looking, hankering after a mythical yeoman and craftsman past, and imbued with the Cobbettite nationalism of the freeborn Englishman'.[18]

By the mid-fifties, then, the main themes of Tichborne populism had a substantial history, further pursuit of which is served better by a topical than by a chronological approach. The movement against compulsory vaccination was probably the most relevant single story.[19] Its roots traced back to the eighteenth century, but an act of 1867 that intensified compulsion stimulated very much greater hostility. Directed against a pet project of Sir John Simon, medical officer to the Privy Council and to the Local Government Board, this hostility represented animus against bureaucracy and centralization—a feeling widespread throughout many social and political groups, but most vehemently expressed by the lower orders. Often, as already noticed respecting Foster and Morgan, it was part of a general resistance to the medical profession, to the overweening claims of science, and especially to doctors allying with the state to impose their views on the community at large. Thus anti-vaccination provided a symptomatic issue on which to anathematize the medical profession, just as did the Tichborne case vis-a-vis the lawyers. As with the poor law and the Tichborne case, family integrity was a banner for protest. Earlier chapters have shown that many Tichbornites were anti-vaccinators, and the situation was reciprocal. The Hume-Rotherys, directors of this crusade, supported the Claimant; an anti-vaccination meeting at Bradford closed with a hymn to Kenealy.

The great themes of the movement found expression in extravagant yet compelling rhetoric. F. W. Newman, brother of John Henry and a famed advocate of eccentric causes, claimed that:

There is a sacred right of insurrection when law is tyrannical; I do not wish to thrust a knife into a surgeon; but I solemnly hold that a surgeon who tries to thrust a poisoned lancet into my child deserves to have a knife held in front of him, and if necessary, thrust into him. Plain, bold speaking, within the limits of the law, will be far more powerful than any vote.[20]

Hume-Rothery demurred against this threat of physical violence. His own use of psychological warfare is more likely to revolt posterity, especially the recital of cases where children allegedly suffered the most appalling illness, usually syphilitic in origin, as a result of the vaccine. Mary Hume-Rothery too was adept at unleashing emotion, as in this invocation to a working-class mother gaoled for defying the law:

God be with thee, poor mother, in thy cruel and most unjust punishment . . . That man should dare to step in with his wicked laws between those whom God has united by the tenderest and holiest of ties is one of the most grievous evidences of human debasement which it is possible to conceive. . . . The poor whom the 'luxurious classes' contemn are wiser far. They knew that they will run no greater risks in performing their duty to those nearest and dearest to them than they would in deserting them. Leave them to their natural instincts and they will cling to, and care for, each other to the last.[21]

Hume-Rothery argued to similar effect before a parliamentary select committee enquiring into vaccination in 1871: he maintained that he 'should prefer the verdict of the unsophisticated working classes on any pending question, to the verdict of an assemblage of so-called educated gentlemen'.[22] Another witness before the committee was J. J. Garth Wilkinson, a homoeopath, spiritualist and Swedenborgian, who wrote numerous pamphlets in the anti-vaccination cause. One, first published in 1871, argued that a sort of 'civil war' would develop between the people and the state over the issue, with doctors becoming identified as spy-servants of the law.[23]

Although the anti-vaccinators included men of name and fame —Newman, Herbert Spencer, A. R. Wallace, P. A. Taylor, George Dawson—the attitude of established respectability to the movement was much the same as to the Tichborne cause. For the *Lancet,* 'the whole class of people who refuse to vaccinate their children, who prefer their own opinion to the judgement of science and the authority of law, are peculiar people'.[24] The *Saturday Review* jeered at anti-vaccinators for showing 'that fanatical resolution which nothing seems to excite so surely as any infringement of an Englishman's sacred right to propagate disease at his pleasure'.[25] Hume-Rothery claimed that 'fool' and 'fanatic' were labels commonly thrown at his followers as they appeared in the courts, but that they had come to discountenance such sneers.[26] Even at this level, the Tichborne cause and anti-vaccination synchronized.

The campaign against the contagious diseases acts had many affinities—personal, ideological, temperamental—with that against vaccination. Statutes of 1864 and 1866 provided that in certain areas, especially where service personnel were garrisoned, police should enforce medical inspection and treatment of alleged prostitutes, to check venereal disease. Opposition was rather slow in developing, but from 1869 it boomed, encouraged by agitation from the other side for nation-wide extension of the acts. Leaders of the opposition were Josephine Butler, wife of a Liverpool pedagogue of some distinction, and James Stansfeld, who thereby forsook the prospect of high political office. The movement broke from the populist syndrome only in that it triumphed, the acts being repealed in 1886.

The movement had many facets. Posterity sees it as important in the development of feminism—itself of interest in this context. But the feminists received male support. Josephine Butler was always anxious to assert, even to exaggerate, the backing of working men: 'they are our chief aids in the matter', she told a royal commission in 1871.[27] The sanctity of womanhood was the fundamental theme of the agitators; they alleged that the acts authorized vicious use of police power to violate this sanctity. Lurid argument to this effect offended Victorian conventions about sex, much as the Tichborne case offended those of class. Not that the latter aspect was wholly absent here, for W. T. Stead and others 'injected a populist, sensationalist element and class argument by asserting that the upper classes, generals, parliamentarians, aristocrats, dons and judges, supported the legislation because they wanted to give prostitution state recognition and extend "the foul and foetid harvest of lust" '.[28] The agitation led also to hostility against the state machine, especially the police. Thus the *Shield,* organ of the movement, insisted that popular feeling against policemen must grow to danger level as a result 'of employing them as *spies* far more than as *protectors* of the people'.[29] The *Shield* suspected all 'welfareism' however benevolent its apparent purpose, once remarking that 'until there are more men in parliament with real sympathy for the poor, and with real knowledge of their difficulties, their wants, and their ways of living, the less we have of "Social Legislation" the better'.[30]

The opponents of the acts denied the inevitability of fornication and saw the provision of clean prostitutes as pandering by the state which encouraged immorality and insulted the common people. The perfectionist strain in populism thus found play. That the acts involved the army and navy sharpened this point. Overall, the majority report of the royal commission disparaged opposition to the acts, but it agreed that their administration by service authorities gave them 'an invidious and offensive character'. To critics it appeared that the nation's virtue was being sacrificed for the benefit of her services, which allied with police and doctors to serve their own venal, carnal ends. One mighty sentence from the *Shield* ran:

We hold that these Acts were passed under the one-sided and professional influence of medical and military authorities, unchecked by any public discussion, to the imminent peril of the best interests of the whole community, and the contemptuous sacrifice of the claims of true social morality, as well as of the inalienable personal rights of every individual English woman, however degraded.[31]

The allegation of underhand dealing—the acts were introduced very discreetly and under a misleading title—was another commonplace of the agitation, making conspiracy as frequent a charge in this connection as in the Tichborne case.

Other associations between the two causes were strong. All factions of the Tichborne movement criticized the acts. Onslow was a vice-president of the national association for their repeal. Southampton was a bastion for this agitation, as for the Claimant. *Reynolds's Newspaper* and the *Morning Advertiser* often alleged police brutality in enforcing the acts. 'Respectable' criticism of Mrs Butler's disciples anticipated that of Kenealy's. F. B. Smith has linked opposition to the acts with wider movements, totalitarian and neurotic, directed against sexual activity that strayed from the narrowest prescriptions: homosexuality, masturbation and child prostitution, all came under this attack.[32] Kenealy's attitude to sex was likewise totalitarian and neurotic, and his attack on Baker anticipated the more famous scandal-crusades of the 1880s and 1890s.

Less emotive than the contagious diseases agitation, yet invoking similar demand for civil liberty, was the campaign for lunacy law amendment. Here again doctors were seen as prompting an over-compliant state to empower them. The Lunacy Law Reform Association was the equivalent of Mrs Butler's organisation. It received a good press from both the *Englishman* and the *Independent*. That Thomas Meyrick allegedly had been whisked into an asylum so that he might not continue backing the Claimant, further symbolized this tie. Mrs Weldon's interest in the question was yet more significant, especially for illustrating how antipathy to the lunacy law naturally cohered with suspicion of the judicial process at large. Another cause of the seventies directed against the medical profession, and sceptical of science, was anti-vivisection. The *Morning Advertiser* saw experiments on animals as 'demoniacal'. In 1876 a royal commission investigated 'the practice of subjecting live animals to experiments for scientific purposes'.[33] Among witnesses critical of vivisection was Sir William Ferguson, a very distinguished surgeon who now deprecated the work of many experimentalists; with wonderful appositeness, Sir William had appeared for the defence in the criminal trial, more or less confirming that body marks on the Claimant accorded with Roger's history. The royal commission did not accept Ferguson's viewpoint, but did recommend supervision of experiments. An act consequently went through parliament, provoking a variety of responses. On one hand the *Englishman* objected to any recognition of these 'heartrending tortures', while the *Times* thought it 'almost monstrous' that doctors, benefactors of civilization as they were, should be treated as 'kind of enemies of the human race'.[34]

The early welfare state had aspects other than medication, and these too suffered considerable criticism. Pelling's argument that perhaps a majority of workers were hostile to 'welfareism', relates mainly to the years around 1900, but with some reference to the 1870s. He stresses that plans for slum rehousing then met resistance and that comprehensive public education often appeared as an injustice. This feeling against national education is especially pertinent to the populist syndrome with its suspicion of the state and of intellect. 'School board tyranny', enforcing pupils' attendance, offended many Tichbornites' ideas of civil liberty; and William Hume-Rothery and Mrs Butler were among those who believed that a state-controlled system demeaned family integrity. Kenealy was extreme when he attacked state education as likely to produce Prussian conformism, but other criticism tended in the same direction. A letter in the *Independent,* purporting to tell the childhood experiences of a Norfolk farm-worker's son, probably expressed genuine sentiment:

We could not afford more than 1 lb. of fat pork per week, with rye bread, for a family of eight. Those were hard times, but if the School Board had compelled the eldest to go to school we must have starved . . . It is a dreadful thing that members of parliament have the making of laws for the ruling of the poor . . . the members are so far removed in society from us that they have not the least knowledge of the difficulties we have to contend with.[35]

The letter ended with plaudits for the Anti-Vaccination League.

Complementing this hostility towards welfare was still stronger feeling against restrictions in the name of morality and order. Perhaps the Contagious Diseases Act took some odium from the view that a man's whoring was his own business, although no direct evidence supports this hypothesis. By contrast the Licensing Act of 1872 provoked physical-force demonstrations. The early seventies also saw vigorous police action against petty gaming and betting, which radical and sporting papers presented as victimization of the poor while the rich continued to indulge their vices. The *Morning Advertiser* alleged too that pugilism had suffered mortally from restriction. The Adulteration Act of 1872 meant for many that government now interfered between a man and his food, just as the Licensing Act did with his drink; widespread resistance to Australian mutton—cheap, good and nourishing, as respectability (but not the *Englishman*) told its underlings—was a current example of popular conservatism on matters of diet. Restrictions on Sunday trading, which back in 1855 had provoked riots similar to those against the Licensing Act of 1872, continued to irritate. The Royal Parks and Gardens Act, yet another statute of 1872, epitomized the government's tendency both to suppress opinion and to deny traditional relaxation. That this was done in the name of royal rights encouraged republican dissidence. For Morgan to have advanced his career by opposition to this measure was very appropriate.

No-one has ever found one simple, satisfactory reason for the defeat of Gladstone in the 1874 election, but hostility to over-government probably was decisive. This hostility ran through a wide social spectrum and against legislation other than that here noted, but populist revolt may have affected the result. Contemporaries recognized the point in stressing the importance of the licensed victuallers' vendetta against the government. Liberals exaggerated the matter as being at once an excuse of self and a vilification of opponent. Yet the *Pall Mall Gazette* was persuasive in arguing:

The simple truth is . . . that the influence of the English publican, like that of the Irish priest, is only great when it is exerted in the popular side . . . The unneccessary and meddling invasion of popular liberties, the foolish and irritating interference in what is or should be each man's private concern—these are the characteristics of the Licensing Act which have made it fatal to the government . . .[36]

In one of the rare parliamentary references to the election result, Hugh Birley argued similarly: 'the late parliament had been too much in the habit of adopting systems of legislation which made that penal which had never before been considered a crime'.[37] The *Morning Advertiser* and the *Licensed Victuallers' Gazette* insisted that it was not yearning for beer but rather antagonism to a police state which moved the voters. When Tichbornites claimed, as they often did, that revulsion at the government's treatment of the Claimant led to its defeat, some symbolic truth lay beneath their words.

Pelling traces hostility to the new police force, 'Peel's bloody gang', from its establishment; but the Licensing Act in particular, and other measures noted above more generally, distinguished the 1870s in this respect. Parliamentary criticism of the force early in the decade was voiced especially by Roger Eykyn, who was also notable for once having asked a question about the Tichborne case.[38] Concerning the London police, he expressed wide opinion that their organization was unduly militarist, and that this caused discontent within the ranks as well as being an infringment of civil liberty. Late in 1872 a mutiny within the force endorsed at least part of Eykyn's argument, while popular support for the mutineers against their leaders might have expressed resentment at the force's ever-expanding activity. Throughout 1873 there continued reports of perjury, collusion, and general loss of morale. In December a lawyer named W. T. Belt successfully prosecuted for wrongful arrest, giving opportunity for many journals from the *Times* to the *Morning Advertiser* to berate the police. Robert Lowe, briefly Home Secretary, protested at this 'dead set' against the force.[39] Also in 1873 began that corruption which resulted in the giant scandal of 1877 involving detectives allied with the Tichborne case.[40] The scandal was another occasion for critics of the police to express themselves, as the *Englishman* and the *Independent* illustrated. Early in the next year a judge at the Leeds assizes rebuked the crowd for applauding the acquittal of a prisoner charged with murdering a policeman; the *Independent* replied that 'we must congratulate ourselves that our labours have not been entirely in vain, and regard it as an omen of a brighter and better future'.[41]

Inexorably hostility to the law and its working obtrudes again. In developing his argument about the continuing force of class law in late-Victorian Britain, Pelling refers to the high cost of justice, the special jury system, the liability of small debtors to imprisonment, deficiencies in compensation for work accidents, and the high cost of divorce. One of Pelling's authorities is Thomas Wright, self-styled 'Journeyman Engineer', who analysed working-class feeling in terms remarkably appropriate to 'the populist context'. Overall, Wright insisted, the tone of the people was republican, in consequence primarily of 'the idea that there is one law for the rich and another for the poor'. The conviction that the rich deliberately legislated to this end was 'the crowning sting of the grievance—the point that maddens'. Wright noticed most of the issues touched upon in the preceding pages, and also the commons question. He did not refer to Tichborne but said of *Reynolds's Newspaper* that it was 'by far . . . more important and influential' than the *Beehive,* the only other paper to have the workers' confidence.[42]

'The English land question', F. M. L. Thompson has argued, was 'central to an understanding of nineteenth-century political history'.[43] The chief radical proposals were the abolition of primogeniture, easier facility for purchase and conveyance of land,

and the ending of privilege over game. Tichbornites generally supported these proposals, although much more significant, at least for some of them, was the commons issue. Sympathy for the Agricultural Labourers Union, for the creation of English Land Leagues, and for Henry George, were other ways through which Tichbornites joined the radical critique of the landed system.

While agricultural reform was a creation of the radical intelligentsia, it still had populist traits and was in great degree a 'symbolic crusade'. Thompson sees the reform planks overall as 'for the most part fantasies, at the basic level of radical intent'; founded on false assumptions, they related little to the true situation. Appropriately and significantly, few of the projected reforms became law. The rhetoric of their supporters was emotional and extreme. P. A. Taylor led parliamentary feeling against the game laws, alleging that among other things they forced rural police to act as gamekeepers and consequently to suffer much odium. Parliament heard too that during the agricultural labourers' mighty protest of summer 1873 there was widespread feeling that police, at the behest of local authorities and farmers, were attempting to 'put down the movement . . . by physical force'.[44] Critics of land reformers alleged that they were ignorant extremists who would destroy all property and distinction. Again the Tichborne debate echoed.

The issues discussed so far were, by definition indeed, at least as interesting for revealing populist temperament as for the objective cause they backed. Yet the objective cause remained. Other aspects of the populist context reversed this balance: temperament dominated altogether.

Victorian politics, like Victorian life generally, were passionate. That applied at every level. The most relevant expression of this passion was the organization of mass movements—against slavery and the corn laws; for temperance, the prosecution of Governor Eyre, and so on. The grand example of the 1870s was the revulsion at the Bulgarian atrocities; R. T. Shannon, historian of the agitation, presents it as indicative of the 'Moral Sensibility of the High Victorian Era'.[45] The agitation, he says—and, one might add, much opposition to the agitation—rested on two self-sustaining principles: 'that states are bound by the same moral laws as individuals; and that it is not merely desirable but essential that decisions of policy should conform strictly and directly to absolute definitions of righteousness'. The emotional quality of the age is also indicated in J. R. Vincent's study of *Pollbooks: How Vic-*

torians Voted, especially in his analysis of the popular radicalism evoked by Gladstone:

What Gladstone was offering was emotional subsistence level— the possibility of participation, antagonism, struggle, commitment, eventual victory, a sense of power and domination—to people normally entirely subject to circumstances and to other people . . . Gladstone offered the psychic satisfaction of ruling to the ruled—not ruling over themselves, but ruling and overruling the traditional holders of authority . . .[46]

Subjective as Vincent's analysis must be, it seems to establish a continuity with E. P. Thompson's *Making of the English Working Class.* Similarly, Donald Richter's study of electoral disturbance from 1865 to 1885, prompts him to argue that 'the illusion of Victorian society, suddenly orderly and serene, first portrayed in contrast by Great War observers, must continue to give way to a truer image of a yet very disorderly people'.[47] The Tichborne agitation seems more and more a representative event, less and less an eccentricity.

Just as populist traces influenced high politics, so too they were present in many public men of the day, eminent and notorious. Vincent's passages suggest that even Gladstone belonged here— that is, his image as created by his followers, rather than his true self. Disraeli was closer to the mark. His romanticism, flamboyance, literary yearnings and Bohemian behaviour all qualified him in this regard; his sympathy for Kenealy testified to affinities between the two. John Pope-Hennessy, also a native of Cork and protégé of Disraeli, behaved like a colonial governor precisely as Kenealy might have done, asserting the rights of his native subjects and arousing settlers to fury. Of David Urquhart no more need be said. One of Urquhart's disciples, T. C. Anstey (whom in 1847 the Irish Confederation had appointed over Kenealy's head as leader of the Repealers in England and Scotland) ended his life as a barrister in India where he was 'an amazing success. His devotion to the causes of his clients generally became a passion which governed his conduct throughout his case; his predominating characteristic was a very exaggerated Kenealyism'.[48] Further to the Left, an outstanding figure was G. W. M. Reynolds who, as Chartist, novelist and journalist, might be the most important populist of all. 'Great, honest and noble-hearted man', read Reynolds's obituary in the *Englishman*; 'he and his paper have done much to disseminate Truth among the Workingmen of this enslaved and impoverished land'.[49] Samuel Plimsoll fitted the populist pattern in his emotion, his tackling of symptoms rather than causes, his evocation of hero-worship; the *Englishman* and the *Independent* both praised him, and one of his agents worked on the Claimant's behalf. H. M. Hyndman was of lineal descent from Kenealy not merely because of his association with the MCA, but by reason of his half-Tory romanticism, his wayward personality, and even his affection for cricket.

For all this, Irish politics and society were more populist than those of England, and the Tichborne movement might be described as having attempted to deploy Irish techniques and attitudes throughout the kingdom. The *Englishman* compared Daniel O'Connell and Kenealy, and maybe Kenealy hoped to emulate, on an even grander scale, the achievements of the man who dominated the political milieu of his early years. Stoke would be a second Clare, the MCA would outstrip the Catholic Asociation, and the Kenealy sons would uphold their father as did O'Connell's. Sympathy for Parnell and for the tactics of Irish political resistance, especially the land leagues, continued the parallel. Whalley was right enough in accusing Kenealy of being an Irish politician. Morgan was even more a man of the two islands.

In mid-Victorian times, sympathy for Ireland often accompanied antipathy to vigorous foreign policy, imperialism, the armed forces, and even the throne. Tichbornites illustrated the continuum, and in so doing linked with more widespread feeling. The Governor Eyre agitation was the most striking instance of hostility to empire and to the service establishment.[50] It prevailed largely among the intelligentsia, but—as Thomas Wright insisted —republicanism had strength among the common people too. The enthusiasm poured upon Garibaldi on his tour of 1864 was one display of this. Anti-monarchical feeling probably reached its peak in about 1870 with the Queen's prolonged withdrawal from public life and the noising of scandal about the sex-life of the Prince of Wales. The granting of a dowry to Princess Louise early in 1871 concentrated antagonism. The *Spectator* offered representative comment:

in every metropolitan constituency the subject is as embarrassing as the Permissive Bill, or the Contagious Diseases Act, or any other topic on which there is a misunderstanding between the electorate and the political classes . . There is no doubt that in her capital Queen Victoria has at last exhausted her long-enduring popularity with the masses. They think it her Majesty's duty to live in her capital, to be the visible chief of her realm; and they resent her preference for remote wildernesses, and her abhorrence of city life as a dereliction of duty. That feeling, however, is confined to London, and it is out of London that opposition to the Princess's dowry is fiercest and most loud.[51]

The traditional belief that late in 1871 the Prince's recovery from grave illness brought Queen and people into new amity may have some force. Nevertheless the civil list remained a hot issue, while the Prince's gambling debts attracted criticism in 1874—as did the Royal Titles Act two years later.

Republicanism helped sustain a pervasive radical subculture through the decades after 1848. This subculture is little known, but Stan Shipley's *Club Life and Socialism in Mid-Victorian London* (1972) offers a model for discovery. Often secularist and educational, the clubs that Shipley describes reflected only a part of the populist syndrome. It was, however, an important part: contempt for Smilesian respectability and deference. Maltman Barry and Morgan moved easily and effectively in this circle, and the clubs' style resembled that of the MCA. Republicans were often the most militant—in F. M. L. Thompson's terms, the most fantastic—of land reformers. In his *Before The Socialists* (1965) Royden Harrison fuses these two causes when describing 'the proletarian left' of the early 1870s.

In counterpoint to these secular movements, a sizeable minority of Britons upheld a primitive religiosity. Even belief in witches persisted: reporting one case in Somerset, the *Daily Telegraph* commented that acts of parliament could no more suppress this conviction than they could faith in the Claimant.[52] Still, witchcraft and its believers were peripheral. The vital expression of popular religion was a grass-roots Protestantism—crude, emotional, and as ready to indulge in hate as in love. In tone, language and personnel, this crusade related especially to the onslaught on the contagious diseases acts. In the latter campaign, sex was the great abomination; for many Protestants, Roman Catholicism evoked the same response. In turn, this antipathy recalled a staple of the Tichborne cause.

Victorian anti-Catholicism was much the same as that of earlier generations. That was its significance: ' "No Popery" agitations were . . . stimulated by men who clung to dying theories of the Constitution, and to social *mores* which were changing faster than they imagined', writes a historian of the subject.[53] Antagonism to the modern, liberal state with its bland tolerance sounded again.

The feeling ran through all classes, and was probably as strong in the seventies as at any other time in the century. Papal infallibility and the Vatican decrees provided the most substantial target, although more striking was the venom that trivial issues occasioned. Among these the conversion in September 1874 of Lord Ripon, erstwhile member of Gladstone's cabinet, was outstanding.[54] Whalley and C. N. Newdegate in the Commons, Lord Oranmore and Brown in the Lords, kept up a parliamentary anti-Catholic crusade; Commoners often jeered Newdegate, but still he managed in 1870 to win a vote—very much against the government's wishes—for an enquiry into convents and monasteries. At a popular level, anti-Catholicism displayed itself most remarkably in the excitement aroused by the lectures of William Murphy. They goaded enemies even more than supporters, and so 'Murphy riots' became commonplace news. 'I should be afraid to trust my memory to state how often I have been applied to by the local authorities to protect them from the presence of Mr Murphy, and by Mr Murphy himself to protect him from his enemies', the Home Secretary told the Commons on 28 April 1871. This was after a meeting at Whitehaven where hundreds of Irish miners attacked, giving injuries from which Murphy never recovered. His death a year later just preceded the early release of the rioters. Newdegate and Oranmore and Brown attacked the release, the latter insinuating that the government was somehow revenging itself for the electoral damage done to it by Murphy in Lancashire.

At Birmingham in June 1867, Murphy-inspired rioters attacked a synagogue and various 'high' Anglican churches, showing that ultra-Protestantism diffused its antagonism. 'Scandals' involving ritualism in the Church of England were very frequent and evoked much feeling. This alleged undercover Romanism may have disturbed more people than did the open enemy. The Public Worship Regulation Act of 1874 showed that such feeling ran strong in official circles, and that Disraeli was ready to beat the Protestant drum in populist fashion. A more positive indication of evangelical Protestantism was the success of the American missioners D. L. Moody and I. D. Sankey as they toured Britain in 1875. Cases of religious mania followed in their wake. Sankey's tunes at once became popular. They were played in the streets and, for example, at agricultural labourers' demonstrations. Respectability stood aghast, especially when the headmaster of Eton permitted the evangelists to address his pupils. The *Examiner* was equally disparaging from the viewpoint of rationalist radicalism: the spokesmen for the Tichborne cause and the evangelists flourished alike as entertainers, exciting followers 'to abandon sober reason for the pleasures of violent emotion'.[55]

The secular movement that owed most to Protestant impulse was temperance. To introduce this as part of the populist context when earlier references have stressed the importance therein of beer, its dispensers and its drinkers, threatens to appear ridiculous. Yet while populism rejected the imposition of respectability from above, it encouraged other forms of moralizing. The temperance movement fitted one such form, being enthusiastic, Utopian, opposed to everyday commonsense and to the inclinations of average sensual man. That Kenealy and some other Tichbornites should support temperance thus had its rationale; that a fundamental cleavage between Conservative and Liberal parties should exist in the support of the Anglican Church and publicans for one, and temperance men and Nonconformists for the other, further told the strength of Victorian populism.

A final element in the populist context was the importance of court cases as occasions for the expression of relevant attitudes. Kenealy's career illustrated this long before he became counsel for the Claimant. His own trial for child-beating was in point: the crowds hissed his alleged brutality as an exemplar of what a father should not do. William Palmer won sympathy from some of his fellow-townsfolk as a promiscuous and profligate sporting man. Above all, the Overened, Gurney agitation vented hostility at finance capitalism and the respectable world. In a narrower frame, it was as much a populist paradigm as was the Tichborne case; Adam Thom the same sort of Messiah-crank as Kenealy himself. Hostility to the police often expressed itself in allegations of their victimizing defendants. One famous case concerned a sixteen year-old girl, Constance Kent, whom in 1860 the police arraigned for the murder of her infant brother. The local magistrates declared that a prima facie case did not exist; popular and press opinion seethed against the police, and especially against Inspector Jonathan Whicher who in 1867 was to work for the Tichborne family and gather vital evidence against the Claimant. In 1871 similar feeling built up around the trial and conviction of one E. W. Pook for murder of his mistress. Such antagonism often merged into insistence that authority was seeking punishment, especially capital punishment, with excessive vengeance: the cases of Palmer and Frederick Hinson were relevant. Divorce proceedings, and especially the Bravo murder case of 1876, invited expression of hate and disgust for upper-class life. Likewise, anti-Catholicism fed on a case of 1869, Saurin *v*. Star, wherein an erstwhile member of a convent alleged persecution against her Mother Superior. The Tichborne case was true to tradition, if transcending it, in causing the courts to provide not merely entertainment, but major socio-political issues.

ASSESSMENT

In the century after the Tichborne case, populism in Britain dwindled. The Labour party there became, by liberal standards, a model of working-class organization, accepting economic change and working purposefully to spread its benefit throughout the community, Republicanism, temperance, land reform—all faded into the limbo of lost causes. Anti-Catholic riots became rare, and secularism more and more profound.

Yet these changes came slowly and were potent at the institutional level rather than in affecting popular attitudes. Pelling's discussion of working-class opposition to the welfare state and suspicion of the law carries well into the twentieth century. The years immediately before 1914 saw violence and emotion more than sufficient to sustain George Dangerfield's study, *The Strange Death of Liberal England* (1935). Those years also saw the crystallizing of the ideas of G. K. Chesterton, whom Kenealy paralleled in many ways and whom a speaker at the 1967 London symposium on populism presented as inheritor of the Cobbett tradition. Horatio Bottomley was a vulgar variant of that tradition; he illustrated that the mass press became the channel for the expression of populist attitudes hardly less vehement than in the past, but less explosive because channelled. Likewise, the wars of the twentieth century offered socially acceptable media for emotional-cum-political catharsis. British fascism, like all fascism, had a strong populist strain.

Accounts of the latter-day poor in Britain reveal persisting populist attitudes. Thus Richard Hoggart in *The Uses of Literacy* stresses the use of the word 'them':

The world of 'Them' is the world of the bosses, whether those bosses are private individuals, or as is increasingly the case today, public officials. 'Them' may be, as occasion requires, anyone from the classes outside other than the few individuals from those classes whom working-people know as individuals . . . 'They' are 'the people at the top', 'the higher-ups', the people who give you your dole, call you up, tell you to go to war, fine you, made you split the family in the thirties to avoid a reduction in the Means Test allowance, 'get yer in the end', 'aren't really to be trusted', 'talk posh', 'are all twisters really', 'never tell yer owt' (e.g. about a relative in hospital), 'clap yer in clink', 'will do y' down if they can', 'summons yer', 'are all in a click (clique) together', 'treat y' like muck'.[56]

Feeling against authority, says Hoggart, is not violent or harsh, but rather suspicious and cynical. The police are still seen as a corrupt agent of class law, especially oppressive towards drinking and betting. Hoggart speaks too of conventional wisdom which insists that 'all politics are crooked', that of political parties 'there's now't to choose between 'em'. Mild xenophobia is constant. As society becomes more complex, the family and the neighbourhood are more rather than less cherished, this being symptomatic of 'a life whose main stress is on the intimate, the sensory, the detailed and the personal'. Hoggart's study is probably the best account of the British industrial proletariat that will ever exist. But similar lessons are taught, for example, by George Orwell's *The Road from Wigan Pier* (1937), with its admiring documentation of how the destitute resist do-gooder advice; or Jeremy Seabrook's *The Unprivileged* (1967), which paints its subjects in more sombre light than does *The Uses of Literacy*, and is more emphatic about popular suspicion of authority and its institutions.

In some degree, such evidence merely suggests that populism is likely to appear at any time, anywhere, and that it expresses an inherent quality of man. The success of twentieth-century fascism points in the same direction, mocking liberal and Marxist views of the true nature of political behaviour. The new Left of the 1960s also has many populist traits. Historians of the new Left, or simply conscious of the new Left, may well discover populisms of one sort or another wherever they look. The work of Pelling, Hobsbawm, Gusfield and others is all evidence that what a populist might call a 'conspiracy' of liberal and academic silence on the subject is ending. The near future might decide that 'expressive' politics are more normal than 'instrumental' politics. This background affects assessment of the populism of the 1870s in Britain. Was it an episode in a more or less constant story, or can this particular populism receive more exact measurement? In any quantitative way, it cannot; and probably the most significant fact is the constancy of populism. Yet further generalizations might be dared: that the populism of the 1870s was more potent than any similar British movement of subsequent years; that it was of about the same calibre as the earlier populist outbursts mentioned in this chapter; and that the Tichborne case was certainly the most bizarre and probably the most important populist episode of the decade. This is not to say that the working class was unanimously populist. The later success of commonsense Labour politics had strong nineteenth-century roots; E. P. Thompson's exaggeration of eccentric, extremist forces in *The Making of the English Working Class* is a warning to be heeded.

Nevertheless other historians have exaggerated in the other direction. Henry Jephson's study of *The Platform* (1892) was a classic example of a high, worthy Whig disdaining that which he felt impaired the dignity of his subject, and so he gave no place at all to the Tichborne cause or other similar movements of the time. General historians like R. C. K. Ensor and W. L. Burn have adopted much the same attitude; Burn's choice of title for the mid-Victorian generation, *The Age of Equipoise*, epitomizing an over-eagerness to make the story of modern Britain too bland and rational. Hobsbawm's Marxism, on the other hand, may have induced him to pre-date and over-stress the end of primitivism; 'in Britain I should put the crucial turning-point somewhere about 1850',[57] he writes, but gives himself the lie by remarking on Londoners' adulation in 1864 of Garibaldi, paramount chief of the primitive urban mob. Perkin has postulated 'the rise of a viable class society' in the generation after Waterloo, and that the 'entrepreneurial ideal' had then won dominance. He qualifies the proposition heavily, yet without reference to Tichborne or other such populism. Taking them into account, the 'viability' of society and the acceptance of middle-class values would have to be modified still more. There was greater resistance to change, more bitterness and anger among the common people, more primitivism and emotion, than the ascendant historiography of Victorian Britain accepts.

To make such a claim entails need to explain why things should be so, and why the seventies especially revealed them. Two disclaimers reduce the obligation, however. First, the counter-question, 'why not?' is more meaningful than usual: it was natural and logical that in a society undergoing profound and unique change there should be some such reaction from below. Second, the rule that description of a phenomenon involves its explanation applies here. Populism flourished in the seventies because

Tichborne, vaccination, common enclosure and so on then arose; they were all causes as much as results. But other circumstances strengthened their force.

For many, economic and social conditions were grim. Perkin himself has extended into the 1870s the argument that most accounts paint too bright a picture of benefits granted the mass by industrialization; poverty, inequality and social rigidity were profound and probably strengthening, he argues. The industrial troubles of the 1870s offer evidence in support of this. 'The numerous strikes which have occurred during the year have produced general anxiety', said the *Annual Register* for 1872. It detailed the strike of gas-stokers in London, in consequence of which five men were found guilty of conspiracy. That caused one great stir, while another was the action by agricultural labourers. Confirmation that the ruling class was ready to use physical force against these dissidents came in 1873 from Chipping Norton, where magistrates imprisoned sixteen women who had attempted to intimidate blackleg labour. A lockout in south Wales in 1875, and a strike in northern cottonmills in 1878, were among other disputes that kept tension high. Repeated railway accidents and industrial disasters, especially in mines, further spelled the cost of change.

Economics pressed from one side, government from another. Never had the executive tried to do so much; never had it possessed the means of doing it so efficiently. The point is most obvious, and most significant, in the field of medicine. From the mid-fifties to the mid-seventies was 'the epic age in English public health', writes one historian; another wrote that 1871 marked a milestone in effective vaccination.[58] The establishment of the Local Government Board in 1871 was both a triumph of centralization and a goad to the anti-centralizers, just as the militarist organization of the police both aimed at greater competence and threatened civil liberty. Education and taxation were other areas where government exerted itself more than ever before. Populism of the seventies had much to react against.

While populism itself was generally hostile to modernity, new techniques strengthened its expression. By report, newspapers sold more heavily during the trial than ever before.[59] Goldwin Smith reminisced that whereas a disputed heirdom of the 1840s had created only local interest, the Tichborne case divided the nation, 'so much more inflammable and excitable has the electric telegraph made the public mind'.[60] The Claimant, Kenealy and Morgan all used the railway to effect their campaigns. They addressed audiences often massed together by the new industrialism.

This mass society lacked amenities, as P. A. Taylor and others were quick to deplore. The greater efficiency and morality of government worsened the situation, as it restricted gambling and drinking. In the same context belong the end of public hangings, in 1868, and of open voting. No wonder that people should seek amusement. Some commentators believed that the passion for betting was on the increase,[61] while the *Vanity Fair Album* for 1872 commented that 'few things are more remarkable than the intense desire that in these times exists among mankind to look upon the faces of each and every individual who has become surrounded with any kind of notoriety'. All these conditions gave populism generally, and the Tichborne case above all, their chance to occupy the public mind.

Others saw the great need as education, not entertainment. The many commentators who deplored Tichbornites as ignorant fools implied that. The *Nonconformist*, grinding an axe, made it explicit:

So long as, in deference to ecclesiastical susceptibilities, we maintain a system which dismisses the bulk of our juvenile population from school barely able to read and write, and without the slightest disciplining of their reasoning powers, there must always remain a grim element of truth in Dr Kenealy's minatory rodomontade. We do live on the verge of a volcano . . .[62]

The one happy aspect of the case, continued the *Nonconformist*, was that not perversity but the warmer feelings of Englishmen led them to support the Claimant. While denied proper training at school, 'in the family and in the street, in the workshop and at the club, their sympathetic and emotional nature is cultivated in an altogether disproportionate degree'. Such argument recognized and complemented the populist suspicion of intellect and education.

Nor did the mass have formal means of political expression.The Reform Act of 1867 broadened the electorate, but many remained outside. That residuum had its traditional role obliterated by the secret ballot. Even the respectable class-conscious working man had to wait for his vote to have full effect. A feature of the 1874 election was the relative failure of labour candidates, sufficient failure to discourage further independent action for twenty years and more.

The declaration of Papal infallibility was one external event that helped to ferment British opinion in the seventies; another was the Paris Commune. The press remarked the sympathetic reaction to the Commune by leading radicals, while Thomas Wright believed that most working men approved its republican and anti-clerical aspects. The most diligent historian of the subject, Royden Harrison, notes that the longer-range effect of the Commune among English radicals was towards

encouraging the revival of lost delusions and traditions . . . By 1873, as the . . . *International Herald* shows, 'Our Commune' had become no more than a return to the old communitarian ideals of the first half of the century: what Whigs, Marxists and other outmoded historians would once have dared to call 'an infantile regression' or a relapse into an 'archaic' form of social protest.[63]

Morgan was contributing to the *International Herald* at this time. As he was the strongest tie between the Tichborne cause and the Commune, Harrison's lament is all the more interesting.

Just as certain factors deepened the vitality of populism in the past, so their modification has caused it to wane and alter direction in recent years. Mass entertainment and professional sport have flourished at the cost of other activities, including politics. The suburb has dispersed potential mobs. Welfare and education may not have been so very acceptable to the working class, but have changed it none the less. Suffrage has been extended, and the Labour party has thrived: in short, democracy has worked, and populism is necessarily pre-, post- or extra-democracy. Civil life has become easier, more relaxed, more bland.

AUSTRALIAN ECHOES

Populism has never been so potent in Australia as in Britain. Notwithstanding bandit Ned Kelly's winning in about 1880 of much the same fame in the New World as did the Claimant in the Old, the development of a 'viable class structure' came earlier and was more complete in the Australian colonies than in the metropolis. The previous chapter has suggested that this difference in social context explained the relative weakness of the Tichborne cause in Australia. Yet just as there was some Australian action on the Claimant's behalf, so there was some populism; just as the Australian cause was largely pursued by individuals, so it was largely through those individuals that the cause and populism were connected.

Historians have used the word 'populist' to describe the milieux of both Henry Parkes and E. W. O'Sullivan. Parkes's political career began in the late 1840s, when he helped unite most of Sydney's radicals. The setting in which these radicals worked has been said to show 'features which have characterized social situations with strong populist elements'.[64] This was in terms of a definition of populism that is somewhat, but not entirely, different from that used throughout this chapter: it fits both definitions that the Australian radicals of the forties were outside Marxist categories and dreamed of rural Utopia. These were characteristics too of the various organizations backed by O'Sullivan, especially the Land and Industrial Alliance. O'Sullivan's biographer has called this 'a populist party in the making'.[65]

The activities of Daniel Smith, that direct import from Britain, were much closer to populism as here defined. Particularly significant was his agitation against government assistance for immigration. Antipathy to immigration has traditionally been the one great populist expression of the Australian working man. Thereby he appears to sacrifice the commonsense needs of development to his own short-term selfishness, usually against the advice of governments and learned men. That Smith, and W. J. Barry too, operated on the Sydney Domain has its interest: such venues, staffed largely by cranks and entertainers, have been on the far edge of the Australian political arena, but have sometimes influenced affairs.

As in Britain, Australian populism linked with liquor, sport, and sensational journalism. The tie became closer in the New World because these interests sided largely with dissident groups, and finally with the Labor parties, in contrast to the British alliance between victuallers and the Conservative party. In Sydney the story was particularly fascinating because the alliance included a nativist interest, often rooted in convict origins. Joseph Eckford, Robert Wisdom, A. G. Taylor, J. C. L. Fitzpatrick, R. D. Meagher, W. P. Crick—all touched this syndrome. The syndrome was very open-ended, and some of these men had but marginal connection with the case. Yet the evidence is sufficient to link the Tichborne agitation in Australia with this area of power and sleazy dramatics.

An Australian sociologist has argued that a recurring type of political leader in Australia is the 'larrikin'.[66] Broadly speaking, the larrikin is a demagogue ready to invoke populism; the term has very much the same meaning as does Ernst Nolte's use of *'condottiere'* to describe Mussolini's life-long style and temperament. Larrikin leaders have often been liquor, sport and scandal men: Taylor, Crick, and especially John Norton, illustrate the rule. But the rule has its exceptions, among them the most able, successful and extreme of the larrikin type: Australia's counterpart to Mussolini was W. M. Hughes. His impingement on the Tichborne case was small, but very nice.

Populism tinged the Australian story at one or two further spots. The unemployed among whom Smith worked not only talked of dynamite but also opposed the acceptance of charity lest the 'perleece' get to know them. Public servants and doctors were accused of conspiring to thwart discovery of Cresswell's identity. W. B. Dalley, a Roman Catholic, and Alfred Stephen, a judge, opposed further enquiry. At the end, Fitzpatrick and others insisted on the right of parliament to release the lunatic against the wishes of bureaucracy and the courts. The very failure of these protests fitted the populist model.

8

KENEALY AFTER DEATH

THE *ENGLISHMAN* CHERISHED the memory of its founder in the months following his death. Work from his pen continued to fill many columns; especially valuable was publication of the autobiography written in the 1850s. Just as subscriptions to aid the man had been a major concern for the *Englishman* during his life, now there was talk of a grand memorial. The pattern continued in that the response fell below aspiration. His grave at Hangleton waited some years for adornment. It proved handsome enough: a tomb patterned with a Celtic cross in brilliant mosaic. A text from Luke 14 : 14 promised 'Thou shalt be recompensed at the resurrection of the just'. Typical contributors to this memorial probably were simple folk who cherished Kenealy's name for his part in the Tichborne saga. That the Claimant himself forever spoke fondly of his counsel symbolized this situation. Even in the *Independent,* which had found much about Kenealy to criticize since 1875, correspondents defended his memory.

As late as 1912 Maurice Kenealy received a letter from one F. E. Stansfield who remembered the doctor in the Wednesbury election of 1868:

My father was a Kenealyite; so was I. I remember with pride the learned Doctor patting me on the cheek, as I stood near the polling booth. From that day to this I have been a Kenealyite, and shall so remain until the grave closes over me. To what extent your father's writings have influenced my life I cannot tell; but I do unhesitatingly declare that had I never come in contact with him through his writings and his speeches I should today, in all probability, be either a gutter-snipe or a mudlark; instead of which I am a fairly respectable member of Society, endeavouring in my own humble way to infuse a little sunshine into the lives of my fellow-men.[1]

Stansfield told how he spent every copper in following the doctor through his circuit of mighty meetings in 1874, and how he exulted in the victory at Stoke. Thereafter the hero suffered many trials, but his fame survived them all: 'and far on in this, the twentieth century, when you and I are mouldering in our graves; when the angry strife of politics disturbs us no more; when all our feuds are hushed, the name of Edward Vaughan Kenealy will be honoured and revered, and the story of his life will be listened to with earnest and deep respect'. Stansfield's forecast scarcely came true, but posterity has paid some attention to each of Kenealy's self-acclaimed roles: politician, poet, seer.

Earlier chapters have mentioned the respect paid to Kenealy's memory by Francis Looney, chartist of 1848, and Alfred Edden, Stafford-born miner who became a Labor parliamentarian in Australia; the recollections of Lord Snell and others as to how the Tichborne case shaped their political education made at least marginal reference to him. The most forthright reminiscence of this type was that of William Collison, 'the apostle of free labour' —that is, foe of trade unions and strikes. In this, Collison was far removed from such upholders of Kenealy's name as Alf Edden, but not so far from Kenealy himself. Born in Stepney in 1865, Collison recalled his political schooling on Mile End Waste. Among the many causes that flourished there, sympathy for the Claimant impressed him especially. Collison peddled the *Englishman* while Kenealy harangued: 'even now I can feel the glow of pride which swept over me when, having sold an extra number of copies, the great little man patted me on the back and gave me sixpence'.[2] In retrospect Collison believed that his champion had become a fanatic, but insisted on the warmth of Kenealy's heart and on his own continuing doubt that the Claimant was Arthur Orton. Collison had close association with Maltman Barry, that dubious but Kenealyesque proponent of Tory socialism.

Kenealy also influenced David Lloyd George. William George discussed the point when writing his brother's biography. He told that Tichborne and Kenealy were lively issues in the discussion group that 'Dafydd' joined as a young lawyer's clerk at Portmadoc in the late seventies. 'Dr Kenealy was very much of a public hero, an advocate who had dared to defend his client at all personal hazard'.[3] Dafydd declared in his diary on 3 April 1880 that he was 'half glad' at Kenealy's electoral defeat, for 'he was an egotistic, self sufficient fanatic'. Yet William George believed that the doctor's influence was greater than this allowed, or than the future Prime Minister ever realized.

From the talks which I had with him at the time I well remember that he was impressed with what I may term the 'Dr Kenealy spirit' in an advocate and his fearless outspoken manner in a cause, which he believed just, and he certainly later on gained for himself, on his appearances at local courts, a reputation for being a fearless advocate in defence of his clients.

The London symposium on populism heard that George and his daughter were 'singularly pure populists'.[4] The judgement was acute, and prompts the speculation that George achieved what Kenealy dreamed of.

S. M. Ellis is the outstanding poetaster of later days who has found Kenealy worthy of interest and admiration. It was as the biographer of W. H. Ainsworth that Ellis had become interested in him, drawing upon correspondence between the two and upon Kenealy's papers generally. These, he said, 'present a vivid picture of early Victorian literary history'.[5] D. J. O'Donoghue, in *The Poets of Ireland* (1912), passed some favourable comment on Kenealy and noted a mysterious publication, *Noah's Ark, a Dream of 1850*. The *Irish Book Lover* published a centenary article showing some knowledge of the Young Ireland context and with an accurate bibliography.[6] The loudest note of praise since Ellis has been Michael Sadleir's appreciation of Kenealy's literary biographies. Miriam Thrall mentioned Kenealy in her study of *Rebellious Fraser's* (1934), being over-generous in attributing articles to him; and W. E. Houghton has blessed this biography by tracing appropriate entries for the *Wellesley Index to Periodicals*. In 1963 the Henry E. Huntington Library purchased five volumes of Kenealy papers from Sotheby's: these tell much of the young man, but they do not include the autobiography, diary, or later correspondence. Why and whither such materials disappeared are intriguing but unanswerable questions.

The burnishing of Kenealy's fame as a divine prophet fell primarily on Charles Wells Hillyear. About the man himself, records tell little. He contributed a poem, very much in the Kenealy nature-worship style, to the *Englishman's Magazine* in 1875; the *Englishman* noted a donation from him in 1878 and published an account of his travels to Niagara five years later. In 1901 Hillyear isued Kenealy's *Testament of Jesus*, an introduction sketching the author's theology and alleging that he had been murdered by poisoning; eight years later there appeared twenty-six copies of *The Prayers, Meditations and Visions of Kenealy (Imaum Mahidi), the Twelfth Messenger of God*. Colophons told that Hillyear lived at Watford; the paper, typography and general presentation of these publications were lavish. Next in 1911, came twenty copies of the *Institutes of Hindu Law, or the Ordinances of Menu . . . by Kenealy (Parasu-Rama)*; and finally, in 1915, Hillyear issued a brief biography, *Kenealy the Twelfth Messenger of God*. This sought to correct the *Dictionary of National Biography* of 1892, the relevant article in which had been rather contemptuous. The odium of the child-beating case was one of Hillyear's targets, and he alleged priestly malice behind the dictionary's animus. Hillyear claimed that 'it was the special mission of the Twelfth Messenger to bring about the re-establishment of a universal monotheism, without the use of militant force', and that Kenealy had achieved this destiny. Greater faith could no man have.

Kenealy made his chief impact on the future through his family. Domestic joy appears to have survived turbulent fortune and regular babies. Several of the children developed talents and traits that not only created interesting careers but echoed their father's life. Not that Elizabeth Kenealy was a passive element in this. Being a girl bride to a man on whom scandal had recently breathed could have been a grim portent for the marriage. Presumably the family home at Portslade was the poorer for Kenealy's purchases on books and art and the expense of his chambers. In so far as harmony prevailed, Elizabeth must have most of the credit. Nor did family concerns drown all other interests. 'Gave my wife her first lesson in Homer', noted Kenealy's diary in August 1858; 'she learned twenty-one lines with perfect ease'.[7] A reference of 1864 indicates that she submitted work to the Royal Academy, without success. Elizabeth's service to Kenealy during the Tichborne years grew from a well-established situation, rather than being a public-relations ploy. On her husband's death she became president of the Magna Charta Association, and tried to maintain its activity. That impossible task failed, she drifted into forty years' obscurity. At her death on 1 or 2 February 1922, she lived in Brighton. For probate purposes, her net personal estate was £124.13.0. At last she joined Kenealy in the grave, the site of which they had chosen together more than fifty years earlier.

The twelve children of the marriage were:

Ahmed John	born	13 April 1854
Charlemagne		2 December 1855
Henrietta Maria		3 January 1857
Maurice Edward		23 April 1858
Arabella Madonna		11 April 1859
Annesley		1 November 1861
Alexander Cockburn Chambers		20 October 1864
Noel Byron		10 June 1866
Edward Wednesbury		26 September 1868
Arthur Plantagenet		19 July 1870
Katherine Vaughan		31 July 1872
Isabel		26 October 1874

Echoing Kenealy's suspicion of systematized education, the children received most of their tuition at home. Otherwise their upbringing seems to have been only a little eccentric. Kenealy's chief interest was to teach ethical virtues and the classics, although he amused them with the violin and supplied all the fairy tales he could: 'the more often we soar into the Realms of Imagination the less we experience the miseries of existence',[8] was his reasoning. Arabella was to recall, or imagine, the children's part in the creation of Kenealy's religious works:

Written at odd moments upon slips of every size and shape, resulting in 'copy' which must have proved a sore puzzle to the printers, written amid the family group, with talk and children's play and chatter buzzing, many indeed of these learned pages were written for an hour at a time with the Baby of the date upon a knee—(there was usually a baby). The little thing would sit as quiet as a mouse, knowing that the penalty of noise or of disquieting movement would be a forfeiture of its proud place. It watched with solemn, interested gaze the lightning passage of the pen and would look up wondering from time to time into the grave, absorbed face and to the eyes full and luminous with the great thoughts fulminating in the brain behind them. Sometimes it would lift a hand to touch with tiny fingers and with awed delight the shining rim of the gold spectacles, which were ever a source of admiring wonder to the infant mind.

Kenealy walked and talked with his children devotedly, the daughter said, bestowing wisdom which they scarcely could appreciate. Allowing for hyperbole, it appears that like many who find difficulty in everyday relations with their peers, Kenealy felt warmth for children and aroused it within them. The memories of Stansfield and Collison are in point; perhaps even Kenealy's marriage to a girl of sixteen, 'my own dearest child and love'.

At eleven, Ahmed reputedly could translate Homer and Virgil 'beautifully', a credit to the private tutoring that constituted his education. He ended schooling at thirteen, going to sea and—he later reported—becoming a captain before his retirement in 1875. In his luckless career as 'Jupiter Junior' it is doubtful how far he was victim of his father's concern to gather all possible pickings into the family maw, and how far he was on the personal make. Either way, he harmed rather than helped the cause. In 1877 Ahmed departed for the Potteries in order to establish a journal in his father's interest, the *Staffordshire News*. This venture too had little success, and it soon ended, whereupon Ahmed transferred to another local paper. In July 1879 the press reported his death by suicide; but this rumour was a hoax, either self-inspired or an act of enmity. The *Englishman* reported the case in terms sympathetic to Ahmed, but in a codicil to his will of January 1879, Kenealy senior had written of the first-born 'having already received and wasted' more than his share of family wealth—evidence in support of insinuations that Ahmed had used the MCA for his own benefit.

In 1880 Ahmed went to the United States and a happier life. He joined the New York *Herald*, and developed expertise as a journalist of yachting. As such he transferred to the magazine *Outing*, and wrote several books. The first was *Yacht Races for the America's Cup* (1894). Ahmed's preface apologized for lack of literary grace, 'as I was brought up from a boy in the forecastle and so never had the benefit of any book learning'. In fact the style is clear and straight. The next year he published *Boat Sailing in Fair Weather and Foul*, which scored seven editions in a decade; no library appears to hold *Yachting Wrinkles* (1899). One —perhaps confused—reminiscence speaks of 'Captain A. J. Keanealy' working with the New York *Recorder* (which ran from 1891 to 1896) and then, prosperously, with the *World* in that city.[9] Ahmed's address in 1907 was Bath Beach, Long Island; after that year he disappeared from *Who's Who in America,* dying some time before 1915.

'That young rogue Charlemagne' might have been the family's favourite through independence of temperament and his bright remarks, but this happiness dimmed with time. When the MCA split into fragments, Charlemagne like Ahmed acted on his father's behalf—and he also incurred suspicion as to his good faith and probity. Moreover the codicil of January 1879 joined him with Ahmed in his father's condemnation. The parallel continued as Charlemagne left England for Cape Colony, South Africa in 1879. On the way he edited the ship's newspaper. Charlemagne became 'a sedate magistrate' at the Cape, but returned to England before his death in June 1922. He sired four children including an Edward.

Maurice was perhaps the most appealing member of the family. For him above all the father's involvement with the Tichborne case was cataclysmic:

it seems to me to be the first thing in life which I remember. The trifling episodes of my first decade are virtually forgotten, The Claimant, his personality, and his wonderful doings having wholly effaced them. Life, indeed, seems to date for me from that morning, early in March, 1873, when Lord Rivers called upon my father . . .[10]

As Maurice was born in 1858 this might have stretched the bow, yet the enthusiasm of adolescence probably did make the case more gigantic for him than for the others. During the trial he and his mother devilled for Kenealy; afterwards he assisted in public meetings and with the *Englishman,* the copyright of which he technically owned by September 1875. Perhaps his organizing skill made possible the massive achievement of publishing *The Trial.* His father responded: the codicil provided that should Elizabeth die without a will, this son should look after the family property, the testator declaring that 'I am sure that Maurice will do what is right just and honourable'.

After Kenealy's death Maurice kept the *Englishman* and the MCA alive, and his political activity expressed genuine humanitarianism and concern for civil liberty. He appeared on the Claimant's platform after the latter's release, but emigrated to North America soon afterwards. Altogether he spent thirteen years in Canada, Mexico and the United States, earning a living as a journalist, and never forgetting the Tichborne mystery. Maurice retained some of his father's papers, especially those concerning the case. From these and from Kenealy's annotated copy of *The Trial* (which Hillyear held) he prepared several articles for the *Weekly Dispatch* in 1907. They in turn became the basis for a book, *The Tichborne Tragedy* (1913). While uncritical in sup-

port of the Claimant, it was a good book; as a study of the case it
is excelled only by Woodruff's. Maurice died in 1921, falling from
the cliffs at Rottingdean. He had gone to gaze at those seas on
which his father so often brooded; it was the eve of the twenty-
third All Fools' Day since the Claimant's death. If ever ghosts
walked, they surely did on the Sussex coast that night. In 1937
A. H. Spencer, a Melbourne bookseller, purchased in London those
Kenealy papers—all of the 1870s, and nearly all concerned with
the case—which are now in the Dixson Library, Sydney.[11]
Maurice's notes for *The Tichborne Tragedy* were among them,
and evidently they derived from his estate. He left no immediate
family, bequeathing all property to his brothers' children.

While Maurice had appeal, Alexander excelled in talent;
whereas Tichborne affairs absorbed one, they scarcely affected the
other. Alex's only major appearance in the *Englishman* before
1880 concerned his being involved in a teenage brawl. He later
described himself as educated at University College school, London, and at Guines, France, and as a graduate of the University of
France. This is rather mysterious. If Alex was not prevaricating,
he must have been precocious, for 1882 saw him in New York
employed on the *Herald*, presumably in company with Ahmed.
Soon Alex moved on to Philadelphia.[12] Between 1884 and 1886
he contributed a few articles to the *Englishman*. The most interesting alleged that John L. Sullivan was drunk at one of his
great prize-fights, with Charles Mitchell; this, Alex wrongly forecast, would end Sullivan's career. He wrote too of the death of
Allan Pinkerton, detective and strike-breaker, stressing the man's
'personal audacity' and 'skill in organization'. Generally these
articles criticized American life, while expressing the hope that
the New World might prove happier than the Old.

Alex returned to the New York *Herald* from 1887 to 1895, and
began to rise in his profession. He joined R. E. Peary's Arctic
expedition of 1891, his reports appearing in the Chicago *Tribune*
as well as the *Herald*; Peary's account indicates personal friendship with Alex, who helped with the scientific work.[13] Other
journalistic highlights were natural disasters and labour riots, including that at Homestead in 1892. Terms as *Herald* correspondent in both Paris and London must have added to life's pleasure.
However Alex left the *Herald* in mid-decade to join the New York
World, bastion of Joseph Pulitzer's empire, then moving into total
war with W. R. Hearst's publications. His particular task was to
edit a comic section of the Sunday *World*, directed by Arthur
Brisbane, who was the popular journalist supreme and also the

son of a famous visionary. Circulation boomed, despite the protest of conservatives and critics. The term 'yellow press' came into use in condemning the journal, the inspiration being the comic's colour. Pulitzer put some restraint on Brisbane, who went over to Hearst in 1897.[14]

Alex stayed with the *World*, and soon the Spanish-American war of 1898 afforded excitement and—judging from his *Who's Who in America* entry—pride.[15] In charge of a despatch boat throughout, he took part in several major incidents. The first offensive action of the American army was to land a group of insurgent Cubans on 3 May; Kenealy reported the story. He came under fire several times. His team, which included Stephen Crane, landed near Santiago early in June and over its camp raised both the flag of Cuba and the banner of the *World*. The Society of the Caribbean, as the international correspondents called themselves, elected Kenealy as their president. Back in civil life, he had a term on Hearst's New York *Journal* before returning to Britain in 1901 as news editor of the *Daily Express*.

In the early years of the new century Alex wrote two books: *The Letters of Alphonse le Mouton* (New York, 1901) and *The Preposterous Yankee* by 'Montague Vernon Ponsonby, Esq.' (London, 1903). No library appears to hold the former. It might have had the same remarkable character as did the work of 'Ponsonby'. Maybe this latter pen-name was part of a hoax, satiricially designed to indulge the conventional Englishman in all his strongest prejudices against the United States. Yet the book is so vehement that the reader can scarcely believe that the author was not giving his own opinions. 'Everywhere is sham'; 'a jerry-built nation'; 'the absolute ignorance of the people'—these were characteristic phrases. In terms somewhat anticipatory of H. L. Mencken's, 'Ponsonby' traced much absurdity to the nation's democratic pretensions, especially the Declaration of Independence:

This nonsensical document, written by democrats for the consumption of country louts, recites the absurd creed that all persons are born free and equal. Of course, since the world began, no person ever was born free, and no person ever was born equal; but the preposterous Yankee imagines that he believes in this freedom and equality nonsense . . .

Belief or pseudo-belief in the declaration opened the way for the 'crank', another bane of the land. 'He is not controlled by any sense of responsibility, by any considerations of heredity, nor by matters of custom or tradition'. In his foolish arrogance, claiming superiority over God and nature, the crank opposed and criticized all, threatening red ruin.

Many aspects of American life came under similar fire. The typical child was a terrorist monster, beyond parental control because parents had themselves never grown into adults. Marriage, especially in California, was often despised, while 'queer' unions produced degenerates. 'It is natural that a nation of neuters should attach little importance to the marriage tie', and so divorce boomed. Shocking diet lifted the death-rate, while quackery dominated medicine. Most interesting of Alex's railings were those against 'American Yellow Journalism—a Preposterous Institution Which Must Be Kept in its own Country'. Whereas in England a plutocrat turned to cultivation of a gentlemanly style, in the United States he started a yellow journal; 'he fills it full of slanderous libels, prevarications, and what he calls "exposures" '.

While critical of democracy, 'Ponsonby' upheld social reform. Three-quarters of the American people were decent and worthy. 'The millionaires, the society snobs, the swindlers, the boasters, the mediums, the quacks, and the politicians are merely the vermin that live on the sons of the soil and the workers'. But these parasites were intelligent, and had organized themselves into trusts which defended their power. In some ways comparable to Britain's House of Lords, this money-interest was much more effective in barring progress. Men of good heart should not despair however: '*Dives* must be suppressed! If necessary, he must be lynched'.

Back in England, Alex showed his competence on the *Daily Express*. *Who's Who* of these years tells that his hobbies were 'loafing, steamer trips, boating'; he belonged to the British Motor Boat Club. After 1904 he would have had less time to indulge these interests, for now came a decade of eminence in the service of Alfred Harmsworth (Lord Northcliffe from 1905). Whatever 'Ponsonby' thought about the yellow press, Alexander Kenealy became significant in developing its British counterpart. Already a tenuous link joined Northcliffe and the Kenealys: one of the former's early ventures was as British agent for *Outing*, through which Ahmed found his *métier* and which anticipated some aspects of popular-magazine format. The vehicle for Alex's achievement was the *Daily Mirror*, which Northcliffe had begun in October 1903. Over the next few months it lost money at a tremendous rate. In January 1904 Northcliffe sought to regain ground by using illustrations on a grand scale, while in size and style the *Mirror* became Britain's first true tabloid. Hamilton Fyfe was appointed editor, with Alex his assistant; but the latter soon superseded his boss. Circulation rose, and Alex won the tag of 'the man who saved the *Mirror*'.[16] He became a director of the Pictorial Newspaper Company (owner of the *Mirror*), and managing director of *Motoring Illustrated* which promoted another of Northcliffe's interests. He also described himself as proprietor of the *Actor Illustrated*, a monthly which appeared in 1905 and 1906; this may have been a personal venture rather than Northcliffe's.

A mild appearance belied the man's power. Fyfe recalled him as one who got much done without apparent effort; smiling benevolently, he thought out new ideas and tactics to keep the *Mirror* ahead of its rivals. Fyfe stressed that Alex made the pace of sensationalism, with Northcliffe remonstrating that this merely produced 'a good paper for cabmen'. Memoranda from 'Chief' to editor confirm that Kenealy often took a path that Northcliffe opposed. Too much on the suffragettes, railed Northcliffe: too many cricket pictures, obviously faked posters, excessive criticism of African missions.[17] 'Someone told me the other day that your people were all Socialists', he complained in November 1910, in tune with his current objections to the overly political nature of the journal. Yet a few months later, in March 1911, Northcliffe pursued a different tack:

It frequently contains news which is below the intelligence of the average fourth housemaid. You can imagine what educated readers think of it. It often does not contain the news at all.

To such remonstrance the editor answered:

I quite agree with your letter about the bad taste and ignorance of some of the things that appear in the *Daily Mirror*. I have been trying to stop them.

Highly-educated men, I find, as a rule have no sense of news. They always want to write about ancient Rome or what happened to Jupiter. They regard the death of King Edward as unimportant because it is recent. We have Oxford men here and Eton men. None of them can write gramatically or spell, and they are woefully ignorant of anything that has happened since 42 B.C.

I heard one of our Eton young men asking a Board School office boy, who hadn't an 'H' to his name, who 'this man Chamberlain' was. The office boy told him. The Eton man hasn't been with us for some time.

Reminiscences tell that Kenealy's exasperation with Northcliffe sometimes became sharper, even prompting an (undelivered) message that he did not mind criticism, so long as it was intelligent.[18]

The 'square-shaped little fat man' aroused affection and enthusiasm among his staff. Northcliffe himself became a friend, and their respective families accordingly. When the editor fell mortally ill early in 1915, Northcliffe showed concern both before and after his death on 25 June. Three days later the *Mirror* printed a large photograph and a long obituary. It referred to his nickname, 'K': 'to us this abbreviation perhaps shows better than any conventional epitaph we could write, how he stood with us, what we felt for him, how human and live a figure he was in his world, which was the world of the daily journalism he knew and loved so well'. Alex, who had never married, was buried in the family grave at Hangleton. Mrs Kenealy, seven of her children, Northcliffe and two of his brothers, were present. The estate had value of almost £15 000.

Vying with Alex as the most notable Kenealy was the second oldest girl, Arabella Madonna. She certainly was precocious. Before her eighth birthday she was teaching the boys their classics. Her schooling was entirely at home. Kenealy complimented 'Madonna' in one of his most affectionate poems. Possibly she wrote certain articles for the Kenealy press as early as 1875: the appreciation of her father's poetry which pondered the nature of 'vital essence', for example; others that discussed the apparent reduction of fertility in highly educated women, 'kindergarten' care of children, and 'our physical degeneracy' as evident among industrial workers.[19] Further references in the *Englishman* tell of her attendance at the Tichborne demonstration of February 1876, and her helping a bazaar in aid of the cause in 1878.

By then Arabella had begun formal study in medicine. She trained at the London School of Medicine for Women, gaining prizes and certificates on the way. To complete her qualifications, Arabella graduated in 1883 as Licentiate of the Royal College of Physicians at Dublin—which alone in Britain offered such facilities for women, three others having preceded her. She topped the class list and also qualified in midwifery. There was talk of her serving in Egypt and of directing a women's hospital at Bombay. Instead she opened a practice in London, later moving to Watford, Hillyear's domicile. She remained in practice until 1894. That Arabella then forsook the profession accorded with her comparative disinterest in physic and her love of ideas; they were rather novel ideas, moreover, although well within the *Zeitgeist*. Her initial concern was for improving human stock, with particular emphasis on the need for men and women to be absolute in the development of their respective, opposed sexual characteristics. Thus the best mothers were utterly feminine, which quality was more a matter of disposition and spirit than physique. Arabella referred to nervous and psychological factors; she came to scorn positivist 'scientific' medicine. While ever insisting on humanity's need to accord with the dictates of evolution, she saw this process more as 'creative', in the Bergsonian sense, than as Spencerian-determined. Part of woman's greatness was that she had a feeling for intuitive moral truth, in contrast to man's cold intellectualism.

Arabella's concern with the feminity of woman prevailed generally among eugenicists of the day. What distinguished her—although not uniquely, as Havelock Ellis the pioneer sex-researcher and Ellen Key, the Swedish-American novelist were among similar thinkers—was the combining of this emphasis with assertion rather than denial of woman's socio-political rights. Arabella created a massive feminine mystique, but it was generally a mystique of superiority. Yet tension inevitably developed between the feminity theme and the women's movement. Arabella retained some association with the latter until about 1912, but then became very hostile to the militant suffragettes. Thus Arabella illustrated the permanent dilemma of those who advocate the rights of a subordinate group. If stress be put on emulation of the master class, then the subordinates lose their identity—this was the nub of Arabella's charges against militancy. But if differentiation is given first priority, the concept of equality becomes redundant, certainly in practice and even in logic. Differentiation means that one group will be superior to the other, according to the task in hand. Arabella's private life mirrored the dilemma, for she never became a wife and mother and so never won that fulfilment of womanhood which her theory proclaimed.

Around these basic themes, Arabella wrote a great deal over more than fifty years. Whatever the truth as to the early *Englishman* articles, she certainly contributed to the paper in the months following her graduation. Then there was silence, apparently in consequence of professional demands. In November 1890 the *National Review* published an article, 'The Talent of Motherhood', which set the future key-note. Another five major articles over the next twenty years, two manuals edited for a *Women's Home Library* (1905), and an essay, *The Failure of Vivisection and the Future of Medical Research* (1909), comprised a relatively homogeneous cluster of Arabella's writings. Its quality is best exemplified in the essay.

In this work, Arabella attacked vivisection as a symbol of modern medicine, especially its failure to come to terms with the real truth about man. 'Every day are being more and more realized (outside Medical Science) the complex nature of man's constitution, the mysterious and incalculable forces with which it is instinct, the immense influence which the mind and environment exert upon physical health'. Developing her argument, Arabella invoked the concept of a 'physical conscience'. This was a force within the human constitution that aspired to lift individual and race to a higher physical level, just as did the moral conscience in its plane. This physical conscience had sway over the whole body; doctors were mistaken in treating particular maladies without awareness of this unity. Localized illnesses often benefited the whole body. Conversely, they might be cured and still some essential trouble grow worse. Medicine must not attempt to override nature, but rather allow the latter's 'Schoolhouse of Disease' to teach its lessons. Next Arabella linked nature with morality, insisting that the great advances in medicine had come from moral conceptions rather than from within science itself. The adage that cleanliness lay next to godliness had inspired asepsis; the temperance movement had prompted study of alcohol's ill-effects; and social reformers forced improvements in treating the insane. Yet still medicine sought to deny the fact, attempting for instance 'to defeat the great moral lessons which Nature teaches . . . by inflicting penalties for violation of her laws'. Arabella meant thus to warn against contraception and ready cure of venereal disease. For her, sex had always to be profound. When reduced, such argument would question any use of science against disease, and Arabella went close to this.

Beyond nature and morality lay yet more fundamental truth:

The aim of modern physiologists is to show that in Physiology there is nothing beyond Chemistry and Physics. And yet it is impossible to explain physiological phenomena without admitting another factor—Vital Force. And no doubt this Vital Force it is which makes blood so Protean and mysterious a fluid, deluding our modern physiologists, as in other ages it baffled and deluded necromancers and alchemists a-search for the philosopher's stone.

The historian sees, even more clearly than did the author, a direct line from this assertion to other dicta: that 'the physiological and the psychological are closely allied', that 'the successful physician is . . . the man of sympathy and intuitive power', that 'in the subconscious plane of mind . . . lies the future of Medical Science and of the Healing Art'. For post-Freudians it is also appropriate that Arabella insisted not only on the profundity of sex, but also that its effect upon health—physical, moral and mental—demanded attention. She attacked 'the hoyden girl' who wasted energy in physical exercise precisely at the time of life when she should be storing her forces, ready for the great task of motherhood. The essay's climax was to call for abandonment of positivist medicine so that man could work with nature to lift his race higher on the evolutionary scale. Arabella did not claim that she had revealed the final mysteries. But one day a second Newton might do so.

Several of the most popular novelists of the twentieth century have had medical backgrounds; the new psychology has found more lucrative and more effective expression in fiction than elsewhere. Arabella was among the first to illustrate these trends. Her novels are interesting not because they show a different side of her, but because their message mirrors that of her journalism. Blood, sex, soul and nature—these will always make keen fiction. D. H. Lawrence was the outstanding exemplar of the rule in contemporary Britain, and Arabella was a lending-library Lawrence. Her description was often vivid, her portrayal of social background acute. Most characters were credible, but the weak plots tended to absurdity and melodrama of novelette type.

Arabella evidently began writing fiction in the late eighties. In May 1890 George Meredith read a manuscript for Chapman & Hall, and two others soon followed. 'Miss Kenealy's book, *Phyllis* (Dr Kenealy I should say) is not of a kind to win the public', he wrote in April 1892;[20] she was 'clever' but had not the skill to influence the reader as she wished. A few weeks later Meredith's comments on *Molly and her Man of War* were yet sharper. However, in 1893 both *Molly* and *Dr Janet of Harley Street* achieved publication, by Bentley and Digby & Long respectively. By 1917 Arabella had published twenty-one novels and three collections of stories, fat volumes all. Publishers ranged from the obscure to Hutchinson, Paul, and, despite Meredith, Chapman. Several of the books were reprinted or had variant editions in Britain, and at least four found American publication. The quality of the oeuvre was even, and any selection would fairly represent it.

A Semi-Detached Marriage was published by Hutchinson in 1899, and had 432 octavo pages. The title anticipated, perhaps inspired, Edith Ellis's description of her union with Havelock. Dedication was 'To The Best Of Mothers', although in fact Elizabeth was not so utterly feminine as her daughter's prescription required. The story was a romantic melodrama. The heroine, Celia, enjoyed that physical beauty which should be the birthright of all but which industrial civilization was denying to its subjects. She was 'like a white flower . . . a flower which love should some day gather for the uses of the race'. From her father Celia inherited an ammunition factory, and managed it herself; Arabella's descriptions of 'this dire Moloch of Demolition' were powerful. Two men came into Celia's life: anti-hero, Coyle, and hero, Strahan. For the one she felt passion, for the other love. But Strahan apparently had a wife, so passion won and Celia married Coyle, accepting his demand that they maintain separate homes. Marriage fulfilled the woman's beauty, but the living arrangements soon proved unbearable: 'I have been my husband's mistress—not his wife'. Coyle bowed to her protest, but soon his villainy appeared. He took her money, and she discovered his crippled child in the attic. Strahan's 'wife' died, and it transpired that in fact the woman had been married to Coyle. Released from her marital bondage, Celia turned to Strahan, but then found herself pregnant by Coyle. Strahan renounced his love, and Coyle remarried Celia. The factory exploded: Strahan's bravery prevented cataclysm but Coyle was killed. True love triumphed.

While the story creaked along, Arabella played with her favourite ideas, especially the role and relationship of the two sexes. Discussion of experimental marriage belonged here: part of Coyle's villainy was in demanding semi-detachment. While a villain, he was yet a true man—intellectual, harsh, even cruel. He would have put his crippled son into a 'lethal chamber', and likewise treat all defectives; for him charity was an evil, sustaining those whom life had beaten. The man, Coyle, thus represented Spencerian evolution; Celia, on the other hand, did not allow harsh intellect to deny intuitive sympathy and feeling for right and wrong. This feminity put her, rather than Coyle, on the side of 'evolving consciousness'. Yet Coyle's behaviour was right *for a man*. In an aside, Arabella remarked that 'I confess to despising a man who is incapable of feeling murderous'; and her last novels, written in the war years, were not to confess but rather to exalt such attitudes. Conversely, Celia herself fell short of total feminity, and paid the price. In pursuit of woman's rights she took over the munition factory, and initially accepted the horror of 'semi-detached marriage'. Her shallowness, Arabella suggested, may have prevented her from bestowing on her son the full masculinity of his father's intellect. Yet the book also expressed women's grievances in a conventional feminist manner.

Reviews of *A Semi-Detached Marriage* illustrated the generally favourable reception enjoyed by Arabella's early books. The occasion prompted *Literature* (a *Times* subsidiary) to remark that 'among the score or so of women novelists who are producing really sane and successful work, Miss Arabella Kenealy impresses one specially as a writer with brains'. The reviewer had some misgivings about her views on the woman question, but found 'verve . . . originality . . . power . . . vivid, clear-cut presentment'.[21] The *Bookman* thought the wit and brilliance so constant that they became monotonous. More realistically, the *Academy* criticized the plot as melodramatic, but placed the book above the range of library fiction. No later work received such extended notice in the ranking journals: probably the critics' taste changed, while Arabella's style—and her audience—stood fixed.

In 1908 appeared *Memoirs of Edward Vaughan Kenealy LL.D.* 'by His Daughter Arabella Kenealy'. It consisted primarily of the autobiography, with snippets from diary and correspondence; perhaps many of these papers then went into the fire. Arabella and her mother provided recollection and comment. The book was of some interest and had good passages. Arabella wrote well about the Tichborne case itself, taking a broader view than did Maurice for example:

in its rushing and conflicting currents were excited every sort of human passion; prejudice, justice, anger, bitterness, heroic disinterestedness, sordid cupidity, ambition, devotion, cowardice, courage—in a word, every man's strength or weakness—the whole gamut of human motive and emotion raging and swirling about one large, melancholy, monstrous, mysterious Figure.

(Her plots had the same sublime absurdity as the Claimant's career.) But the *Memoirs* rarely achieved this standard. Very much the work of piety, they glossed over the uglier parts of Kenealy's life, ignoring the most revealing passages of his correspondence and even the agony of 1850, as the autobiography published by the *Englishman* in 1880 had not. Arabella professed to believe that but for the Tichborne case her father would have become an eminent judge.

The journals were divided in their reception of the book. At one extreme the *Academy* complimented Arabella's editing and remarked that the excerpts of Kenealy poetry, 'if not of the highest literary merit, are quite startlingly refreshing in their way'.[22] The *Irish Law Times* hailed this 'biography of a great advocate'. But the *Times Literary Supplement* and the *Athenaeum* pointed to factual and other weaknesses. Old hate-fear echoed as the *Times Literary Supplement* insisted that Kenealy was a crank, in both his philosophy and his life, and that the Stoke election 'for a time did more harm to the democratic cause than anything that ever happened in this country'. The authoress answered such criticism with more heat than effect. However, she did advance strong evidence for her claim that John Bright *had* offered to introduce Kenealy into the House of Commons well before the newcomer appeared at the Speaker's table.

In 1920 and 1934 Arabella published two works of commentary-cum-speculation, *Feminism and Sex-Extinction* and *The Human Gyroscope*. The title of the former bespoke its theme: a denunciation of the militant suffragette movement for having perverted the cause of woman by attempting to minimize sexual differentiation and therefore denying the feminine capacity to sustain higher values. The temper of the times appeared in Arabella's diatribes against socialism, anarchism and Bolshevism. *The Human Gyroscope* redeemed the half-promise of the 1909 essay that the author might some day unlock the secret of evolution. In very opaque prose she argued that gravity and rotation had moulded living forms into human shape. This was super-positivism, apparently reversing the Bergsonian emphasis of earlier years. But Araballa went on to stress that this physical process was but part of the whole; the interaction of male and female had injected spirituality into the story, with woman playing the nobler part. So repetition rather than novelty characterized this work.

It had some interesting by-ways, however. More clearly than ever before, Arabella presented her view of the ideal society: all should have decent living conditions, but differentiation of individuals, classes, race, as well as sex, should prevail, in rejection of the current trend towards homogeneity. The world was in a fearful state, evolution's trend notwithstanding. Violence had become the norm, largely because women had aped masculinity. The sickness applied at every international level, from politics to sport; bodyline bowling was one sign of the violent times. (From a woman of seventy-five this was an interesting thought.) Over-education was another contemporary ill, as teachers stifled that 'natural faculty' which inspired creative effort. The text referred specifically to Bergson, Freud and Jung, and developed its own version of a collective unconscious. This led in turn to Arabella's vindication of telepathy, supported by personal experiences including communication with her late fiancé, both before and after his death. Another personal note was the book's dedication to Alex, 'in affectionate remembrance of his sterling lovable character and brilliant intellect'.

Arabella died on 18 November 1938 at Portland Place, London. She left over £45 000. Having inherited from Alex and from her sister Katherine, who died in 1934, Arabella's will was scrupulous in redistributing 'the family finances'. Bequests went to widows of her brothers Edward and Noel, and to Charlemagne's children and their offspring, while the residuary legatees were her remaining niece and three nephews—progeny of Edward and Noel. The last of Kenealy's children to die, Arabella also chose Hangleton as her burial-place. Altogether the churchyard holds four Kenealy tombs, housing husband, wife and seven children.

To trace Arabella's influence would entail much work and some reward. No major library in Australia holds her novels today, yet by 1915 came a call from Australia from one W. J. Chidley. He sought endorsement of his answer to the world's troubles: that man forswear erection and have intercourse only when his mate's vagina drew him, inert. Chidley also sought backing from Havelock Ellis, who praised the reformer's autobiography as a major literary, social and sexual document, but spurned his nostrum. Arabella saw in it some good: 'sex should be duly and properly cultivated in woman, not suppressed and dwarfed as it is liable to be under our present upbringing'.[23] In 1926, W. S. Sonnenschein included *Feminism and Sex-Extinction* among his *Best Books* on sex. That work also had praise from A. M. Ludovici whose *Enemies of Women* (1948) argued very similarly, as part of a latter-day Nietzschean crusade. *The Human Gyroscope* likewise appealed to a neo-Bergsonian, G. C. Bowden, author of *F. Matthias Alexander and the Creative Advance of the Individual* (1965). Bowden saw Arabella as echoing Alexander's message— favoured also by Ludovici and others more famous, including John Dewey, Aldous Huxley, G. B. Shaw and William Temple— that man's psychic and bodily ills resulted from bad posture.

Annesley Kenealy suffered the curse of having aspirations similar to those of her siblings, but far less ability. Whereas Arabella became a doctor, she qualified as a nurse. An *Englishman* report of May 1886 told that Annesley, a 'remarkably handsome type of the higher class of young English women' was in Philadelphia— presumably following Alex—as matron of an orthopaedic hospital. A home-nursing manual she published in 1893 was sensible, and indicated that she had won professional status in London. But in time, Annesley took to journalism, 'the most fascinating though the most strenuous branch of the world's work'.[24] From early in the new century she worked for the domestic magazine *Lone Chat*, and did other freelancing including a spell on Northcliffe's *Daily Mail*. For Northcliffe himself, Annesley had an infatuation, which ended in anger; there is even a suggestion that she attempted suicide. Early in 1910 Annesley sued Northcliffe for wrongful dismissal from the *Daily Mail*.[25] This resulted, she said, from her criticism of vivisection, while the defence argued that general eccentricity was the cause. Annesley admitted having 'threatened that she would go to every meeting of the anti-vivisectionists, suffragists, and unemployed and make it a labour question'. Northcliffe disparaged Annesley's claim to have had an important post on the *Daily Mail*, in charge of women's and social issues; he admitted having been interested in one of her articles— on juvenile prisons—but insisted that he employed her out of benevolence to the family. The case divided the Kenealys: Arabella and Henrietta gave evidence in Annesley's favour, but she was estranged from Alex (although—as Arabella virtually announced in court—he had resisted Northcliffe's pressure to silence the litigant). The judge intervened to save one witness from what he termed Annesley's 'vivisection', and the jury quickly decided against her.

Frustrated in love and journalism, Annesley produced some books. They were *Thus Saith Mrs Grundy* (1911); *A Modern Magdalen* (advertised 1911; probably not published); *The Poodle Woman. A Story of 'restitution of conjugal rights'* (1913); *A 'Water-Fly's' Wooing: A Drama in Black and White Marriages* (1914), and *'Do the Dead Know?'* (1916). Annesley's themes were plagiarized from Arabella, save that in her case the feminine mystique mattered less and everything else mattered more. Especially was she more ardent in support of women's rights. *The Poodle Woman* was first in a projected series of 'Votes for Women Novels' which she herself had persuaded Stanley Paul to publish. She sat on the committee of the Women Writers' Suffrage League.[26] All her work was heavily didactic: against the marriage laws, against a code which prescribed different rules for the two sexes, against poverty, against Little Englandism, against the middle class, against the classics (Virgil and Homer presented women falsely), against almost everything.

It is hard to decide which book is the oddest and worst. *Mrs Grundy* was extraordinarily turgid, the story-line submerged in floods of rhetoric which primarily concerned prostitution. On one hand Annesley defended, or even exalted, prostitution as the product of that passion which England feared and shunned—to the nation's cost; on the other she saw it as a nasty product of double sexual standard and capitalist exploitation. The protagonist of *The Poodle Woman* was Mrs Hawk-Hawkings, an upper-middle-class lady of debased morality: 'filled as she was with the goulish instinct of her type to prey upon the homes and happiness of other women, Mrs Hawkings was a bitter enemy to the high-aiming Feminist movement'. '*Water-Fly*' took its name from Annesley's term for half-caste; she was very fashionable in her slang. The book berated miscegenation, with a vehemence extreme even in that peak age of Anglo-Saxon racism:

Pure-bred, black-skinned men have often shown themselves to be noble and brave. They did so in the Indian Mutiny. Some negroes have been men of fine character. But the half-breed—never. He has the vices of the black and white races, and the virtues of neither. He is a crime against nature.

But, alas, English girls were tumbling into the lustful arms of colonial 'dusky sons' who came to London (Kensington saw the problem at its most rampant); hence the rot of empire threatened. Annesley's last novel avoided ideology and politics but excelled in macabre fantasy: the heroine revived from apparent death, escaped from the coffin, and saw her world through spectral eyes.

Annesley returned to the courts late in 1915, suing W. H. Smith & Sons for having slandered '*Water-Fly*' by putting it among their immoral books.[27] Conducting her own case, Annesley opened with a 100-minute speech. She claimed that the novel had sold 75 000 copies as a *Tit-Bits* serial, but that Smith's action had stopped her income. All this, she alleged, was in revenge of her father's criticism of Smith's for not selling the *Englishman*. Defending counsel quoted *Mrs Grundy* and *The Poodle Woman* to show Annesley's scorn of marital obligations. 'Do you think that those books are fit to fall into the hands of young girls?', he asked. Yes, replied Annesley, she wished they would read more of them. That the cover of '*Water-Fly*' showed a black man and a white girl embracing was presented as an incitement rather than as the doom-threat it was. The judge was B. J. S. Coleridge, son and heir of the Claimant's antagonist. He ruled that there was no case for the jury to consider, upon which Annesley rose and announced that she had taken poison. She collapsed, and a few days later appeared in a lower court charged with attempted suicide. Evidence that the incident was a stunt aroused her anger and honour. Annesley was released on her brother's paying a £50 bond for good behaviour over the next six months.

Litigation alone distinguished Annesley's last years. In 1918 one William Chorley, proprietor of an old persons' home, won £500 damages in consequence of her allegations—themselves part of a general harassment—that he ill-treated patients. The cost may have bankrupted Annesley; she was on suspended discharge from that state when her mother drew up a will in February 1919. Her next victim was her brother Edward, whom she accused of stealing family property and maintaining a bastard. She died in October 1926. Her estate had a gross value of over £12 000, a very surprising amount. Henrietta was to enjoy life interest in the property, but on her death it should endow two funds: one, 'In Memorial of Elizabeth Kenealy, the Mother of Many Writers', to maintain a ward at the Royal Free Hospital; the other, the 'Annesley Kenealy Bequest' to be distributed by the Royal Literary Fund among needy women writers. In the event, Henrietta arranged that a bed at the hospital commemorate Annesley herself, while the literary fund declined its bequest.[28]

Less is known of the other children. Henrietta may have been the still-centre of the family, a true eldest daughter. To her, 'whose unfailing affection has been one of the best things in my life', Annesley not only left money but dedicated '*Water-Fly*'. Not one of the sisters married. The mother's will implied that Isabel—conceived in the final weeks of the criminal trial and born as her father's fame reached its peak—was mentally defective. Edward and Noel were primarily journalists, both working at one time with *Motoring Illustrated*.[29] Perhaps they rode on Alex's wagon, although Noel at least had some ability. He studied art at the Slade and other schools, and his engravings were exhibited at the Royal Academy in 1891, 1892 and 1893. Married in 1905, Noel also lived in Watford; *Who's Who* described him as editor of periodicals dealing with automobilism, adviser on art matters, founder of the Hertfordshire Automobile Club and of the British

Motor Boat Club (Alex's only club allegiance). Noel died in December 1918; both he and Edward had at least two children. The youngest brother, Arthur, had died before 1915. Edward Hyde never returned to the historical record after the storm of 1850.

The above biographies not only have intrinsic interest, but fulfil Kenealy's own story. Annesley smote her father's ghost when attacking Homer and Virgil; Noel's art obviously derived from his mother. With such small exceptions, the children stayed true to their paternity. This applied even to trivia: Alex owned *Actor Illustrated* sixty years after Kenealy's stage-struck phase; Edward junior had his own bastard scandal; Arabella denounced bodyline just as the *Englishman's Magazine* lamented professionalism in cricket. But it went much deeper. To interpret the children's lives risks distortion, but this is the father's biography.

The family was introverted, notwithstanding Annesley's quarrels with her brothers. For kindred to dedicate books to each other is common enough; as is following the same profession, or sharing ideas, wealth and the tomb. But the clustering of such features is noteworthy. The Kenealys' low marriage rate and fertility bears out the impression that generally they were happier with each other than with outsiders. To have been the child of Dr Kenealy was probably a badge of differentiation, even before Tichborne times. The force of the man's personality must have created an unusual domestic atmosphere. The boys escaped, in some degree, by migrating; but the girls stayed behind and remained Kenealys all their days. Moreover the children followed their father's path to eccentricity. Whatever Isabel's deficiency, Annesley would seem to have been unbalanced, at least in later years. Arabella was scarcely that, but the gap between the feminine mystique which she preached and the barren spinsterdom of her practice must have been the cause and result of considerable tension. Alex's diatribe as 'Ponsonby' against the yellow press, and his service to it as aide of Pulitzer, Hearst and Northcliffe, was a similar phenomenon.

Yet the inheritance included ability, even brilliance. Annesley emulated Kenealy's ability at giving 'a slashing speech' in court, while—strange episode though it was—his own joust with medical studies set the pattern for Arabella's and Annesley's achievements. He left a greater legacy as wielder of the pen than of the scalpel. 'The man who saved the *Mirror*' was truly a son of him who directed the *Englishman*, with its vast sale and its fierce power to shock the bourgeoisie. Those good Tichbornites, the cabmen, must have bought the *Englishman*, and Alex—so Northcliffe complained—met their taste a generation later. The new press talked about sport more than law suits or politics, and as much about sportsmen as criminals. But thirty years on, the Claimant, with that splendid pigeon-shooting eye of his, would have won fame as a professional athlete, his exploits maybe selling an unprecedented number of newspapers just as the criminal trial did in its day. Ahmed rang the changes with equal harmony: whereas love of the sea was Kenealy's poetic inspiration, it became the livelihood of this son, as sailor and sporting journalist.

The children's more ambitious writing was equally true to the Kenealy tradition. Sex, procreation, passion, exploration of the psyche and spirit—most poetry and fiction draw upon these themes, but the link between Kenealy's use of them and his daughters' was markedly direct. His worship of nature had its equivalent in Arabella's equation of nature with morality and her insistence that from it came better healing than that of medical science. Father and daughter both scorned intellect and positivist science as against intuition and emotion. As counsel for the Claimant and for the Dowager's memory, Kenealy developed a version of feminine mystique which his daughters generalized and expanded. Arabella, and to a lesser extent Annesley, also joined their father in seeking absolute answers to life's issues. When writing the *Memoirs* in 1908 Arabella condescended somewhat to his metaphysical ponderings, but *The Human Gyroscope* had the same tortured mysticism, the same conglomerate of quotations, the same mixture of banality and ambition.

In political terms Kenealy and his children were critics of social wrong; their responses to it were later to coalesce as fascism. Kenealy's protests against the ills of his world had their counterpart in the books and journalism of Alex and Annesley. The three offered similar remedies. Kenealy wanted a populist republic, with himself as leader. Alex, as 'Ponsonby', made a similar diagnosis of American society as that propounded by his fellow-hero of the war of 1898, Theodore Roosevelt; and as editor of the *Daily Mirror* he was to apply similar rhetoric to Britain, especially to aid in the war-time rise of Kenealy's erstwhile admirer, David Lloyd George. Annesley wanted the master race to achieve a new intensity of imperialism and social reform. In retrospect all these ideas have a fascist tang. To say this means not that the Kenealys would have supervised the Nazi gas ovens, but that they rejected liberal-democratic capitalism, and hoped for some strong-armed elite to guide the worthy but inert masses into a happier future. Those Kenealyesque heroes, Roosevelt and Lloyd George, were Mussolini's English-speaking counterparts. Alex's work for the popular press, using propagandist techniques, strengthened the family's contribution to proto-fascism; so did Arabella's contempt of egalitarian homogeneity, intellect and science, her sympathy for eugenics, and her hatred of Bolsheviks.

To end on this note is indeed to confirm Shakespeare's adage about man's posthumous fate. Yet it accords too with Kenealy's whole story. Tragi-comic absurdity was his life's consistent theme, and the children fulfilled their heritage in playing some small part in the madness of the early twentieth century. The historian can enjoy the congruence, and bestow some pity.

NOTES

AUTHOR'S NOTE

[1] Letter to G. Onslow, evidently mid-1877, Dixson papers 248; *Commons Debates*, 9 Feb. 1877.

1 KENEALY

[1] C. G. Duffy, *Four Years of Irish History* (London, 1883), p. 423.
[2] A Kenealy, *Memoirs of Edward Vaughan Kenealy LL.D.*, p. 28. This is the chief source for the following paragraphs and generally for Kenealy's life to 1860.
[3] Memo, Aug. 1845, Huntington papers.
[4] A printed version is among the Huntington papers, but its provenance is not indicated.
[5] Letter, 12 Dec. 1840, Huntington papers. Unless otherwise indicated, all Kenealy correspondence of the 1840s derives from this source. References are given only in cases of particular importance.
[6] Letter, 27 Dec. 1840.
[7] The Huntington papers document this, and much else of Kenealy's early literary career.
[8] Kenealy's relations with Bentley are documented in both the Huntington and Bentley papers. For assistance concerning the latter, I thank Dr Scott Bennett, University of Illinois.
[9] This is the most important point at which the version of Kenealy's autobiography published in *Memoirs* must be supplemented by the fuller account given in the *Englishman* after his death. The issues for Oct. 1880 relate to this passage.
[10] The Bagshawe papers also complement Huntington material.
[11] E. Downey, *Charles Lever. His Life in his Letters* (2 vols, Edinburgh, 1906), vol. 1, pp. 183-4.
[12] M. A. Oliphant, *William Blackwood and his Sons* (3 vols, Edinburgh, 1897-8), vol. 2, p. 360.
[13] M. H. Spielmann, *The History of 'Punch'* (London, 1895), p. 336.
[14] The slip remains in a copy held by the University of Cambridge Library.
[15] Vol. 7, pp. 173-4.
[16] *Critical Dictionary of English Literature* (3 vols, Philadelphia, 1859), under name.

17 *Mainly Victorian* (London, 1925?), pp. 174-7.
18 July-Dec. 1845, p. 11.
19 Letter to T. J. Ouseley, 3 Sept. 1844.
20 The address was published contemporaneously: see Bibliography.
21 *Cork Constitution*, 18 Sept. 1845. For assistance with Cork sources, I thank Mr David Barry of that city.
22 Address to Kenealy, Huntington papers.
23 J. McCarthy, *The Story of an Irishman* (London, 1904), p. 38. McCarthy's chronology is somewhat awry.
24 *Memoirs*, pp. 113-14; the daguerrotype faces p. 114 there. See plate facing p. 18.
25 Memoranda concerning Kenealy held by National Library of Ireland, Dublin.
26 *Four Years*, pp. 422-3. The attack on Davis occurred in Kenealy's article on Maclise, for which see Bibliography.
27 Letter, 22 Jan. 1848.
28 The *Times* reported the case, 10, 11 July 1848.
29 *Englishman*, 30 Apr. 1881.
30 J. Macdonnell and J. E. P. Wallis (eds), *Reports of State Trials. New Series* (8 vols, London, 1888-98), vol. 8, pp. 381-466.
31 Cork newspapers reported his campaign; the quotations are from *Examiner*, 8 Oct. 1849 and *Constitution*, 3 Nov. 1849. See also *Memoirs*, p. 129.
32 'Dublin University Magazine', *Bibliographical Society of Ireland Publications*, vol. 5, 1938, pp. 59-81, at p. 76.
33 16 Feb. 1850; the *Times* fully reported the subsequent proceedings.
34 Jan.-June 1850, p. 90.
35 *Englishman*, 9, 16 Oct. 1880.
36 [H. W. Lucy], 'The Member for Stoke', *Gentleman's Magazine*, vol. 14, 1875, pp. 698-709, at p. 701; I cannot find the reference in *Punch* to which Lucy attributes the story.
37 Quotations are from pp. 113, 153, 380.
38 Vol. 36, p. 583.
39 The diary merges with the autobiography in the 1850s, as presented both in *Memoirs* and the *Englishman*; other pertinent documentation comes at the end, chronologically, of the Huntington papers.
40 E. F. L. Gower, *Bygone Years* (London, 1905), p. 59; W. W. Vernon, *Recollections of Seventytwo Years* (London, 1917), p. 206; R. E. Francillon, *Mid-Victorian Memories* (London, n.d.), p. 122.
41 *Memoirs*, especially pp. 151-60, give some information on this story, but most derives from the Beaconsfield papers. Relevant letters from Kenealy are dated 15 Jan. 1851 (mis-dated 1850), 25 Feb., 21 Oct., 5 Nov. 1852, 20 Sept. 1853. The *Press* has a series to itself: see especially Lucas to Disraeli, 20 Oct. 1853.
42 *Tablet*, 5, 26 Apr. 1856; see also *Law Times*, 6 Dec. 1873, and letters from Ouseley, 24 Mar., 25 Apr. 1856.
43 The pamphlet is republished in G. H. Knott and E. R. Watson, *Trial of William Palmer* (London, 1952), appendix 1.
44 M. S. Hardcastle, *Life of John, Lord Campbell* . . . (2 vols, London, 1881), vol. 2, p. 345.
45 21 June 1856; the *Times* commented 5 June 1856.
46 Letter, 14 May 1858, Beaconsfield papers; see also that of 27 Feb. 1858.
47 *Englishman*, 17 Jan. 1880.
48 Knott and Watson, *Trial of William Palmer*, p. x.
49 M. Horgan, *Cahir Conri* (Cork, 1860).
50 In *The Prayers, Meditations and Visions of Kenealy (Imaum Mahidi)*, and *Englishman*, generally.

[51] Letter, 26 Oct. 1866, Beaconsfield papers.
[52] 17 Jan., 19 Dec. 1863.
[53] T. H. L. Leary, 'Dr Kenealy as a Poet', *Gentleman's Magazine*, vol. 12, 1874, pp. 220-7, especially pp. 222-4.
[54] *Memoirs*, p. 211.
[55] Notation on Kenealy's letter, 12 Oct. 1866, Beaconsfield papers; see also letters, 18, 24, 26 Oct. 1866.
[56] G. A. H. Sala, *The Life and Adventures of George Augustus Sala, Written by Himself* (2 vols, London, 1895), vol. 2, pp. 272-3.
[57] Letter, 6 Mar. 1867, Beaconsfield papers.
[58] *Englishman*, 17, 24 Jan. 1880; J. F. Ede, *History of Wednesbury* (Wednesbury, 1962), p. 360; D. C. Murray, *Recollections* (London, 1908), p. 68.
[59] The *Times*, 2 Feb. 1869.
[60] Ibid., 23 Dec. 1869.
[61] 25 Dec. 1869.
[62] *Law Journal*, 1 Jan. 1870. Finlason's book was *A Report of the Case of the Queen v. Gurney and Others* (London, 1870).
[63] *Englishman*, 4 Dec. 1880; E. H. Coleridge, *Life and Correspondence of John Duke Lord Coleridge* (2 vols, London, 1904), vol. 2, p. 150.
[64] Dixson papers 249.
[65] *Enoch, the Second Messenger of God*, vol. 1, p. xv.
[66] *Apocalypse*, p. 340.
[67] Ibid., p. 636; the subsequent quotations are from pp. 81-2, 6.
[68] *Memoirs*, p. 244.

2 THE TICHBORNE CAUSE

[1] Douglas Woodruff made available to me his copy of the Australian Commission (In the Court of Common Pleas. Tichborne vs Lushington), and the University of Tasmania Library holds a microfilm copy.
[2] J. Holmes to A. Norris, 16 Nov. 1867, Dixson papers 259.
[3] There is a 6 vol. version, Tichborne vs Lushington. The set used was that in the University of Cambridge Library.
[4] Correspondence, especially Kenealy's letter, 11 Apr. 1873, Dixson papers 249.
[5] *Law Journal*, 14 July 1871; for following verses, M. E. Kenealy, *The Tichborne Tragedy* (London, 1913), pp. 90-1.
[6] 21 Feb. 1872.
[7] E. Partridge, *A Dictionary of Slang and Unconventional English* (London, 1937).
[8] C. McInnes, *Sweet Saturday Night* (London, 1967), p. 92. The baby was Harry Relph, later to become famous in the music halls as 'Little Tich'.
[9] An example is in D. Woodruff, *The Tichborne Claimant* (London, 1957), p. 319. There is a good collection in Dixson papers 256.
[10] Dixson papers 256.
[11] J. F. Stottlar, 'A Victorian Stage Censor', *Victorian Studies*, vol. 13, 1970, pp. 253-82, at p. 273.
[12] Cutting in Maugham scrapbook, Lincoln's Inn papers.
[13] These examples come from Dixson papers 256 and from the British Museum ephemera.
[14] The Brighton Museum holds a set, for the sight of which I thank the director.
[15] J. F. Tussaud, *The Romance of Madame Tussaud's* (London, 1920), pp. 141-3. I must thank Tussaud's archivist, Lady Chapman, for assistance. Her information has prompted me to conclude that J. F. Tussaud's chronology is somewhat awry, and I have modified this reference accordingly.

[16] *Law Journal*, 14 July 1871; *Public Opinion*, 29 July 1871.
[17] J. W. Cross, *George Eliot's Life as related in her Letters and Journals* (3 vols, New York, 1885), vol. 3, p. 107. References concerning the other literati derive from standard biographies.
[18] (Melbourne, 1970), p. 152.
[19] This and following item are from Dixson papers 256.
[20] E. V. H. Kenealy (ed.), *The Trial at Bar of Sir Roger C. D. Tichborne*, Introduction, p. 84.
[21] E. H. Coleridge, *Life and Correspondence of John Duke Lord Coleridge* (2 vols, London, 1904), vol. 2, p. 206.
[22] *The Trial*, Introduction, p. 23.
[23] 13 Mar. 1872.
[24] *Law Journal*, 14 July 1871.
[25] *The Trial*, Introduction, pp. 86, 99.
[26] 1 Feb. 1873.
[27] For example, the *Times*, 8, 20 Apr. 1872.
[28] 29 Mar. 1872.
[29] The *Times*, 25 May 1872.
[30] (2 vols, London, 1903), vol. 1, p. 149.
[31] *Tichborne News*, 17 Aug. 1872.
[32] Summary of letter, 31 Oct. 1868, Dixson papers 222. 'Onions' is a meaningless scrawl in this version, but the reading is confirmed by Mr C. W. Ringross, Librarian of Lincoln's Inn, working from papers there.
[33] Dixson papers 233.
[34] 9 Mar. 1872, 22 July 1871.
[35] *Public Opinion*, 18 May 1872.
[36] 10 June 1871.
[37] *Commons Debates*, 7 Mar., 8 Apr. 1872.
[38] Ibid., 7 May 1872.
[39] 'Copy of the Application to the Treasury for Aid . . .', *Parliamentary Papers*, no. 297, 1873, vol. 54; *Commons Debates*, 9 Aug. 1872.
[40] *The Trial*, Introduction, p. 239.
[41] Ibid., p. 241; the subsequent pages document the aftermath.
[42] 1 Feb. 1873; Finlason expressed his view in 'Contempt of Court', *Law Magazine and Review*, vol. 2, 1873, pp. 164-72.
[43] 'Report of the Select Committee of the House of Commons on Public Petitions', 1873. These sessional reports were printed, but sets are very rare; I used that in the British Museum. They document all my statements concerning petitions.
[44] G. S. Layard, *A Great 'Punch' Editor: being the life, letter and diaries of Shirley Brooks* (London, 1907), p. 468.
[45] The *Times*, 25 May 1872.
[46] *The Trial*, Introduction, p. 107. I have switched the order of the last two phrases.
[47] 10 Mar. 1872.
[48] *Saturday Review*, 30 Mar. 1872.
[49] Tichborne vs Lushington, p. 347; see also pp. 4366-7.
[50] Letter to Sedgefield and Allport, 24 Dec. 1867, Holmes correspondence, Lincoln's Inn papers.
[51] *The Trial*, Introduction, p. 119.
[52] Coleridge, *Life of Coleridge*, vol. 2, p. 207.
[53] The *Times*, 7 Mar. 1872.
[54] J. Gormley, 'Reminiscences', *Wagga Wagga Express*, 4, 11 Sept. 1915; 'An Old Commercial Traveller', *The Tichborne Case* (Brisbane, 1882).
[55] Letter, 20 Oct. 1866, Dixson papers 236.
[56] *The Trial*, vol. 3, p. 8.

[57] Letter to E. Rous, 16 Apr. 1869, Dixson papers 235.
[58] Item, 27 Aug. 1867, Dixson papers 222.
[59] *The Trial*, vol. 1, p. 118. The passage gives other statistics, for what they are worth.
[60] 24 Jan. 1875.
[61] *Examiner*, 18 May 1872.
[62] *The Trial*, Introduction, p. 101.
[63] 9 Aug. 1872; for consequent court proceedings, the *Times*, 29 July, 8 Aug., 11, 12, 13 Dec.; for Napper case, 26 Aug., 7 Sept.

3 KENEALY RIDES THE WAVE

[1] E. V. H. Kenealy (ed.), *The Trial at Bar of Sir Roger C. D. Tichborne*, vol. 3, pp. 156-9. For further reference to the writ, which evidently was pursued by McMahon rather than Kenealy, see attorney-general's speech, *Commons Debates*, 23 Apr. 1875.
[2] The *Times*, 25 Oct. 1873.
[3] *The Trial*, vol. 3, p. 259. For an exposition of the trial, see D. Woodruff, *The Tichborne Claimant* (London, 1957).
[4] *The Trial*, vol. 7, p. 69.
[5] Ibid., vol. 3, p. 259.
[6] Ibid., vol. 7, p. 200; see also vol. 7, p. 190, vol. 3, pp. 129-30.
[7] Ibid., vol. 3, p. 10.
[8] Ibid., vol. 2, p. 46; vol. 6, pp. 326-7.
[9] Ibid., vol. 7, p. 340.
[10] Ibid., vol. 3, p. 274; see also vol. 3, p. 117.
[11] Ibid., vol. 8, p. 2.
[12] Ibid., vol. 3, p. 256.
[13] Ibid., vol. 6, p. 71.
[14] Ibid., vol. 8, p. 85; see also vol. 8, p. 123.
[15] Dixson papers generally.
[16] *Law Journal*, 7 Mar. 1874; F. H. Maugham, *The Tichborne Case* (London, 1936), pp. 322-3, 330-1; J. B. Atlay, *Famous Trials of the Century* (London, 1899), pp. 364-6.
[17] R. Harris (ed.), *The Reminiscences of Sir Henry Hawkins* (London, 1904), p. 223.
[18] *The Trial*, vol. 5, pp. 233-4.
[19] J. Gray to Inspector Denning, 11 July 1873, National Library of Australia item NK713.
[20] *The Trial*, vol. 5, p. 155.
[21] 20 Sept. 1873.
[22] *Public Opinion*, 7 Mar. 1874; Woodruff, *The Tichborne Claimant*, p. xiii; the *Times*, 2 Mar. 1874; *Saturday Review*, 7 Mar. 1874.
[23] E. H. Coleridge, *Life and Correspondence of John Duke Lord Coleridge* (2 vols, London, 1904), vol. 2, p. 223.
[24] 'Trial of the Claimant', Birmingham ephemera.
[25] 'The Tichborne Belief', Dixson papers 256. The lady evidently received £5 from her husband, Captain Harvey, that she might travel to meet Bellew.
[26] 1 Nov. 1873.
[27] *Pall Mall Gazette*, 7 Mar. 1874; for the *Advertiser*, see especially 20 Sept. 1873.
[28] The James correspondence is in Dixson papers 249, and the 'Bolt' letter in 248.
[29] 'Reminiscences of the Tichborne Case', *Englishman* supplement, 1886, p. 22. In the British Museum file of the *Englishman* this supplement is bound at the end.

[30] H. Snell, *Men, Movements, and Myself* (London, 1936), p. 18.
[31] *The Trial*, vol. 5, pp. 66, 254.
[32] 'Trial of the Claimant', Birmingham ephemera; this is also source of next item.
[33] The *Times*, 25 Sept. 1873, 19, 23 Jan. 1874.
[34] *Commons Debates*, 2 May 1873.
[35] *The Trial*, vol. 6, p. 79.
[36] Most newspapers gave long accounts. Probably the best, and that quoted, is from the *Observer*, 1 Mar. 1874. For the account of Wapping, see *Morning Post*, 2 Mar. 1874.
[37] G. E. Buckle (ed.), *Letters of Queen Victoria . . . between . . . 1862 and 1878* (2 vols, London, 1926), vol. 2, pp. 329-30.
[38] *The Trial*, vol. 1, p. 399.
[39] British Museum ephemera.
[40] Bodleian Library, Oxford.
[41] *Commons Debates*, 23 July 1874; the return was 'Account of the expenditure . . . in . . . Regina v. Castro', *Parliamentary Papers*, no. 358, 1874, vol. 54.
[42] Tussaud reference, *Sunday Times*, 25 Mar. 1895; lecture tour, *The Trial*, vol. 8, p. 680.
[43] *Standard* (and other journals), 9, 10 Mar. 1874.
[44] M. Hilbery, 'The Kenealy Scandal', *Graya*, vol. 62, 1965, pp. 125-37; *The Trial*, vol. 8, pp. 676-710; the *Times*, 20 Apr. 1874.
[45] Quotations in this paragraph are from the issues for 20 June, 29 Aug., 12 Sept. 1874.
[46] H. G. Gill, *The Life and Forensic Career of E. V. Kenealy* (London, 1874). The British Museum catalogue indicates that the pamphlet quickly went into a second edition.
[47] Kenealy to Evans, 26 Jan. 1874, Dixson papers 250. For information on Evans, I am indebted to Mr Rupert Evans, University of Leicester.
[48] 12 Sept. 1874.
[49] A. Kenealy, *Memoirs of Edward Vaughan Kenealy LL.D.*, p. 291.
[50] *The Trial*, vol. 8, pp. 745, 748.
[51] *Life of Coleridge*, vol. 2, p. 246.
[52] Buckle (ed.) *Letters of Queen Victoria 1862-78*, vol. 2, pp. 357-8.
[53] *The Trial*, vol. 8, pp. 716-28; *Englishman*, 20 Feb. 1875 and generally.
[54] H. E. Litchfield, *Emma Darwin* (2 vols, Cambridge, 1904), vol. 2, p. 274. The reference does not appear in the public edition (London, 1915).
[55] 'Politics Before Easter', *Blackwood's Magazine*, vol. 117, 1875, pp. 526-8, at p. 526.
[56] D. A. Wilson and D. W. MacArthur, *Carlyle in Old Age (1865-1881)* (London, 1934), p. 353.
[57] The facts in issue remain in some dispute. I have used especially Mr Speaker Brand's diary; *Times Literary Supplement*, 28 May, 4 June 1908; D. C. Murray, *Recollections* (London, 1908), p. 125; and H. W. Lucy, *Sixty Years in the Wilderness* (London, 1909), p. 414. See also p. 215.
[58] Murray, *Recollections*, p. 127; see also *Public Opinion*, 13 Mar. 1875.
[59] The Marquis of Zetland (ed.), *The Letters of Disraeli to Lady Bradford and Lady Chesterfield* (2 vols, London, 1929), vol. 1, p. 214.
[60] Ibid., vol. 1, pp. 232-3.
[61] *Commons Debates*, 25 June, 3 Aug. 1875.
[62] Ibid., 5 Aug. 1875.
[63] *The Trial*, vol. 7, pp. 370-1.
[64] For a detailed account, G. Playfair, *Six Studies in Hypocrisy* (London, 1969), pp. 45-78. The duel story derives from Brand's diary.
[65] The *Times*, 25 Sept. 1875.
[66] 31 July 1875.

[67] *Public Opinion*, 3 Apr. 1875.
[68] Letter from G. Wayte, 29 June 1875, Dixson papers 250.
[69] *Leicester Evening News*, 24 July 1875.
[70] *Englishman*, 10 Apr. 1875.
[71] Ibid., 17 July 1875.
[72] For the ideal, 6 Mar. 1875; for the reality, 17 Apr. 1875.
[73] *Leicester Evening News*, 7 Aug. 1875.
[74] 30, 31 Mar., 24, 26 Apr. 1875.
[75] 3, 24 Apr. 1875.
[76] 'The Member for Stoke', *Gentleman's Magazine*, vol. 14, 1875, pp. 698-709, at pp. 707-9.
[77] 1 May 1875.
[78] *Letter to Edward Vaughan Kenealy* (London, 1875), p. 8.
[79] For Dawson, see the pamphlet report of his speech on *The Tichborne Trial* (Birmingham, 1884—the speech was a decade older, however); for Plimsoll, *Englishman*, 15 May 1875.
[80] *Judy*, 5 May 1875; broadsheet, British Museum ephemera; *Punch*, 4 Sept. 1875.

4 KENEALY IN DECLINE

[1] *Englishman*, 24 June 1876; C. Hiatt, *The Cathedral Church of Chester* (London, 1897), pp. 31-2, and Illustration 4.
[2] Vol. 14, 1878, pp. 436-7.
[3] *Commons Debates*, 26 June 1877.
[4] *Englishman*, 11 Mar. 1876.
[5] Leaflet dated 5 Nov. 1878, Dixson papers 248.
[6] *Englishman*, 1 July 1876.
[7] L. Edel, *Henry James. The Conquest of London 1870-1883* (London, 1962), p. 278.
[8] 9 Feb. 1876.
[9] 4 May 1878.
[10] 17 June 1876.
[11] Little of this ephemera has survived, save some pamphlets by Onslow, for which see D. Woodruff, *The Tichborne Claimant* (London, 1957), p. 463.
[12] The man's name is often spelled with one 's'. I use two, except where quoting official documents which use one.
[13] *Englishman*, 1 Dec. 1877; E. V. H. Kenealy (ed.), *The Trial at Bar of Sir Roger C. D. Tichborne*, vol. 8, p. 276.
[14] *The Trial*, vol. 8, p. 483.
[15] Ibid., pp. 571, 371.
[16] Ibid., vol. 2, p. 310.
[17] *Englishman*, 21 Oct. 1876.
[18] Letter from S. C. E. Goss, 16 Aug. 1876, Dixson papers 250.
[19] *Englishman*, 13 Dec. 1879.
[20] *Independent*, 23 Sept. 1876.
[21] *Englishman*, 1 Jan. 1876.
[22] Letter, evidently mid-1877, Dixson papers 248; see also that of 15 June 1877, Dixson papers 249.
[23] *Commons Debates*, especially 1, 26 Mar., 9, 22 Feb., 5 June 1877.
[24] *Englishman*, 22 Apr., 8 July 1876.
[25] For Kenealy's speech, *Commons Debates*, 9 Mar. 1876; for Disraeli's comment, the Marquis of Zetland (ed.), *The Letters of Disraeli to Lady Bradford and Lady Chesterfield* (2 vols, London, 1929), vol. 2, p. 47.
[26] *Englishman*, 21 Dec. 1878. For the subsequent references, 29 Mar., 27 Sept. 1879.

[27] Ibid., 14 Dec. 1878.
[28] *Commons Debates*, 26 Feb. 1878.
[29] 11 May 1877; see also 13 Apr. 1877.
[30] I follow the outstanding study, R. T. Shannon, *Gladstone and the Bulgarian Agitation 1876* (London, 1963).
[31] 4 Aug. 1877.
[32] 6 Nov. 1875.
[33] 9 Sept. 1876.
[34] *Englishman*, 26 May 1877.
[35] In assessing this situation, as in studying Kenealy's career in parliament generally, I have been fortunate that these years are covered by T. N. Roberts, *Parliamentary Buff Book* (London, annual). I used the set at the University of Cambridge Library.
[36] P. 355.
[37] Pp. 401-3.
[38] *Englishman*, 12 May 1877.
[39] *Dublin University Magazine*, vol. 28, 1846, p. 236.
[40] M. Sadleir, *Bulwer: A Panorama* (London, 1931), pp. 433-4.
[41] There are two versions, which I have conflated: *Englishman*, 29 Sept. 1877, and *The Prayers, Meditations and Visions of Kenealy (Imaum Mahidi)*, p. 122.
[42] G. Keynes and B. Hill (eds), *Letters between Samuel Butler and Miss E. M. A. Savage 1871-1885* (London, 1935), pp. 118-19.
[43] 9 Dec. 1876.
[44] *Fo*, p. 110.
[45] P. cxxi.
[46] *Englishman*, 14 Sept. 1878.
[47] The *Staffordshire Sentinel* and *Potteries Examiner* give good accounts.
[48] *The Story of His Life . . . Told by Himself* (London, 1901), pp. 94-8.
[49] A. Kenealy, *Memoirs of Edward Vaughan Kenealy LL.D.*, p. 300.
[50] *Englishman*, 1 May 1880; this issue also documents the funeral.
[51] *Public Opinion*, 24 Apr. 1880; *Pall Mall Gazette*, 17 Apr.; *Potteries Examiner*, 24 Apr.
[52] *Public Opinion*, 17 Nov. 1877.
[53] C. Y. Lang (ed.), *The Swinburne Letters* (6 vols, New Haven, 1959-62), vol. 3, p. 7.
[54] 2 Feb. 1878.
[55] *Prayers, Meditations and Visions*, p. 52.

5 OTHER SUPPORTERS OF THE CAUSE IN BRITAIN

[1] *Independent*, 24 Apr. 1875; see also the same, 27 May 1876.
[2] *Morning Herald* (Dunedin), 26 Nov. 1881; see also *Otago Daily Times*, 8 Dec. 1881. For assistance concerning Barry's career I thank the staff of the Alexander Turnbull Library, Wellington, New Zealand. See also the (somewhat inaccurate) article in the *Encyclopaedia of New Zealand*, under name.
[3] *Glimpses of the Australian Colonies and New Zealand* (Auckland, 1903).
[4] *Englishman*, 4 Sept. 1875.
[5] *Independent*, 30 Oct., 13 Nov. 1875.
[6] Ibid., 17, 24 June, 1 July 1876.
[7] *Englishman*, 12 Jan., 23 Feb. 1878. The Woodruff papers include some documentation of Biddulph's activities.
[8] It has not been seen.
[9] *Independent*, 15 Dec. 1883.
[10] 13 Jan. 1880.

[11] *Independent*, 18 Dec. 1875.
[12] A. Griffiths, *Fifty Years of Public Service* (London, n.d.), p. 214.
[13] *Englishman*, 9 Mar. 1878.
[14] *Public Opinion*, 18 Apr. 1874.
[15] *Englishman*, 29 Mar. 1884.
[16] *Bulwer Lytton* (London, 1913).
[17] See G. F. W. Lees, *Dr Frederick Richard Lees: A Biography* (London, 1904).
[18] *Tichborne Gazette*, 29 Aug. 1874.
[19] 19 June 1875.
[20] 5 June 1875.
[21] 29 May 1875.
[22] 10 July 1875.
[23] 19 Aug., 30 Sept. 1876; Spencer's comment, *Social Statics* (New York, 1954), pp. 335-6.
[24] 20 Apr. 1877.
[25] *International Herald*, 30 Aug. 1873.
[26] Ibid., 29 June 1872; K. Marx and F. Engels, *Werke* (39 vols, Berlin, 1960-8), vol. 33, see index; Institute of Marxism-Leninism of the C.C., C.P.S.U., *The General Council of the First International 1871-1872: Minutes* (Moscow n.d.), see index.
[27] H. Collins and C. Abramsky, *Karl Marx and the British Labour Movement* (London, 1965), p. 73, and generally.
[28] *Unorthodox London* (second series, London, 1875), pp. 211-23.
[29] 10 July 1875.
[30] Lefevre, *English Commons and Forests* (London, 1894), p. 2.
[31] *Annual Register*, 1875, p. 121.
[32] Speech of F. W. Knight, *Commons Debates*, 25 May 1876.
[33] Lefevre, *English Commons and Forests*, p. 78; see also speech of G. Hardy, *Commons Debates*, 8 Aug. 1876.
[34] *Independent*, 8 July 1876.
[35] 28 Oct. 1876.
[36] *Commons Debates*, 23 Feb. 1877.
[37] *Independent*, 25 Jan. 1878.
[38] Letter to G. Onslow, evidently mid-1877, Dixson papers 248; 'against me' is scored out in this draft.
[39] *Englishman*, 28 Apr. 1883.
[40] *Independent*, 28 Oct., 4 Nov. 1876.
[41] Ibid., 30 Sept. 1876.
[42] 11 Aug. 1877.
[43] *Independent*, 23 Aug. 1878.
[44] 15 Apr. 1876.
[45] Interesting references to Barry appear in *Reynolds's Newspaper*, 8 Feb. 1874; W. Collison, *The Apostle of Free Labour* (London, 1913); A. E. P. Duffy, 'Differing Policies and Personal Rivalries in the Origins of the Independent Labour Party', *Victorian Studies*, vol. 6, 1962, pp. 43-65; H. Cunningham, 'Jingoism in 1877-78', *Victorian Studies*, vol. 14, 1971, pp. 429-53, at pp. 431-2; Marx and Engels, *Werke*, vols, 33, 34, see index; Institute of Marxism-Leninism, *First International 1871-2: Minutes*, see index; Collins and Abramsky, *Karl Marx and the British Labour Movement*, generally.
[46] 24 Nov. 1877; see also the *Times*, 17 Nov. 1877.
[47] Apart from the *Englishman*, see M. S. Wilkins, 'The Non-Socialist Origins of England's First Important Socialist Organization', *International Review of Social History*, vol. 4, 1959, pp. 199-207.
[48] Dixson papers 256; D. Woodruff, *The Tichborne Claimant* (London, 1957), pp. 423-4.
[49] There is a poor biography, P. Treherne, *A Plaintiff in Person* (London,

1923); see also the *Times*, 13 Jan. 1914 (obituary), and *Groves's Dictionary of Music and Musicians*, under name.

[50] Griffiths, *Fifty Years of Public Service*, p. 215.
[51] *Leaves from a Prison Diary* (London, 1885), pp. 54-9.
[52] *Englishman*, 10 Jan. 1885.
[53] J. B. Atlay, *Famous Trials of the Century* (London, 1899), p. 391.
[54] 30 Oct. 1884.
[55] *Englishman*, 25 Oct. 1884, 24 Jan. 1885.
[56] *Independent*, 10 Oct. 1885 ff.
[57] C. Pearl, *Morrison of Peking* (Harmondsworth, 1970), p. 60.
[58] Collison, *The Apostle of Free Labour*, p. 8.
[59] The confession was published in the magazine *People*, and then as a penny booklet, *The Entire Life and Full Confession of Arthur Orton*. Maurice Kenealy criticized the account in *The Tichborne Tragedy* (London, 1913), and W. A. Frost in *An Exposure of the Orton Confession of the Tichborne Claimant* (London, 1913). I scrutinize relevant parts of the confession in my 'Arthur Orton, the Tichborne Case, and Tasmania', *Tasmanian Historical Research Association. Papers and Proceedings*, vol. 18, 1971, pp. 115-36. Copies of the booklet *Confession* are held by the National Library of Scotland and the Mitchell Library, Sydney.
[60] L. C. Collins, *Life and Memoirs of John Churton Collins* (London, 1912), p. 192.
[61] Woodruff, *The Tichborne Claimant*, pp. 443-4.
[62] G. F. W. Lees, *Dr Frederick Richard Lees*, p. 190.

6   THE TICHBORNE CASE AND CAUSE IN AUSTRALIA

[1] Letter from Sedgefield and Allport, 11 June 1869, Holmes correspondence, Lincoln's Inn papers; see also D. Woodruff, *The Tichborne Claimant* (London, 1957), p. 40.
[2] See chapter 2, note 1.
[3] Letter from J. S., 3 Oct. 1871, 'William Creswell' paper, *Votes and Proceedings of the Legislative Assembly of New South Wales*, 1878-9, vol. 3, pp. 221-48, at p. 8.
[4] After previous temporary confinement, Cresswell entered Tarban Creek asylum in August 1871 and transferred to Parramatta the following April.
[5] *The Sydney Assassins* (Melbourne, 1964). Mr Cotton himself died soon after his book was published. I therefore was unable to check his material.
[6] S. Baker to E. Hopkins, 24 Oct. 1867, Holmes correspondence, Lincoln's Inn papers.
[7] E. V. H. Kenealy (ed.), *The Trial at Bar of Sir Roger C. D. Tichborne* (9 vols, London, 1875-80), vol. 1, p. 179.
[8] On this matter I have received help from Dr John Atchison, University of New England.
[9] The original is published in the edition of P. D. Edwards and R. B. Joyce, *Australia* (St Lucia, 1967), pp. 412-13.
[10] A. B. Peirce, *Knocking About* (New Haven, 1924), p. 153.
[11] For background, see K. Swan, *A History of Wagga Wagga* (Wagga Wagga, 1970), pp. 78-80.
[12] Quoted in *Mercury*, 13 Mar. 1868; see also *Launceston Examiner*, 9 Feb. 1869.
[13] Quoted in *Launceston Examiner*, 25 May 1872.
[14] H. Cornish, *Under the Southern Cross* (Madras, 1880), pp. 238-9.
[15] J. A. Reid, *The Australian Reader* (Melbourne, 1882), pp. 75-7.
[16] *Wagga Wagga Express*, 4, 11 Sept. 1915.
[17] *Riders of Time* (Melbourne, 1967), pp. 149-50.

18 File CSD 13/76/1438, Tasmanian Archives; see also Jackson's pamphlet, *Sir Roger Tichborne Revealed!* (Sydney, 1885).

19 'An Old Commercial Traveller', *The Tichborne Case* (Brisbane, 1882).

20 *Englishman*, 9 Oct. 1875.

21 21 Oct. 1876 ff.

22 Statement, 11 Oct. 1877, 'William Creswell' paper, *Votes and Proceedings of the Legislative Assembly of New South Wales*, 1878-9, vol. 3, p. 6. This paper plus a brief supplement printed 26 Nov. 1878 and published at pp. 249-50 of the same volume document the subsequent paragraphs.

23 Some correspondence is in the Parkes papers, Mitchell Library manuscript A921; see also P. Loveday and A. W. Martin, *Parliament, Factions and Politics* (Melbourne, 1966), especially p. 96. The *Englishman*, 10 June 1882, refers to Parkes's visit.

24 Speech of D. O'Connor, *N.S.W. Assembly Debates*, 5 Oct. 1881.

25 *Votes and Proceedings of the Legislative Assembly of New South Wales*, 1883-4, vol. 6, pp. 593-622 (with petition at pp. 623-4).

26 Letter, 18 Dec. 1882, Mitchell Library manuscript A921.

27 *Independent*, 12 Oct. 1877. I have corrected some typographical errors.

28 *Sydney Mail*, 14 Apr. 1883.

29 *Sydney Morning Herald*, 27 Apr. 1883; *Independent*, 28 July 1883.

30 *Independent*, 7 July, 23 June 1883.

31 J. E. Cunningham, The Sequel to the Tichborne Case, National Library of Australia manuscript 760/3/3.

32 F. Clune, *Scandals of Sydney Town* (Sydney, 1957), especially pp. 76-9.

33 Evidence of Mrs Smithers, Royal Commission on 'Case of William Creswell', *Votes and Proceedings of the Legislative Assembly of New South Wales*, 1900, vol. 6, pp. 997-1073, at pp. 12-13.

34 B. E. Mansfield, *Australian Democrat* (Sydney, 1965), p. 52. The book is of general relevance at this point. See also A. A. Hayden, 'The Anti-Immigration Movement, 1877-1893', *Royal Australian Historical Society, Journal and Proceedings*, vol. 48, 1962, pp. 25-43.

35 *Democrat* (Sydney), 3 May 1884. This item is held in the Ferguson collection, National Library of Australia.

36 *Sydney Morning Herald*, 13 May 1884.

37 Ibid., 28 May 1884.

38 *Australian Encyclopaedia*, under name; C. Pearl, *Wild Men of Sydney* (London, 1958).

39 File CB 12/1, Tasmanian Archives; see also file Con 33/99. Several variants of Brown's name appear from place to place.

40 *Monitor*, 5 Jan. 1895. I thank Dr R. P. Davis, University of Tasmania, for this reference.

41 File 4/924.1, New South Wales Archives; see Clifton's obituary, the *Times*, 1 Nov. 1900.

42 Mitchell Library manuscript At20/1. The petition to the governor-general is in the Commonwealth Archives, Canberra, series A1, file 03/2159. See also M. Gilmore, *Old Days: Old Ways* (Sydney, 1963), p. 21.

43 Mansfield, *Australian Democrat*, p. 149.

44 For the royal commission, see note 33; the select committee's progress report is part of the paper cited there.

45 E. C. Rickards, *Zoe Thomson of Bishopthorpe* (London, 1916), pp. 135-7. Rickards was also Moorhouse's biographer.

7 THE POPULIST FACTOR

1 *Symbolic Crusade: Status Politics and the American Temperance Movement* (Urbana, 1963).

[2] D. MacRae in G. Ionescu and E. Gellner (eds), *Populism* (London, 1969), p. 158.

[3] P. Wiles in Ionescu and Gellner (eds), *Populism*, p. 167.

[4] E. T. Cook and A. Wedderburn (eds), *The Works of John Ruskin* (39 vols, London, 1903-12), vol. 29, p. 480.

[5] 24 Apr. 1875.

[6] *The Tichborne Trial* (Birmingham, 1884), p. 13.

[7] P. Wiles in Ionescu and Gellner (eds), *Populism*, p. 167.

[8] *Primitive Rebels* (Manchester, 1959), pp. 22-3. I must admit to finding Hobsbawm's acclaimed study, *Bandits* (London, 1969) a confusion rather than a development of his earlier work.

[9] *Primitive Rebels*, p. 123.

[10] *The Pursuit of the Millennium* (New York, 1961), p. 308.

[11] *Gladstone and the Bulgarian Agitation 1876* (London, 1963), p. 202.

[12] D. MacRae in Ionescu and Gellner (eds), *Populism*, p. 161.

[13] See *The Crowd in History* (New York, 1964) and more detailed studies cited there.

[14] (London, 1963), pp. 12-13.

[15] Quoted in H. Jephson, *The Platform* (2 vols, London, 1892), vol. 1, p. 564.

[16] *The Origins of Modern English Society 1780-1880* (London, 1969), pp. 216-17.

[17] *Popular Politics and Society in Late Victorian Britain* (London, 1968), p. 2. This is also illuminated in N. C. Edsall, *The Anti-Poor Law Movement 1834-44* (Manchester, 1971) and D. Roberts, *Victorian Origins of the British Welfare State* (New Haven, 1969).

[18] 'Jingoism in 1877-78', *Victorian Studies*, vol. 14, 1971, pp. 429-53, at p. 432.

[19] The classic account from within is W. White, *The Story of a Great Delusion* (London, 1885).

[20] *The National Anti-Compulsory Vaccination Reporter*, Dec. 1877.

[21] Ibid., Apr. 1877.

[22] 'Report from the Select Committee on the Vaccination Act (1867)', *Parliamentary Papers*, no. 246, 1871, vol. 18, at question 2756.

[23] *Compulsory Vaccination. Its Wickedness to the Poor* (London, n.d.). The copy seen (at the Public Library of New South Wales) is of a second edition.

[24] *Public Opinion*, 27 Apr. 1872.

[25] Ibid., 26 Aug. 1876.

[26] *Reporter*, Nov. 1879.

[27] 'Royal Commission upon the Administration and Operation of the Contagious Diseases Acts', *Parliamentary Papers*, no. 408, 1871, vol. 19, at question 12 920.

[28] F. B. Smith, 'Ethics and Disease in the Later Nineteenth Century: the Contagious Diseases Acts', *Historical Studies*, vol. 15, 1971, pp. 118-35, at p. 129.

[29] 18 Oct. 1873.

[30] 29 Mar. 1893.

[31] 13 June 1870.

[32] Smith, 'Ethics and Disease'.

[33] *Parliamentary Papers*, no. 1397, 1876, vol. 41.

[34] *Public Opinion*, 12 Aug. 1876.

[35] *Independent*, 6 Nov. 1875.

[36] *Public Opinion*, 14 Feb. 1874.

[37] *Commons Debates*, 1 July 1874.

[38] Ibid., 12 Aug., 9 May 1873; Eykyn asked his Tichborne question on 7 Mar. 1872.

[39] *Public Opinion*, 13, 20 Dec. 1873.

[40] See G. A. Minto, *The Thin Blue Line* (London, 1965), ch. 8.

[41] 25 Jan. 1878.

[42] *Our New Masters* (London, 1873), pp. 153, 156, 334.

43 'Land and Politics in England in the Nineteenth Century', *Transactions of the Royal Historical Society*, vol. 15, 1965, pp. 23-44, at p. 23; the subsequent quotation is from p. 39.
44 Speech of Lord Edmond Fitzmaurice, *Commons Debates*, 23 July 1873.
45 *Bulgarian Agitation*, p. 27.
46 (Cambridge, 1967), p. 45.
47 'The Role of Mob Riot in Victorian Elections, 1865-1885', *Victorian Studies*, vol. 15, 1971, pp. 19-28, at p. 28.
48 *Law Times*, 13 Sept. 1873.
49 28 June 1879.
50 See B. Semmel, *The Governor Eyre Controversy* (London, 1962).
51 *Public Opinion*, 4 Feb. 1871. This journal documents well the current republican feeling.
52 Ibid., 9 Jan. 1875; see also 25 Dec. 1875.
53 E. R. Norman, *Anti-Catholicism in Victorian England* (London, 1968), p. 21.
54 *Public Opinion*, 12 Sept. 1874; see also 6 Sept. 1873, 15 July 1876.
55 3 Apr. 1875.
56 (Harmondsworth, 1963), pp. 72-3; following quotations are from p. 103.
57 *Primitive Rebels*, p. 108.
58 R. Lambert, *Sir John Simon 1816-1904 and English Social Administration* (London, 1963), p. 577; H. J. Parish, *A History of Immunization* (Edinburgh, 1965), p. 30.
59 H. Paul, *A History of Modern England* (5 vols, London, 1904-6), vol. 3, p. 431; A. L. Thorold, *The Life of Henry Labouchere* (London, 1913), p. 106.
60 *Reminiscences*, edited by A. Haultain (New York, 1910), p. 70.
61 *Manchester Guardian*, quoted in *Public Opinion*, 5 Apr. 1873.
62 28 Apr. 1875.
63 *The English Defence of the Commune 1871* (London, 1971), p. 279. Harrison republishes Wright's article on the Commune.
64 T. Irving and B. Berzins in R. Gordon (ed.), *The Australian New Left* (Melbourne, 1970), p. 79.
65 B. E. Mansfield, *Australian Democrat* (Sydney, 1965), p. 55.
66 S. Encel, 'The Larrikin Leaders', *Nation* (Sydney), 25 May 1868.

8 KENEALY AFTER DEATH

1 M. E. Kenealy, *The Tichborne Tragedy* (London, 1913), pp. 367-8.
2 *The Apostle of Free Labour* (London, 1913), p. 8.
3 *My Brother and I* (London, 1958), pp. 12-13.
4 P. Wiles in G. Ionescu and E. Gellner (eds), *Populism* (London, 1969), p. 170.
5 *W. H. Ainsworth and his Friends* (2 vols, London, 1911?), vol. 2, p. 5.
6 'Edward Vaughan Kenealy', *Irish Book Lover*, vol. 11, 1919, pp. 3-6.
7 A. Kenealy, *Memoirs of Edward Vaughan Kenealy LL.D.*, p. 201.
8 *Memoirs*, p. 234; the subsequent quotations are from pp. 219, 138, 231.
9 D. C. Seitz, *The James Gordon Bennetts* (Indianapolis, 1928), p. 220. The confusion could be with Alex Kenealy, but Seitz should have known his facts.
10 *The Tichborne Tragedy*, pp. 3-4.
11 A. H. Spencer, *The Hill of Content* (Sydney, 1959), pp. 156-7.
12 *Englishman*, 22 May 1886; the articles by Alex are in issues of 26 July 1884, 9 Jan., 13 Feb. 1886.
13 R. E. Peary, *Northward over the 'Great Ice'* (2 vols, New York, 1898), vol. 1, pp. 48, 58; see also P. Kinsley, *The Chicago Tribune* (3 vols, Chicago, 1943-6), vol. 3, p. 182.
14 D. C. Seitz, *Joseph Pulitzer* (London, n.d.), pp. 229-32.
15 See also C. H. Brown, *The Correspondents' War* (New York, 1967).

[16] R. Pound and G. Harmsworth, *Northcliffe* (London, 1959), p. 282 and generally; see also H. Fyfe, *Sixty Years of Fleet Street* (London, 1949), p. 117.

[17] Relevant manuscript material has been made available by Sir Geoffrey Harmsworth, Bt: for this and other help my warm thanks are due. Kenealy's only extant reply to Northcliffe is in Pound and Harmsworth, *Northcliffe*, p. 416. The spelling of 'gramatically' is as given, at least in that version.

[18] B. Falk, *Bouquets for Fleet Street* (London, 1951), p. 395; the subsequent quotation is from the same source.

[19] *Englishman*, 14 Aug., 4 Sept., 6 Nov. 1875.

[20] C. L. Cline (ed.), *The Letters of George Meredith* (3 vols, Oxford, 1970), vol. 2, p. 1078. Other references are from Meredith's reports as reader for Chapman and Hall, in the H. S. Huntington Library; Cline is somewhat astray in his editorial comments.

[21] 6 May 1899; *Bookman*, Sept. 1899; *Academy*, 27 May 1899.

[22] 13 June 1908; *Irish Law Times*, 8 Aug. 1908; *Times Literary Supplement*, 21, 28 May, 4 June 1908; *Athenaeum*, 18, 25 July 1908.

[23] W. J. Chidley, *The Answer or the World as Joy* (Sydney, 1915), endpaper.

[24] *The Poodle Woman. A Story of 'restitution of conjugal rights'* (London, 1913), p. 48.

[25] The *Times*, 20, 21 Jan. 1910; see also P. Ferris, *The House of Northcliffe* (London, 1971), p. 166.

[26] *The Suffrage Annual and Women's Who's Who* (London, 1913) has several references to the Kenealy sisters.

[27] The *Times*, 19, 20, 30 Nov. 1915.

[28] Personal communication from the secretaries of these bodies, to whom my thanks are due.

[29] J. F. S. (Earl) Russell, *My Life and Adventures* (London, 1923), p. 293.

BIBLIOGRAPHY

MAJOR WRITINGS OF E. V. H. KENEALY

The following list is not complete. As mentioned in the text, the location of Kenealy's very first publication is unknown, and so too are the details of some of his articles in the 1840s and still more the 1850s. In a letter to Disraeli of 16 January 1861 (Beaconsfield Papers), Kenealy remarked that he was about to issue a pamphlet in the form of a letter to Lord Palmerston by a major of the Volunteers. This has not been indentified, and there may have been other similar items. I also exclude the Greek version of the Palmer trial (see p. 20). Nor does this bibliography attempt to describe Kenealy's individual contribution to the *Englishman* and the *Englishman's Magazine*.

1841
'Specimens of the Table-Talk of the late John Boyle, Esq.', *Fraser's Magazine*, vol. 23, pp. 574-83, 731-48. All contributions to *Fraser's* were anonymous.

1842
'A Letter from Ned Hyde', *Ainsworth's Magazine*, vol. 1, pp. 191-2. Anon.
'The Songs of Italy', ibid., vol. 1, pp. 313-14, vol. 2, pp. 48-50.
'A Farewell', ibid., vol. 2, p. 41.
'The Late William Maginn, LL.D.', ibid., pp. 218-20.
'Three Songs', ibid., pp. 436-7.
'A Venetian Romance', ibid., pp. 519-23.
'Memoirs of . . . Henry Flood', *Dublin Review*, vol. 13, pp. 100-54. Anon.

'A Letther from Mr Barney Brallaghan', *Fraser's Magazine*, vol. 25, pp. 65-80; 'A Second Letther . . .', pp. 160-81.

'The Last of the Homeric Ballads by William Maginn . . . with an introduction and notes by The Templar', ibid., vol. 26, pp. 439-46.

'The Love Epistles of Aristaenetus', ibid., pp. 661-7.

'To a Fountain in Hymettus', *Bentley's Miscellany*, vol. 11, pp. 327-8.

'The Greek Poet's Dream', ibid., p. 497.

'To ********** *****', ibid., p. 510.

'Life and Songs of Anacreon, edited by Barney Brallaghan', ibid., vol. 11, pp. 479-93, 644-55; vol. 12, pp. 254-61, 466-77.

'Lines on Lord Ashley's Motion', ibid., vol. 12, pp. 31-2.

'Song', ibid., p. 156.

1843

'A Venetian Romance', *Ainsworth's Magazine*, vol. 3, pp. 45-50.

'The Shepherd Paris', ibid., p. 30.

'Stanzas', ibid., p. 149.

'Lines to—', ibid., p. 234.

'The Story of Pygmalion', ibid., vol. 4, pp. 141-6.

'Arundines Cami', *Dublin Review*, vol. 14, pp. 121-40. Anon.

'Memoirs of the Life and Times of . . . Grattan', ibid., vol. 15, pp. 200-52.

'A Polyglot Paper. By Barney Brallaghan', *Dublin University Magazine*, vol. 21, pp. 425-32.

'Oliver Yorke at Home', *Fraser's Magazine*, vol. 27, pp. 1-35.

'The Love Epistles of Aristaenetus', ibid., pp. 578-83.

'A Continental Tour', ibid., vol. 28, pp. 681-94.

1844

'While the Dews Fall over the Mulberry-Tree', *Ainsworth's Magazine*, vol. 6, p. 154.

'William Maginn, LL.D.', *Dublin University Magazine*, vol. 23, pp. 72-101. Anon.

'A Continental Tour', *Fraser's Magazine*, vol. 29, pp. 449-64.

'The King of the Cannibal Islands', *Punch*, vol. 6, p. 79. Anon.

1845

Brallaghan, or the Deipnosophists. London.

The Inaugural Address to the Members of the Temperance Institute, Cork.

'To Some Withered Flowers Dearly Loved', *Ainsworth's Magazine*, vol. 7, p. 57.

'Enjoy thy May of Life', ibid., p. 253.
'Hymns of the Catholic Church', ibid., vol. 7, pp. 451-3; vol. 8, pp. 72-4.
'On a Favourite Walk', ibid., vol. 8, p. 462.
'Lyric Poem' *Dublin University Magazine*, vol. 25, pp. 187-8.
'Personal Recollections of Thomas Campbell, Esq.', ibid., pp. 557-63, 679-89. Anon.
'Beauteous Little Mary', *New Monthly Magazine*, vol. 74, pp. 380-1.

1846
'Shelley', *Ainsworth's Magazine*, vol. 9, p. 66.
'Swedish Anthology', ibid., pp. 111-22.
'Sonnet to Dr D. M. Moir', ibid., p. 143.
'Sonnet to W. Harrison Ainsworth', ibid., p. 161.
'Edith Carleton', ibid., vol. 10, pp. 179-86, 289-96, 373-8.
'Scraps from Brallaghan's Common-Place Book', *Dublin University Magazine*, vol. 27, pp. 463-79.
'Three Sonnets', ibid., vol. 28, p. 236.
'Laman Blanchard', ibid., pp. 509-24. Anon.
'Sonnet to Serjeant Talfourd', *New Monthly Magazine*, vol. 76, p. 49.
'Byron', ibid., p. 184.
'Fionn: An Irish Romance', ibid., pp. 281-2.
'A Thought', ibid., vol. 77, p. 57.
'On Revisiting Trinity College', ibid., pp. 439-42.

1847
'Edith Carleton', *Ainsworth's Magazine*, vol. 11, pp. 509-14.
'Travels in Central America', *Dublin Review*, vol. 23, pp. 78-89. Anon.
'History of the Conquest of Peru', ibid., pp. 322-40. Anon.
'Homer's Hymn to Hermes', *Dublin University Magazine*, vol. 29, pp. 296-314.
'Daniel MacLise, R.A.', ibid., pp. 594-607. Anon.

1848
'The Ballad of Gunhild', *Dublin University Magazine*, vol. 31, pp. 12-14.

1850
Noah's Ark, a Dream of 1850. See p. 200 and next entry.
Goethe: A New Pantomime. London. All copies seen bear the imprint, 'second edition'. I long supposed this to be bluff, but

possibly the preceding item was identical save for title and so constituted a first edition. It may have been an Irish imprint.

1856
A Letter to the Lord Chief-Justice Campbell. London. Anon.

1860
English translation of M. Horgan, *Cahir Conri*, Cork. John Windele referred to Kenealy's authorship in his preface.

1861
Prayers and Meditations. Anon. Not seen.

1863
A New Pantomime. London.
Poems and Translations. London. As remarked in the text, the title-page bears the date 1864. There was an identical printing, described as a second edition in 1865.

1866
The Book of God: The Apocalypse of Adam-Oannes. London. Anon. The title-page bore the hieroglyph of a circle, with a central dot. This reappeared in the religious books issued during Kenealy's lifetime.

1868(?)
The Book of God: An Introduction to the Apocalypse. London.

1869
Edward Wortley Montagu. An Autobiography. 3 vols, London. Anon. The Library of Congress catalogue indicates that a one-volume edition was published in Philadelphia in 1870 and again, probably in 1877.

1870
The Book of God: A Commentary on the Apocalypse. London.

1872 (?)
Enoch, the Second Messenger of God. 2 vols, London.

1875-9
The Poetical Works of Edward Vaughan Kenealy. 3 vols, London.

1875-80
(Editor) *The Trial at Bar of Sir Roger C. D. Tichborne.* 9 vols, London.

1878
Fo, the Third Messenger of God. London.

1901
The Testament of Jesus. Edited by C. W. Hillyear. Watford.

1909
The Prayers, Meditations and Visions of Kenealy (Imaum Mahidi), the Twelfth Messenger of God. Edited by C. W. Hillyear. Watford.

1911
Institutes of Hindu Law, or the Ordinances of Menu . . . by Kenealy, Parasu-Rama. Edited by C. W. Hillyear. Watford.

MAJOR WRITINGS OF ARABELLA KENEALY

1890
'The Talent of Motherhood', *National Review*, vol. 16, pp. 446-59.

1891
'The Physical Conscience', *National Review*, vol. 17, pp. 477-93.
'A New View on the Surplus of Women', *Westminster Review*, vol. 136, pp. 465-72.

1893
Dr Janet of Harley Street. London.

1894
Some Men are Such Gentlemen. London.

1895
The Honourable Mrs Spoor. London.

1897
Belinda's Beaux and Other Stories. London.
'How Women Doctors are made', *Ludgate*, vol. 4, pp. 29-35.

1898
Woman and the Shadow. London, New York and Chicago.

1899
A Semi-Detached Marriage. London.
'Woman as an Athlete', *Nineteenth Century*, vol. 45, pp. 636-45, 915-29.

1900
Charming Renée. London, New York.

1901
The Love of Richard Herrick. London.

1903
His Eligible Grace the Duke, and Other Stories. London.

1904
The Marriage Yoke. London.
'The Curse of Corsets', *Nineteenth Century*, vol. 55, pp. 131-7.

1905
(Editor) E. L. Coolidge, *The Mother's Manual*. London.
(Editor) E. E. Walker, *Beauty through Hygiene*. London.

1906
An American Duchess. London.
Lady Fitz-Maurice's Husband. London.

1907
Dr Smith of Queen Anne Street, and Other Stories. London.

1908
Memoirs of Edward Vaughan Kenealy LL.D. London.
The Whips of Time. London, Boston.

1909
The Failure of Vivisection and the Future of Medical Research.
   London.

1910
King Edward Intervenes. London.

1911
The Mating of Anthea. London.
My Beautiful Neighbour. London.
'A Study in Degeneracy', *Eugenics Review*, vol. 3, pp. 37-45.

1912
The Irresistible Mrs Ferrers. London, New York.
The Woman-Hunter. London.

1913
The Painted Lady. London.

1914
The Way of the Lover. London.

1915
This Thing We Have Prayed For. London.

1917
Woman's Great Adventure. London.

1920
Feminism and Sex-Extinction. London.

1934
The Human Gyroscope. London. This was published in two versions, one presenting the argument more briefly.

A GUIDE TO SOURCES

To achieve uniformity and order in this task is difficult. My notes give locations if the material concerned has very specific and/or isolated significance. In these paragraphs, arranged alphabetically and according to a key word, I comment upon materials and repositories of more general relevance. One purpose of this identification is to make clear my debt to librarians, archivists and others.

Australian archives The Archives Office of Tasmania is integrated with the State Library of Tasmania, Hobart; the Archives Authority of New South Wales is associated with, and its documents largely housed in, the Public Library of New South Wales, Sydney.

Bagshawe Papers The papers of H. R. Bagshawe, relating to his work for the *Dublin Review*, are at the Archbishop of Westminster's house, London.

Beaconsfield Papers This rich store, under the administration of the National Trust, is at Hughenden Manor, Buckinghamshire. A guide is available. As indicated in the text, there is a run of Kenealy's letters to Disraeli and a separate file concerning the *Press*.

Bentley Papers The papers of Richard Bentley, publisher, are at the University of Illinois, Urbana.

Birmingham ephemera I thus refer to the important collection of Tichborne ballads at the Public Library of Birmingham.

Brand's Diary The diary of Mr Speaker Brand is in the House of Lords Library.

Brighton Museum Here is held not only the set of figurines mentioned in the text, but also the most notable item of fine art inspired by the trial: a group modelled in terra cotta by Randolph Caldecott showing the three criminal trial judges as owls, the Claimant as a turtle, Hawkins as a hawk, and Kenealy as a cock.

British Museum ephemera The museum holds a fair collection
of ballad and other such material, catalogued under 'Orton,
Arthur'. Some material, including unique pamphlets, was destroyed by enemy action in World War II.

Cambridge ephemera The University of Cambridge Library
also holds a small sample of such items.

Dixson Papers The Dixson Library is part of the Public Library
of New South Wales. It holds an extremely rich collection of
Tichborniana, deriving chiefly from the estate of Maurice
Kenealy (see p. 205). The material came originally from varied
sources, including several solicitors for the Claimant, and
Anthony Norris, solicitor for the Dowager. This material con-
stitutes by far the greatest part described in a splendid guide:
J. D. Hine, Tichborne Checklist: A Classified List of Materials
connected with the Tichborne case in the Public Library of
New South Wales (typescript, Sydney, 1958). It includes manu-
scripts, pamphlets, legal documents, and all kinds of ephemera.

In the notes, reference to these papers is by way of a three-
figure numeral. This numeral identifies the item as a Dixson
'additional manuscript'. To describe each item further is desirable but difficult, as most are heterogeneous. The following list
refers to all items specifically cited and generally follows the
binder's title or equivalent.

222 Holmes's Bill of Costs re Tichborne.
233 Chilian Commission in the Tichborne Case, with
     solicitors' annotations.
234 Various Letters and Documents.
235-6 Various Letters.
248-9 Notes by Dr Kenealy in pursuit of his brief.
250 Extracts, Newspaper Cuttings, etc.
256 Printed Affidavits and Printed Pamphlets.
259 Affidavits.
261 Pictorial Material.

Huntington Papers The H. S. Huntington Library, San Marino,
California, holds five volumes of papers relating to E. V. H.
Kenealy. They derive almost entirely from the period 1836-55,
and are chronologically arranged save that volume 5 includes
some material from earlier years. They consist primarily of
inward letters and outward drafts, with some newspaper cuttings and other miscellanea. See L. B. Jones, 'The Kenealy Collection at the Huntington Library', *Victorian Periodicals News-
letter*, vol. 14, 1971, pp. 20-2.

Lincoln's Inn Papers   The major item in this important collection in London is the Holmes Papers, in eight volumes. These include Holmes's accounts, and the correspondence in which he engaged concerning the case. There is considerable overlap with the Dixson Papers; my notes refer to that source from which my transcription is fuller. Also at Lincoln's Inn are several volumes of newspaper cuttings, and an album of photographs etc. relating to the case. They include material deriving from Lord Maugham, author of a book on the case.

Mitchell Library   The Mitchell Library is part of the Public Library of New South Wales. As the richest and best-catalogued repository of Australiana, the Mitchell has relevant holdings of books, newspapers, and manuscripts. My notes refer to specific items of particular importance.

National Library of Australia   This library, in Canberra, holds various items of which the most important are:
Item NK713   The Tichborne Trial 1871-4. This comprises representative ephemera, an extensive collection of photographic portraits, and other material collected by Inspector Denning, the policeman in charge at Westminster.
Item NK9595   The Tichborne Trial: Original Drawings, Photographs, and Caricatures.
Manuscript 760/3/3   J. E. Cunningham. The Sequel to the Tichborne Case. Arthur Orton or William Creswell. The Proceedings in New South Wales. This most useful document, prepared by a court reporter, details the legal proceedings of 1884 and their background. Obviously Cunningham meant to publish his work as a pamphlet, but I have no evidence of its appearance.

Newspapers and Periodicals   My guides to this material were the *British Union Catalogue of Periodicals,* the British Museum catalogue under 'Periodical Publications', and *Newspapers in Australian Libraries,* National Library of Australia. Any follower in my footsteps should discover locations by reference thither.
I was fortunate in that the weekly anthology, *Public Opinion,* was current during the Tichborne years. My notes cite this source rather than the original, when in fact my acquaintance with the item concerned came thereby.

Wills   These are available through Somerset House, London. The *Times* reported the more substantial ones.

Woodruff Papers   Douglas Woodruff made available the archive he had gathered in pursuit of his Tichborne studies. Especially interesting was material relating to A. J. W. Biddulph and the Claimant's post-prison years.

INDEX

[C = Claimant; K = Kenealy]

247